AUSTRALIA'S RED TAPE CRISIS

THE CAUSES AND COSTS OF OVER-REGULATION

Edited by Darcy Allen and Chris Berg

AUSTRALIA'S RED TAPE CRISIS

THE CAUSES AND COSTS OF OVER-REGULATION

CONNOR COURT PUBLISHING 2018

First published in 2018 by Connor Court Publishing Pty Ltd

ISBN: 9781925501902

Connor Court Publishing Pty Ltd
Suite 2, 146 Boundary Street
West End, Queensland, Australia, 4101

sales@connorcourt.com
www.connorcourtpublishing.com.au
Phone 0497 900 685

Contents

Introduction   1
Darcy Allen and Chris Berg

Part one: The economics and politics of red tape

1   Regulation in a small open economy   9
    Chris Berg

2   The big picture   28
    David Kemp

3   Australia's economic malaise   48
    Michael Potter

4   Some (micro)economics of regulation   69
    Sinclair Davidson

5   The politics of red tape   80
    Georgina Downer

Part two: Red tape: history and culture

6   A regulatory culture?   97
    Matthew Lesh

7   1901: Federation as bureaucratisation   114
    William Coleman

8   Red tape: Tethering Australia to the world   128
    Gregory Melleuish

Part three: Case studies

9   Environmental regulation and red tape   143
     Daniel Wild

10   Housing affordability and red tape   160
     Ashton De Silva

11   Over-criminalisation as red tape   175
     Andrew Bushnell

12   Over-regulation in public services   189
     Aaron M. Lane

13   Red tape reduction: A new approach   208
     Darcy Allen

14   Regulation and technological change   222
     Darcy Allen and Chris Berg

References   235
Contributors   293

Introduction

DARCY ALLEN AND CHRIS BERG

Regulation is one of the main ways that governments affect our day-to-day lives. Regulation can be used to eliminate or mitigate market failures, prevent or compensate for externalities, protect consumers and smooth market exchange. In an ideal world, governments would intervene in the market when there was clear evidence that consumers and producers would be significantly worse off in the absence of that intervention.

But determining exactly when and how to intervene is difficult. Knowing what problems can be fixed through law and what problems should be solved by individuals isn't always clear. At the same time we know that political incentives can push governments into intervening more than the optimal. The result of these knowledge problems and perverse incentives is over-regulation and red tape: regulation which exceeds the minimum amount of intervention necessary to tackle an identified social or economic problem.

One estimate suggests that red tape costs the Australian economy an estimated $176 billion in foregone economic output each year. This book offers an overview of the scope and consequences of red tape and over-regulation in Australia, and is structured in three main parts: politics and economics, history, and case studies.

The first part looks at the politics and economics of red tape. Chris Berg provides an outline of the economic significance of regulation and over-regulation for a small, open economy such as Australia's. Regulation calcifies an economy, fixing business models and practices in place. Australia's trade and demographic challenges mean that red tape reduction should be focused on making it more resilient to future structural change.

In Chapter Two, David Kemp provides an overview of the political significance of red tape and its reduction. Focusing on the role of leadership, Kemp explores the relationship between populism and economic control, and argues that policymakers need to recapture responsibility for regulation from the administrative state.

Michael Potter looks at how over-regulation and red tape is manifesting itself in a malaise in Australia's economic performance. Weak wage growth and sagging business investment can be attributed to the growing tax and red tape burden. Potter also explores how misaligned tax incentives have driven red tape growth at the state level.

In Chapter Four, Sinclair Davidson provides a framework to understand the relationship between regulation and open markets. Citizens demand new regulation when they perceive the costs of allowing the market to control economic activity as too high. However these perceptions are not always correct, and suffer from a grass-is-always-greener fallacy. Davidson concludes that rather than increasing regulation, governments should seek to empower the civil litigation system as a more targeted method of satiating the fears of the market.

In her chapter, Georgina Downer explores the ideological and political dimensions of red tape and red tape reduction policies. Observing political demands for action in the face of crisis, Downer looks at the role risk culture, the precautionary principle, and new ideas like the 'social licence' play in regulatory growth.

The second part of the book covers the history and politics of red tape and regulation. Matthew Lesh's chapter argues that Australia's regulatory framework is fundamentally a Benthamite one, inspired by the utilitarian ideas of the nineteenth century philosopher Jeremy Bentham. Lesh argues that the Benthamite standard of 'the greatest happiness for the greatest number' systematically favours the growth of the regulatory state.

In Chapter Seven, William Coleman explores the Australian federation's bureaucratic impulse. As he argues, 'an aura of gratuitousness' surrounds the decision to bring the Australian colonies together into a nation in 1901. Coleman identifies the desire for a federal bureaucracy, and the deep integration of ideas of bureaucracy as part of Australia's colonial administration, as one of the main reasons for federation.

In Chapter Eight, Gregory Melleuish explores the relationship between Australian outback culture and the culture of the city, which was archetypally seen to be characterised by red tape. Melleuish focuses on the literary evidence for this relationship, and argues that as the frontier closed, so bureaucracy and control expanded.

The third part of the book offers some case studies of red tape and regulation in key sectors of the economy. Daniel Wild details the growth of Commonwealth environmental law and the effect this has on economic development and particularly major projects. Wild then looks at three particularly significant environmental controls: Section 487 of the *Environment Protection and Biodiversity Conservation Act 1999*, which gives privileges to environmental groups for litigation, the 'water trigger', which gives the Commonwealth environmental jurisdiction over large coal and coal seam gas projects, and state-based native vegetation restrictions.

In Chapter Ten, Ashton De Silva identifies connections between Australian housing prices and red tape in the planning system. Drawing on three focus groups conducted in 2016 with participants in land development, the housing industry and planning regulators, the chapter explores the roles that bureaucratic ignorance and ideological opposition to development play in increased housing costs.

In Chapter Eleven, Andrew Bushnell looks at how red tape manifests itself as over-criminalisation. As he argues, the use of criminal sanctions for regulatory offenses does little to support the health of the economy. Bushnell explores the normative basis for these criminal regulatory offenses and finds that this class of economic control is both inefficient and speaks to an underlying suspicion about the morality of market exchange.

Aaron Lane's chapter scrutinises the role red tape plays in the delivery of public services. While the bureaucracy creates regulation, it is also subject to regulation. Over-regulation in public services matters because we rely on the public sector to provide many central economic functions such as education and health. Lane looks at the education sector, finding increasing regulatory complexity.

In Chapter Thirteen, Darcy Allen presents a new approach to red tape reduction. Governments seeking to reduce red tape systematically need a metric on which they can measure their success or failure to do so. While previous red tape reduction programs have focused either on the calculated cost of over-regulation or other measures such as pages of regulation, a new method looks at the notion of 'regulatory restrictiveness clauses' to more carefully identify the effect of a new regulation. This approach has been successfully used in British Columbia and was for a short time used in Queensland.

Finally we conclude the book by exploring the relationship between technological change and the red tape burden. New technologies such as artificial intelligence, machine learning, and distributed ledgers are likely to drive structural changes in decades to come, not least in the way firms comply with regulation and how regulators enforce regulation. Regulatory technology, or 'RegTech', presents opportunities to reduce the regulatory burden on firms and make regulation more efficient and less harmful. On the other side, regulators need to come to terms with new technologies that may challenge existing business models or regulatory constructs, and we propose policymakers adopt a 'permissionless innovation' principle in response, ultimately allowing experimentation with new technologies by default unless direct harms can be demonstrated.

This book came from research papers presented at a workshop at RMIT University in June 2017 on regulation and red tape in Australia. The workshop was supported by the Cut Red Tape to Unleash Prosperity Project of the Institute of Public Affairs. We'd like to thank the IPA for its generous support. We'd also like to thank all the contributors to this volume, Peter Gregory for his editorial assistance, and Anthony Cappello at Connor Court Publishing for his enthusiasm for the project.

PART ONE

The economics and politics of red tape

CHAPTER ONE

Regulation and red tape in a small open economy

CHRIS BERG

Every new Commonwealth government elected in Australia
in the last two decades has done so declaring it would tackle Australia's regulatory and red tape burden. At the 1996 election John Howard promised to 'reduce the amount of regulation
and red tape enveloping small business by 50 per cent, during
the first three years of government'.[1] In opposition, Labor leader
Kevin Rudd stated that 'the quantity and complexity of business
regulation today is eating away at the entrepreneurial spirit of
Australian business', and created the Commonwealth government's first minister of deregulation.[2] The 2013 election saw the
Coalition under Tony Abbott promise to cut the red tape costs
on business and the community by $1 billion a year.[3] Promises

and policies to reduce red tape are also regular features of state politics. Each state and territory has its own form of regulatory reduction program, such as a Red Tape Commissioner (Victoria), a Red Tape Reduction Coordinator (Tasmania), ministers for Better Regulation (New South Wales) or a Better Regulation Taskforce (Queensland).

Despite this abundance of work at the political level, there is a large gap between the political attention paid to regulation, over-regulation, and red tape and the scholarly attention.

This chapter provides an overview of the significance of regulation and red tape for a country such as Australia. Australia is a 'small, open economy'.[4] Australia's macroeconomic performance has no significant effect on global macroeconomic performance. It is for the most part a global price-taker. Australia's external trade appears to be driven less by specialisation and more by classical comparative advantage such as its mineral and agricultural resources.[5] The implications of this are that Australia's industrial mix is highly concentrated. Australia has a unique mix of public policy settings that have developed in line with these economic characteristics.[6]

It is the argument of this chapter that for a small, open economy such as Australia's, red tape and regulation plays a significant role in the sources of, and constraints on, prosperity, and that red tape reduction and regulatory reform offer Australian governments substantial opportunity to strengthen the Australian economy.

Understanding the red tape burden

Red tape and regulation is a social institution by which governments seek to control the activities of the businesses, organisations and individuals in their jurisdiction. Since the reform era of the 1970s-1990s, regulation has displaced direct government ownership as the primary mechanism by which the government imposes control on economic activity. The emphasis that developed world governments now place on regulation has led to the situation being described as the 'regulatory state'—neither the nightwatchman state nor the mid-twentieth century welfare states.[7] There are nearly 500 entities, bodies, and administrative relationships at the Commonwealth level alone involved in the design or enforcement of the regulatory system.[8] While regulatory economics is a vibrant field of microeconomics, given the dominance of regulation in modern economic systems it is well past time to look at regulation from a macroeconomic perspective: the consequences of regulation and red tape as an institutional mode for growth, stability, and resilience.

Regulation imposes costs on an economy, but those costs are diffuse. The costs of regulation are borne largely on economic actors rather than the government, and these costs do not appear in the government budget. They include the direct costs of compliance—such as the time spent applying for licences, the paperburden—the opportunity costs of regulatory compliance—such as investments not made because of the compliance costs of regulation or prohibitions embodied by those regulations—and the costs of the burden on international competitiveness and growth. Estimating those costs is fraught. As the Competitive Enterprise Institute's Clyde Wayne Crews writes, 'The difficulty of regulatory cost measurement is inherent, stemming from basic subjectivity and the slipperiness of measuring costs and the more profound reality that no "objectively identifiable magnitudes" are available to the third-

party regulator or analyst'.[9] Nevertheless, as Crews notes, the
fact that it is hard to estimate regulatory costs does not mean
the task should be abandoned—particularly given the deep
significance of regulatory intervention in the economy. The
Australian government estimates that the direct compliance
burden of Commonwealth government regulation on
businesses and individuals is approximately $65 billion
per year.[10] This estimate was arrived at through a non-
comprehensive stocktake by government departments of the
estimated compliance costs of individual regulations. This
'bottom-up' approach has a number of shortcomings. First,
the estimates of costs are highly subjective, highly dependent
on the judgement of the bureaucrats that administer them.[11]
Second, those bureaucrats are subject to incentives that might
drive them to underestimate the costs of regulation relative
to the benefits.

Other approaches have led to significantly higher
estimated red tape and regulatory costs. Deloitte has
estimated the regulatory burden imposed by all levels of
government—Commonwealth, state, and local—comes to
$94 billion a year.[12] Using a 'top-down' method developed by
W. Mark Crain and Nicole V. Crain, Mikayla Novak finds
an Australian regulatory burden of $176 billion a year in lost
economic output—approximately 11 per cent of GDP.[13]

Both the concepts of regulation and red tape are rarely
defined. Regulation is 'the intentional restriction of a
subject's choice of activity, by an entity not directly party to
or involved in that activity'.[14] Here we use regulation to refer
to regulation by state actors. The definition is more expansive
than statutory or black-letter regulation however. Much
of the regulatory burden in Australia is imposed through

'grey-letter law' or 'quasi-regulation', developed at arms length by state agencies and industry and administered by a combination of both.[15] While often described as 'voluntary' or 'self-imposed', the implied state power behind these controls and rules mean they should be treated as regulation for analytical purposes.

In the new comparative institutional economics, regulation exists on a continuum of institutional choices that represent a balance between dictatorship costs and disorder costs.[16] A market ordering minimises dictatorship costs while risking high disorder costs while a state ordering— such as the nationalisation of the means of production— minimises disorder costs while risking high dictatorship costs. Regulation is an approach to social control that exists between these two extremes on the institutional possibilities frontier, attempting to strike a balance between disorder and dictatorship costs. The institutional possibilities frontier framework has been applied to a wide variety of public policy questions, including productivity, innovation, free speech, environmental and prudential regulation, and governance.[17]

The comparative institutional economics approach is useful for characterising broad regimes of social control. However, each point—that is, each institution—on the institutional possibilities frontier can be subject to a more fine-grained approach. In mainstream welfare economics, the state imposes regulation in order to correct market failures and for other social goals.[18] But regulation can be imposed in a more or less efficient manner. The term red tape attempts to capture the distinction between efficient social control and inefficient social control. While 'red tape' is pejorative, its political importance means that many analyses of red tape use it synonymously with regulation.[19] However we need a more analytically useful conception of red tape. Red tape consists of regulation that is imposed where an increase in dictatorship costs results in no decrease in disorder costs. Red tape under this approach is neutral to the purpose of social control. More formally, red tape is the 'rules, regulations and procedures that require compliance but do not meet the organization's functional objective for the rule'.[20]

The next sections of this chapter describe Australia as a small open economy. It then goes on to present Australia's challenging current economic position. The chapter provides an overview of the institutional economics of regulation, and applies those economic principles to regulation in Australia. In conclusion, the chapter offers some thoughts on a red tape and regulatory reduction agenda.

Trade openness

Australia's reputation and view of itself as a highly open, trade-exposed economy is not evident in one of the most common measures of trade openness. The OECD measures trade openness as a sum of the imports and exports of goods and services against national gross domestic product. On this measure, Australia is the third least trade exposed nation in the OECD, just behind New Zealand—another apparently trade exposed nation for whom imports and exports account for a surprisingly small share of gross domestic product. Nevertheless, what the OECD is measuring is less a measurement of 'openness' as it is 'exposure' to trade. This is a surprising finding, particularly given the widespread perception that Australia has low formal barriers to trade. The effective rate of assistance—that is, a calculation of the effect of tariffs, non-tariff barriers and subsidies—applied to Australian manufacturing has declined from 35 per cent in 1970-71 to around 4 per cent. Likewise, the effective rate of assistance to the agricultural sector has fallen from 25 per cent in 1970-71 to around 2.5 per cent.[21] Nevertheless, the Heritage 2017 Index of Economic Freedom only ranks Australia's openness to trade as the 48th highest in the world. Australia's average tariff rate on all products is 1.8 per cent—higher than the uniform European Union tariff of 1.02 per cent.

As Simon Guttmann and Anthony Richards show, when matched to a gravity model of international trade, Australia's involvement in foreign trade is roughly what we would expect from a country with its economic and institutional characteristics.[22] Participation in and reliance on trade is predominately explained by a country's population and geographic location. Smaller countries tend to be more reliant on trade as their lower populations offer fewer opportunities for domestic production and sales (the implications of Australia's population will be discussed in the next section). Australia's geographic location has led to higher transport costs than many of its developed world competitors. While transport costs decline over time, as Geoffrey Blainey's *Tyranny of Distance* famously demonstrated, the economic implications of that decline are ambiguous.[23] In a world with few tariff barriers and cheap communications—which reduces the coordination costs of long distance trade—transport costs have assumed a more significant role in the allocation of trade than was the case in the past.[24]

Australia's relatively low trade openness/exposure is significant for a number of reasons. The first is the relative attention policymakers should place on expanding

Australia's trade integration. The empirical evidence for a causal relationship between free trade and economic growth is mixed but the preponderance of the evidence suggests a positive relationship.[25] Productivity and growth enhancing reform would focus in part on transport costs, ensuring that these costs are no higher than Australia's geographic position demands. Aaron Lane and I have looked at the heavy regulatory barriers placed on Australian coastal shipping by cabotage and industrial relations restrictions.[26] Restrictions on foreign investment in culturally sensitive transport sectors—such as Qantas' status as a 'national carrier'—also have a secondary effect of reducing the efficiency of transport services.[27]

The second reason for the significance of geography is the implications of the evolution of the world economy for Australia's domestic economy. As Guttmann and Richards point out, Australia is far from its traditional trading partners in the United States and Europe but close to the middle income and rapidly growing economies of southern and south-east Asia.[28] The Gillard government's *Australia in the Asian Century* white paper identified the increasing engagement between Australia and Asia in the next century.[29] Australia's economic location will improve as those countries grow in importance in the global economy, increasing Australia's trade openness and the importance of trade to domestic markets. This integration will likely place heavy pressure on firms and patterns of trade and production that have been relatively unaffected by Australia's traditional trading patterns.

Population, prosperity and demography

Australia's trade exposure—partly a function of its geographic characteristics—should be seen in the context of two other features: its middle ranked population and its high level of economic development. With its population of 24 million people, Australia ranks around fiftieth in terms of size, occupying a position near Cameroon, Madagascar, South Korea and Romania. It is smaller than all but two of its top ten trading partners (Singapore and New Zealand). China, Australia's number one trading partner, is 57 times Australia's size. The United States is 13 times and Japan is more than five times Australia's size respectively.

While Australia is middle ranked for size, it is in the upper echelons of economic development. It is consistently in the top ten countries of GDP per capita, among city-states like Singapore and Luxembourg, resource rich countries like Qatar and Norway, and global powers like the United States. Despite its modest population this means Australia has an outsized position in the global economy, ranking in the global top twenty for absolute GDP. The consequence of this wealth is a high ranking along other measures of development.

GDP is a useful but partial indicator of economic and social achievement.[30] All measures of development have to be weighted according to values individuals place upon them. For example, not all people equally weight equality or political participation against health and education. The OECD has developed a 'Better Life Index' website which allows users to adjust the relative importance according to their subjective views.[31] On almost all possible adjustments of the OECD's approach, Australia is in the top ranks of the OECD, which is itself a narrow set of the more highly developed economies.

This rosy picture should not obscure Australia's demographic challenges. As with all developed economies, Australia has an aging population. In 1975 there were 7.3 people between the ages of 15 and 64 for every person who was 65 years or older. By the mid-twenty-first century, this will have declined to just 2.7 people. Average life expectancy is expected to grow from 91.5 years for men and 93.6 years for women today to 95.1 years for men and 96.6 years for women by 2054-55.[32] Australia's fertility rate has remained below 2.1 babies per woman since 1976, meaning that Australia's fertility has been below replacement rate for forty years. Net migration to Australia has ensured that population growth has remained positive. As I have explored with Jason Potts in a previous essay, the long run economic consequences of population stagnation or decline are both significant and concerning.[33] An aging population is potentially a less dynamic and entrepreneurial population, and the top-heavy burden of older workers or pensioners will put substantial pressure on Australia's social security system.

Economic challenges

Australia has enjoyed the longest economic expansion in historical record—recording 104 quarters without a recession in the second quarter of 2017. This has led to a vaguely Panglossian sense that sustained economic growth is a reward for Australian policy genius. It is just as likely, however, that the combination of economic characteristics identified above have given Australia particular historical and geographic advantages in the period in which this was achieved. For example, Griffith University's Tony Makin has convincingly demonstrated that the fact that Australia did not experience a technical recession during the Global Financial Crisis in 2008-09 was as likely due to the combination of low interest rates, exchange rate depreciation, the labour market framework that prevailed at the time of the crisis, and foreign demand, particularly from China.[34] This contrasts with the popular and political view that it was the Rudd government's fiscal stimulus which accounts for Australia's success during the crisis.

If Australia's success is specific, particular and not driven by any innate Australian propensity for successful management, the country is more economically vulnerable than that record might make it appear. In this context, it is important to recognise a number of signs of weakness in the Australian economy that might well be indicators of that vulnerability. First, Australia's fiscal settings are extremely poor. Since the stimulus package of 2009, Australia has run a persistent deficit to cover recurrent expenditure.[35] Despite the declared intentions of a series of governments to return the budget to surplus, the deficit shows every sign of remaining fixed into the future. Sustained budget deficits have a corrupting influence on the fiscal responsibility of democratic governments, as James Buchanan and Richard Wagner have shown, particularly where an institutional norm of returning to surplus is not strong.[36] The reduced political attention paid to that deficit in recent years indicates a steady weakening of that norm.

Coupled with poor fiscal settings, the Australian economy is exhibiting a number of signs of weakness. Non-mining investment has failed to take up the slack after the end of the mining boom. As a consequence, business investment is currently at just 12.2 per cent of GDP, the lowest it has been since the recession of the early 1990s.[37] Non-mining investment is the lowest it has been for fifty years.[38] Other indicators suggest a declining dynamism in the economy. For all the significance of entrepreneurship to economic growth, it can only be measured by proxy. One such measure is the rate of business start-ups and closures (entrepreneurial activity is likely to be indicated by business collapse and creation). Australia's business entry rate has declined from 17.4 per cent in 2003-04 to 13.4 per cent in 2014-15, despite a substantial increase in both population and GDP.[39] The International Monetary Fund has described Australia as suffering from the 'new [global] mediocre', which it attributes to the risks of weak domestic consumption, housing market vulnerabilities, and the risks of global protectionism and the slowdown in Australia's trading partners.[40] These latter two underline Australia's exposure to global economic challenges and emphasise the need to tailor Australian policy to that condition.

The economics of red tape and regulation

The costs of regulation and red tape can be quantified, as discussed above, but regulation and red tape has important influences on the shape and nature of the economic system. Traditional neoclassical economics sees a role for regulation as resolving market failure in a way that seeks to imitate the results of a perfectly or reasonably competitive market. In such a conception, competitive markets approach equilibrium where supply and demand is balanced, subject to the judicious intervention of state regulation. By contrast, evolutionary and institutional economists emphasise the dynamic nature of an economic system. Following Joseph Schumpeter and Kenneth Boulding, in this conception, markets are a process rather than a place in which exchange occurs.[41] Through experimentation and failure, economic actors create new knowledge that results in economic growth. Schumpeter's 'creative destruction' is only the most visible result of that knowledge and wealth creation.

An evolutionary and institutional approach emphasises different effects of regulation and red tape than the straightforward market failure approach. Taking the neoclassical assumptions of rationality and maximisation as given, from the 1960s onwards the public choice school of economics applied the economic analysis of incentives to political markets. By treating political actors, bureaucrats, and special interest groups as rational agents seeking to maximise their own welfare—as traditional analysis did with economic actors—the conclusions these analyses came to were strikingly different from that of the traditional school. Political decision making is highly susceptible to capture by special interest groups.[42] Firms seek regulation in order to suppress competition.[43] Bureaucracies tend towards self-interest rather than public interest.[44] It is hard to align the incentives of political representatives with those who they claim to represent.[45] Apart from bringing a much more cynical approach to government intervention in the economy—including, but not limited to, regulation and red tape—the lesson of the public choice school emphasised the division between the principles under which regulation should be imposed in welfare economics and the practices by which regulation actually was imposed.

Under this framework, regulation limits competitive pressure in the economy with the subsequent effect of lowering living standards. Regulatory burdens tend to be supported by large economic actors, for whom regulatory compliance is relatively less costly than new entrants. For this reason, firms find it profitable to invest in lobbying politicians and bureaucrats. Not all entrepreneurial activity is productive—when funneled by the institutional environment into rent-seeking and political behaviour it can be unproductive.[46] One estimate of the economic return on lobbying in the United States during the passage of the American Jobs Creation Act of 2004 found that for every $1 invested, firms received a return of $220.[47] Other studies have consistently found that political engagement was translated into better operating performance.[48] The more complex the regulatory web, the more opportunities there are for rent seeking behaviour.

A more recent advance in the study of economic processes has been the downgrade of the assumptions of rationality and maximisation for an emphasis on learning and knowledge. The implications of this new approach are significant for the study of the effects of regulation. Firms need to constantly adjust to factors including changes in the price of inputs, competitor behaviour, consumer tastes and preferences, technological shifts, and general macroeconomic factors such as inflation and interest rates—of which they have negligible influence over. Successful firms display adaptive behaviour to these changes. Regulation and red tape place legal constraints on that adaptation. A telling and pressing example is a country's industrial relations framework. Labour markets have recognised imperfections such as high search costs, asymmetrical information between employers and employees and downward wage rigidity.[49] These features make the redeployment of labour assets—that is, the movement of workers from one job to another—slower and less efficient than in a hypothetical market for widgets. On top of these 'natural' features of the labour market, the industrial relations framework can impose further rigidities. Regulation that makes it more expensive to hire and fire workers, that prevents wages from reaching an equilibrium during an economic downturn, and that impose additional costs on employment slow or prevent the necessary adaptive behaviour to external market changes. John

Haltiwanger, Stefano Scarpetta and Helena Schweiger find that 'stringent labor market regulations may have an important adverse impact on allocative efficiency and in turn productivity levels and growth'.[50] Another prominent example of this effect can be seen in occupational licensing—which makes it hard for workers to move into more profitable industries. However, this is an effect which applies to all regulatory restrictions. Regulation that prevents business activities that would have otherwise been pursued, or red tape which imposes inefficient burdens on otherwise lawful business activities presents a limitation to the adaptive capacity of firms.

In an important study, Christian Bjørnskov shows the macroeconomic effects of a high regulatory burden on this adaptive process.[51] Looking at 212 economic crises in 175 countries between 1993 and 2010 against the Heritage Foundation's Index of Economic Freedom, Bjørnskov finds that while economic freedom does not prevent economic crises from occurring, economic freedom has a positive effect on the recovery of countries from those crises. The ability of firms to redeploy and reorientate in the context of macroeconomic changes facilitates a faster recovery from an economic crisis.

Australia's red tape and regulation problem
These macro-level effects of regulation are most problematic in times of economic crisis: when there are clear global downturns that effect country-wide aggregate economic data which can be measured against aggregations like the Index of Economic Freedom. The dynamics in question are, however, contextual and particular. As Friedrich Hayek wrote, while statistical aggregates are the dominant tool of economic analysis, we must

not 'forget about the constant small changes which make up the whole economic picture'.[52] Regulatory burdens vary significantly between industries, and affect firms and workers in specific and individual ways. Not all external shocks are macroeconomic. For an individual employee, an external shock might be a death in the family that requires a change in employment or industry. For a firm, that external shock might be the creation of a new competitor, process or change in input prices. The effect of red tape and the regulatory burden is experienced at the individual and firm level first and foremost.

There is abundant reason to believe that these micro-level burdens are being felt in Australia. A survey conducted by the Australian Chamber of Commerce and Industry of 709 of its members found that 74 per cent of respondents believed government regulatory requirements had either a 'moderate negative impact' or a 'significant negative impact' on their business. Forty-seven per cent of respondents reported that regulation had prevented them from making changes to grow their business, and 68 per cent believed that their industry was either 'somewhat over-regulated' or 'very over-regulated'.[53] National Australia Bank research has found that future business growth needs to be supported by 'less red tape, less regulation and a simpler taxation system'.[54] Research by Sensis concluded that small and medium businesses were 'worried about excessive bureaucracy and red tape'.[55] Of course, most developed countries suffer from a heavy regulatory burden. One estimate finds that the regulatory burden on American business comes to $1.8 trillion.[56] This is around 9 per cent of United States' GDP and is therefore in the same ballpark as the Australian estimate by Mikayla Novak. It is the argument of this chapter however that Australia's characteristics should make red tape a more significant problem and worth political focus. Australia has a small population, policy settings which encourage foreign trade, high living standards but (potential) demographic stagnation. It has a relatively open economy that exposes firms and individuals to changes in consumer preferences and technology. It is a global price taker: highly exposed to global macroeconomic conditions. Finally, it has a highly concentrated economy, which has come to be structured around a small number of world-competitive sectors.

While there are a number of (imperfect) ways to measure economic diversification, the most widely accepted is export concentration.[57] This measure seeks to proxy the concentration of a domestic economy by the mixture of goods exported. In this index, the closer a country is to one the more concentrated its exports are. Australia has significantly more concentrated exports than the average among developed economies. The mining boom has increased that concentration further, although since the peak of the boom that concentration has begun to ease off.

Concentration is significant because, in concert with Australia's other characteristics, it suggests that Australia is vulnerable to external shocks that might harm key sectors. The easing off of the mining boom has been one such shock. A further global economic downturn would be another such shock—without the support of Chinese demand for mineral resources, or the shock absorbers of a budget in surplus, or a flexible industrial relations framework, Australia's relative prosperity would be at risk. Regulation and red tape increases this vulnerability. A dynamic economy needs to reallocate capital and labour to its highest value use in response to external changes. Regulation and red tape slows that process.

Conclusion

This chapter has only been able to touch lightly on the economic, political, and social consequences of the regulatory state. The reforms to the structure of government that have accompanied the imposition of regulation as the primary mode of social control have separated regulators from the chain of democratic control and reduced political accountability.[58] In most cases this has been a deliberate decision to remove regulation from the control of politicians but the consequences have been to create a separate institutional structure whose democratic legitimacy is questionable and—in its most extreme forms, such as the European Union—has created a technocratic class that are now the target of a populist backlash. The burden of red tape and regulation is a common theme among voters attracted to populist or alternative parties. An Essential Poll taken in February 2017 found a striking difference between major party (Labor, Liberal/National and Green) voters and those who were planning to vote 'other' on the question of whether 'Australia has too much or not enough Government regulation'. While only 33 per cent of Labor voters, 31 per cent of Liberal/National voters and 20 per cent of Greens voters answered 'too much regulation', 52 per cent of 'other' voters answered similarly.[59]

The menu of approaches to red tape and regulatory reduction is substantial. The regulatory problem can be divided into a 'stock' and a 'flow' approaches: regulatory reduction needs to tackle both the existing stock of regulation and reduce the flow of new regulation. For the former, reduction has been tackled with policies such as systematic audits of the stock of regulation, regulatory reform programs focusing on individual industries or economic problems, and targets such as the Abbott government's promise to reduce the compliance burden of regulation by

$1 billion a year. Policies seeking to reduce the flow of new regulation include institutional requirements such as enhanced scrutiny of the impact of new regulations. Other approaches, such as the 'one-in, n-out' that have been introduced in many jurisdictions around the world, attempt to tackle both stock and flow simultaneously. Many of these policies are highly sensitive to the measurement of regulatory cost and quantity.

More generally, if scholars of the 'regulatory state' are correct, the effect of policy initiatives such as these will be limited in the absence of a cultural change among policymakers. Observing the weaknesses and costs of Australia's current regulatory regime, Sinclair Davidson has proposed that Australian policymakers adjust their approach to social control of economic activity along the institutional possibility frontier. Rather than favouring regulation as the 'default' option in response to demands for increased control, Davidson argues that a:

> system of private enforcement of public rules would substantially reduce the amount of make-work regulation that currently burdens Australian business. Regulatory action that was initiated by actual individuals who had actually experienced some harm and who had standing to bring an action would see regulation evolving is such a way to enhance economic efficiency.[60]

There is still some low hanging fruit available for economic reform in Australia. But the primary focus of future Australian governments should be on red tape and regulatory reduction, eliminating those unnecessary and excessive rules which prevent businesses, individuals and entrepreneurs from adjusting to macro and microeconomic changes.

CHAPTER TWO

The big picture

DAVID KEMP

Political leadership will fail unless it can make the case for its policies. As governments inexorably grow, the case for limited government, and hence for the importance of individual freedom to achieving the good society, seems today to be failing by default.

It was Robert Menzies, the great advocate of liberal thought in our politics, who said that:

> The art of politics is to convey ideas to others, if possible, to persuade a majority to agree, to create or encourage a public opinion so soundly based that it endures, and is not blown aside by chance winds; *to persuade people to take long-range views.*[1]

Understanding regulation—its sources and its consequences—lies at the very heart of the debate about the desirable role of government, for it is the basic tool of government. Governments exist to regulate the social world. Without regulation governments can neither tax nor spend. The nature of regulation—its capacities, characteristics and limitations—tells us much that we need to know about what government can and cannot do. There is no activity of government with respect to which it is more important to take long range views, and to persuade people of their value, than regulation, including law-making.

The purpose of this chapter is to attempt to highlight some important elements of such a case that seem to be absent today from much of the public and parliamentary debate. Democratic government ensures that regulation is accepted by the largest possible proportion of the population, but does not guarantee that that regulation is optimal for the public interest.[2] In this chapter I consider some lessons about the nature of regulation and its impacts from history and from theory, and conclude with some observations about how we can define good government and how we might improve government's success rate.

The starting point is the recognition that government rule-making is a blunt tool that can affect the functioning of the social order in profound ways. Successful regulation achieves its objectives and, hopefully, helps people towards better lives. Regulatory failure creates disorder and damages lives. It can undermine respect for the law, for political parties and even democracy itself. Government leaders need to know this and be able to explain it.

Though the growth of government is often indicated by the proportion of government spending to GDP or by the number of people employed by government, or by the number of politicians and agencies, perhaps the most important dimension of 'big' government is the enormous expansion of government's attempts to regulate the social world. The case for and against big government depends heavily on how we evaluate the impact of regulation on the working of the economy, social institutions, the environment and on politics itself.

There are sound practical and theoretical reasons for thinking that much of the measured decline in recent times in people's satisfaction with democracy, and in trust in government, has been a response to the policy failures and unintended consequences of unwise regulation, which disrupts the working of markets and communities and distorts the incentives on which individuals take decisions.[3] Government failure, loss of confidence in the major parties, and ineffective, or damaging, regulation are intimately linked. One of the biggest dangers to democracy today is the overreach of its governments and the absence of a satisfactory framework within which this overreach may be analysed.

As the ambitions of those who control government grow, the capacity of our elected politicians to understand, or even see, what government is doing, and to hold government servants and agencies accountable, or to be adequately accountable themselves, is necessarily eroded. As government expands the use of central authority, the accountability problem becomes massive, and the resentment of citizens in the face of policy failure grows.

Populism or popular revolts?

Much attention is being given currently to so-called 'populist' revolts within the democracies, with 'populism' commonly interpreted as voting support for illiberal or authoritarian policies motivated by xenophobia and policy ignorance. But the extent to which the electoral revolts in the cases of Brexit or Trump have been 'populist' rather than more broadly motivated 'people's revolts' is an open question. In Britain and America voters rejected the Conservative/Labor and Republican/Democrat leadership in favour of Brexit or Trump/Sanders by substantial majorities, suggesting a broad distrust of established parties. Macron's victory in France, in particular, suggests that 'popular revolt' may be a better characterization than 'populist revolt', for the populist leader in France was Le Pen. A feature of Macron's platform was reducing regulation (particularly of the French labour market). Australian micro-parties also seem motivated by a broad anti-establishment feeling overlaying populist messages.

But if anti-establishment attitudes are behind these electoral revolts, what might be the nature of the policy or other failures of the best-educated political class in history that are alienating voters? It seems evident that leaders advocating more regulatory policies have been very much in the frame. In particular, how far might their failures be connected to the growing difficulty of achieving policy success in the ambitious regulatory states that the West now seeks to operate?

Democratic policy making is a matter of trial and error, and finding the optimal mix of regulation and activity unregulated by government has been the main item on the agenda of democracies for generations. Significant public debates about how far big government is compatible with democracy, prosperity and social harmony have been held before—in the nineteenth century, and during the socialist push of the 1940s. The issue is re-emerging again.

Historic debates

The debate about regulation is—at its core, and rightly— the time-honoured debate about freedom and control: the extent to which the good society and the pursuit of happiness are better achieved when people are generally free to pursue their own missions in life or whether the good society can be brought forward by extending government regulation of behaviour.

This debate has been raging since the Enlightenment of the late eighteenth century, but the classic formulae attempting to define the appropriate balance between freedom and control are not proving strong enough to resolve current controversies about whether to regulate or not. The evolution of our language and the complex issues of a modern society mean that old formulae, while still providing useful frameworks, need to be interpreted in light of new meanings and the experience of a complex and technological world. Key terms used in such formulae such as 'harm', 'oppression' or 'justice' are today more often the starting points of debate than its resolution.

Adam Smith, for example, in 1776 defined the role of government (and hence its desirable regulatory scope) as protecting citizens from invasion by other states, preventing citizens oppressing each other, providing justice, and doing things of public benefit that individual citizens for lack of incentive would not undertake.[4] There is much that remains profoundly helpful about such a framework, but it leaves considerable room for debate if 'oppression' is widely defined to include psychological harm or undue exposure to risk or discrimination as it is by many today, and if 'justice' is extended to include not only equal procedural justice (as through the courts), but distributive or social justice.

Again, John Stuart Mill in 1859 suggested a test of 'harm to others' to define when the state was justified in interfering with individual liberty, but like 'oppression', 'harm' is a concept that can be endlessly debated.[5] Again, Mill's proposition that the state is never justified in interfering with a person simply for that person's own good does not have quite the same clarity in an age when we are much more conscious of the importance of the social environment and the social sources of identity, and the impact of individual characteristics on others, though the concept of personal responsibility as a goal of policy, as I will argue, remains vital to successful policy outcomes.

Defining the optimal balance between regulation and freedom cannot therefore depend on finding a verbal formulation that adequately and unambiguously defines the role of government. But nor is it the case that the only alternative is the need to mount unique arguments in relation to each individual instance of proposed regulation, for the really important arguments have a general character, and the specific arguments will turn out in most cases to be simply applications of the general case. These are arguments from experience and from theory.

Ensuring that the option of freedom is weighed adequately in the balance depends largely on an understanding of the benefits for individual people and for society as a whole that arise from the empowerment of individual purposes under the rule of law, based on the recognition that these generally (but not always) lead to more positive outcomes. Negatively the case for freedom relies on an understanding of the risks, and indeed of the individual and social damage that arise from inappropriate regulation. Government education departments that use their authority to impose special interest curricular without consulting parents and community values invite resistance. One of the features of good regulation is that it empowers the individual within a framework of rules that provides adequate certainty and protects the individual against the uncertainty that arises from the exercise of arbitrary discretion by partisan and interested parties. It is in this sense that we speak of the importance of the rule of law and its supporting interpretative institution—an independent judiciary.

The broadest possible argument for freedom is that it is the foundation for the good society, and as Menzies argued in the Australian context, of civilization itself.[6] The good society we can define as that in which people can have the greatest chance of achieving happiness or fulfillment for themselves. Equal rights to pursue happiness can be considered the only truly egalitarian goal, for regulation in practice and in theory very often ends up empowering the few over the many. Communism argued that the happiness of all would be achieved if all were committed to the same goals, if they had the same resources, and gave up their individuality, and that the state in the economic sphere should organize them to be so, replacing prices and markets with bureaucratic decisions imposed by authority on what should be produced. The result was concentrated power in a few. The reality has proved to be that individuals achieve happiness in different ways and that society and economies can barely function without allowing people to act on the information they alone possess about their own values and the lessons they have derived from their individual experience.

Underpinning this reasoning is the recognition that a society in which people have the capacity to live peacefully and in freedom is an orderly society governed by custom, and habit, and based on trusting social relationships of affection, reciprocity and peaceful exchange. It is a world of mutual adjustment dominated by the process of people making decisions influenced by their desire for validation from their fellows.[7] It is a world certainly not free from rules, but rules which are generally unwritten norms, conventions and moral injunctions. It is in short the peaceful natural order pictured by the philosopher John Locke,[8] and not the 'war of all against all' of Thomas Hobbes[9] and his seeming disciple the Human Rights Commissioner Tim Soutphommasane,[10] which sees order only being achieved through the imposition of central authority. Perhaps one of the best examples of how such a spontaneous social order has come into existence and functioned in historical times is the emergence of the moral and peaceful society of Australia as the children of convicts and immigrants from depressed Britain, in conditions of unequalled economic, social and political freedom, set out to build decent lives for themselves in mid-nineteenth century Australia.[11]

The lessons of history

It is against the benefits of economic and social freedom that we are able to test what have been the costs of regulation that inhibits that freedom. Our own historical experience as a nation provides us with some guidance on this point, and our national history is but a subset of a global history whose lessons were unambiguously taught with enormous human cost during the twentieth century when wars were fought to open markets closed by self-defeating protectionist regulation, and communist utopias crashed under ideological attempts to insist that society operate without the information provided voluntarily by markets, prices, individuality and choice.

The regulatory initiatives of nineteenth century governments in Australia were largely aimed at finding an appropriate balance between freedom and control, with a bias towards freedom. They embraced the establishment of the economic framework for private enterprise, especially through partnerships and limited liability companies, the legalization of voluntary trade unionism, factory, mining and sweated labour acts to protect workers from exploitation by employers; public health, banking, primary education equally for boys and girls, land settlement, and of course legislation to do with voting rights and the structure of government including local government.

By 1890 Australians were per capita the wealthiest people in the world. The generalization can be made that the regulation of the era had generally sought to empower and protect while letting people get on with their own lives. The cause of equal rights for women made steady progress. The great exception was the treatment of Indigenous people, whose right to happiness was discounted, who were discriminated against and often violently attacked, and ultimately confined by paternalistic laws. The squatters, despite their appeal to the deep belief in private property of the era, failed to gain title to the vast tracts of land on which they grazed their herds and flocks, as liberally and democratically minded governments gave priority to the need to establish a regulatory framework that would allow the development of an agricultural society and rural towns. Flawed for reasons outlined below, such regulation nevertheless achieved its general purpose.

Even in such a liberal era, the power of selfish self-interest was loud. Manufacturers sought protection from competition and unions argued for compulsory membership. By the 1890s, with the aim of abolishing industrial conflict, compulsory intervention of courts into the workplace, a privileged place for unions (over individual workers) before the courts, and race-based immigration policies were being set in place. Though public interest arguments were heard and often believed for each of these regulatory interventions, the enactment of such policies pushed employers and unions apart, led to discrimination against individual workers, damaged the Australian workplace and fed class war. The export capacity of Australian manufacturing was undermined through rising costs and protectionism's built-in incentive to inefficiency, while a powerful parochialism and isolationism began to infuse Australian nationalism.

The regulation attendant on industry protection, as the Brigden Inquiry pointed out in the 1920s, proved impossible to contain and it spread inexorably throughout the economy. The constantly extending protectionism of the Tariff Board provided a classic demonstration of how ambiguous rules could be interpreted by a tribunal whose discretion was barely guided by vague objectives.[12] Australia's level of industry protection was second only to that of the United States, and was accompanied by licensing of entry to some rural industries, organised marketing, and what was claimed to be the largest government enterprise sector outside the Soviet Union.[13]

Eventually, the economy was so hamstrung by regulation that even the Bruce-Page government committed to growth could scarcely produce any. When the Depression came

Australia suffered some of the highest unemployment in the world. As other countries followed down the same disastrous path, world wide protectionism led to a collapse in world trade, and was a contributing factor to the onset of the Second World War. The world learned the bitter lesson that special interest regulation of economic life could fatally damage prosperity and security. As a result, during the post-war years, freedom of trade began to resume, and the scope of the discretionary authority of tariff, industry and arbitration tribunals and boards was wound back. Not until the 1980s and 1990s was the privatization of large government monopolies substantially achieved.

In economic life the need for a significant level of freedom, competition and deregulation for enterprise and trade was thus powerfully demonstrated, and was understood to have been learned by both sides of Australian politics. After two decades of policies withdrawing decades of unwise economic regulation, Australia by 2000 had become what some referred to as 'the miracle economy of the Western world'. In 2008 Australia was ranked first of all developed countries (excepting the city states of Singapore and Hong Kong) on the Heritage Foundation's *Index of Economic Freedom*. In 2017 it had slipped to third.[14]

The virtues of economic freedom, however, are matched by the virtues of social freedom. If people have the opportunity to determine their life's missions and pursue their enterprises— whether economic, religious, philosophical, artistic—they are much more likely to be motivated and purposeful, and to achieve a greater level of happiness than would be possible if their goals are frustrated or prohibited. If the state does not prohibit to people the use of economic mechanisms such as markets and prices to aggregate their values and express their choices, and does not deprive them of the right to reward for their efforts, they will be motivated and able to use their experience and preferences to achieve what they want more effectively than through the discretionary decisions of officials.

The limits of authority and rules

The theoretical frameworks that allow us to understand such a history are derived from the disciplines of economics and political science, and it is through such frameworks that public interest policies empowering individual preferences can begin to be adequately defined.

The principal mechanism of social coordination that allows complex economies to achieve order is freedom of exchange through markets and prices that reflect the marginal values of people. The optimal role of regulation here is to provide a framework of just rules, not to replace this mechanism. Two hundred years of economic theorising and failed policy experiments have helped policymakers to broadly understand this. The other side of this picture, which is less widely understood, concerns the capacities and limitations of the principal mechanism underlying regulation, which is the authority relationship. Yet the last century, going back at least to the 1920s, and the work of Max Weber, has led to some fundamentally important understandings of the nature of authority that are essential to a more comprehensive assessment of how government and other organisations function.[15]

This body of social theory helps us to understand not only why some economic regulation can produce large-scale destruction, but why every attempt to engineer society by regulation has the potential to be undermined by side-effects outweighing any benefits that the regulation may achieve. In coming to conclusions about the appropriate role for government in particular we need to consider:

- the nature of authority as a mechanism of social control;
- the inherent characteristics of rules as exercises of authority; and
- the nature of political processes in general and of democratic processes in particular as they impact on policy-making and seek to guide government in the exercise of its authority.

While there are always those who seem to assume that government regulation is mostly effective in achieving good social outcomes, and those who wish to make their own mere opinions rules of conduct for others,[16] there are in fact severe limitations to the capacity of government authority—to such an extent that the American political economist Charles Lindblom in the 1970s summed up the problem of government policy making in today's complex world as 'small brain, big problems'.[17] Lindblom provided a telling metaphor that government was 'all thumbs, no fingers'. It could pass laws and move big quanta of money around and hand out money with ease, it could build pyramids and space rockets (not cheaply), but could not effectively regulate to achieve the detailed outcomes which might satisfy the needs and values of individual citizens or indeed the society as a whole. He linked this problem to the fundamental character of government, and the weaknesses of the instruments available to it. Its limitations demand a new perspective on what the role of the state should be.

Briefly, the identified limitations of authority and rules to achieve intended social outcomes include the following:

- Authority to be effective relies heavily on the identification with its perceived values of those who accept it. As Chester Barnard pointed out long ago, authority ultimately rests with those subject to it. Authority ceases to be legitimate in the eyes of citizens, indeed ceases to operate within a certain scope, when its exercise conflicts with their deeply held values, even in a democracy. One of the greatest policy failures illustrating this limitation of government was the legal prohibition of alcohol in America during the 1920s. It was an example of authority extended far beyond its legitimate scope, with the outcomes being crime and disrespect for the law on a massive scale. The collapse of the Soviet bloc 1989-90 shows that the attempt to assume authority of limitless scope to mould behaviour and thought cannot succeed for this reason.

- A related limitation of government authority—arising from the variety of the values of citizens and their pressure groups—is the difficulty of establishing clear objectives for policy, because the political reasons for accepting policy are diverse. As a consequence, attempts by those using authority to clarify objectives in major policy areas tends to result in conflict and even policy paralysis.[18] The propensity of governments to leave policy objectives unclear is in part a response to this fundamental feature of authority. It is obvious today that a central factor in explaining why Australia has some of the most expensive housing and energy in the world has been the central government's inability so far to align multiple conflicting objectives in social and environmental planning. Stable public interest policy needs objectives which have the coherence that only effective political leadership can give them.

- Unlike markets, which aggregate and signal vast amounts of information about values and preferences at the margin, systems of authority are information bottlenecks.[19] Government rulemakers are ignorant of much of the information that is required to achieve good social outcomes. The information available about specific contexts and impacts is always much less than that possessed by the individuals whose actions are regulated. Rulemakers are fundamentally ignorant of matters that may be essential for policy success. This is why attempts at comprehensive central economic planning always fail, and why tax and spend policies readily lead to misdirection and waste of resources. This inevitable ignorance counsels humility to would-be regulators.

- Rules impose uniformity, yet intelligent responses to complex situations may need to be flexible and diverse. Regulation is at best a blunt response. The Rudd/Gillard government's imposition of school halls across the nation exemplified both ignorance of what local communities needed in their schools and an inability to centrally obtain the necessary information to underpin a rational policy. The monopolistic National Broadband Network with its mandated technology struggles in an era of rapid technological change. The regulatory state attempts to impose an expanding blanket of uniformity/conformity on society, when social and economic innovation and growth, and effective mutual adjustment by citizens, require the flexibility to address constantly changing circumstances. Attempts to achieve this flexibility by empowering subordinate agencies with discretion erode democratic accountability and feed the belief that government is unjust and a source of uncertainty.

- Rules need interpretation, because language is ambiguous. The wider the regulatory ambition of the state, the more government relies on an ever-expanding set of tribunals whose discretionary power to interpret rules constantly creates uncertainty for private decision makers. The Federal Human Rights and State Equal Opportunity Commissions administering inevitably ambiguous laws, have eroded the rule of law, freedom of speech and today threaten religious liberty. The power of these tribunals provides a strong incentive to their capture by partisans and the diversion of their objectives into partisan campaigns. The attempt to impose regulation of social behavior through tribunals exercising discretionary authority is fraught with danger, and explains why such approaches to cultural reform evoke strong resistance. Persuasion through free debate remains an alternative strategy without these side-effects.

- The inevitable ambiguity and unforeseen consequences of rules leads to their proliferation in attempts to clarify or close loopholes, with the result that regulatory solutions tend to create more regulation, i.e. more imposed uniformity, more discretionary power, more limitations on individual judgement and the use of individual knowledge, more rigidity. The continuing growth of regulation over time is the inevitable consequence. Non-regulatory solutions do not have this consequence.

- Regulations create their own incentives, and these may be quite destructive, leading individuals into perverse decisions or empowering selfish interests. Exploiting rules becomes an aim rather than rational outcomes. This is particularly the case where the regulatory solution is a tax and spend solution. The availability of unearned money to enterprises, unions, institutions and individuals can massively distort decision-making. As Indigenous leaders have testified, welfare lies at the heart of the violence, abuse and family breakdown in remote indigenous communities, but it is equally wreaking havoc in the welfare-dependent areas of large cities.

It is not surprising in light of these adverse consequences that regulation is almost always a second best solution, not a straightforward cut-through instrument to policy success. Labor's need to placate the powerful union interests on which it depends, and to entice back into the fold the radical professionals with their agenda of moral regulation and identity politics, is leading to the re-regulation of the workplace and new adventures in industrial and social regulation. Adverse effects are already obvious in diminished social harmony, motivation and morale.

It is the general characteristics of regulation that explain why government is clumsy in its approach to social, economic, technological and environmental problems, why it is 'all thumbs, no fingers', and why policies that rely heavily on regulation and disempower individuals to express their values and use their unique knowledge fail through the unanticipated consequences of imposed uniformity, while simultaneously creating both rigidities and uncertainty, and distorting incentives. These are the fundamental reasons why socialist regimes, assaulting widely held values and the individuality of citizens with ambitious regulatory goals, fail and why a country such as Venezuela has descended into chaos as the government resorts increasingly to coercion as its authority crumbles.

It is scarcely surprising that there is increasing dissatisfaction with government as the state expands its efforts and multiplies its failures in its efforts to control economic and social outcomes. The democratic process can encourage or dampen these consequences, depending on the character of its leadership.

Problems arising from the nature of democratic policy making

It would be a mistake to ignore the fact that democracy has its limits. Winston Churchill reminded us that democracy is the 'worst form of government except for all those other forms that have been tried from time to time'. The default position of democracy (in the absence of political leadership that can define, and argue for, a public interest policy direction) is that policy is made by special interests—those with the loudest voices and the greatest political clout. Party discipline in Westminster systems is in theory a protection against these pressures as applied to individual members of parliament, but only if parties are capable of defining the public interest, and currently this is now in question.

Organised special interests seeking benefits for themselves from the state are more numerous in democracy than in any other system as a result of the freedoms of association, speech and the press. This is unquestionably a benefit because all are heard, while in authoritarian regimes only a few have access to power. But in the absence of public interest leadership it can lead to policy paralysis, and the struggle to find leadership and direction in democracies is a constant one.

De Tocqueville thought that the drive of private interests to regulate others and receive benefits in their own interests would eventually lead to a government despotism as the web of regulation tightened. This would happen because the authority of democratic government was so extensive, that citizens would accept its demands and allow the chain they had resisted from kings and tyrants to be put around their necks.[20] But de Tocqueville surely overlooked the limits of central authority, and the drive of citizens to control their own lives. Despotism may be attempted, but disorder and political revolt seems the more likely outcome.

Moreover, in the era of big government, politicians, the agencies of the state and those dependent on favourable state action have joined in profusion the army of the special interests, with manifold opportunities to pursue selfish goals. The democratic process can amplify the inherent difficulty of rule making by central authority noted above, a fact exemplified in the current agony experienced by government in resolving the 'trilemma' of energy policy objectives (security, affordability and sustainability, each pushed by conflicting interests). Another policy failure with similar origins is the persistence of the long tail of students with inadequate literacy and numeracy skills. This disaster, which has denied millions of Australians opportunities and blighted lives has arisen through the unwillingness of bureaucratic and union interests to take decisions that will ensure that well-known and proven solutions that conflict with their interests are adopted. Interest appeasement clearly lies at the heart of the difficulties of balancing budgets and cutting regulation.

The accountability problem
The reality is that much of the state is now well beyond any effective system of accountability and is not in any effective

way answerable to the people. The state in its manifold ambitions has outrun the mechanisms that make representative government work, and its agencies are increasingly open to occupation by special interests. The picture increasingly emerging across the developed world is one of people who increasingly feel they have lost control of their government, and of elected governments that have lost control over policy outcomes. This is the context in which major long-established democracies and political parties are experiencing popular revolts.

An important part of the answer is for policymakers in democracies to recapture the sense that the role of regulation is to empower citizens within a system of just rules, and to be as clear as possible about the objectives of policy. The need for a leadership with a philosophy of government which puts the citizen above organised interests is inescapable. In the short term, institutions supporting reasoned policy need to be stronger, policy reasoning needs to take into account the limitations as well as the capacities of the regulation through which it hopes to achieve a better world, and party leaders need to spend more time and energy making their public interest case. In the longer term, there needs to be a much stronger public understanding of what government can reasonably be asked to do, and what it is better to leave to the personal responsibility of citizens themselves.

CHAPTER THREE

Australia's economic malaise

MICHAEL POTTER

After many years of strong economic performance com-pared to other developed countries, Australia is now showing many signs of weaker performance.[1] As Australia is performing worse than other similar countries, the causes of this malaise are most likely Australia-specific. This chapter fo-cusses on one likely cause—the substantial and growing red tape burden on the economy.[2]

There are many reasons for the growth in poor quality regulation in Australia, including the benefits of regulation being identifiable and concentrated while the costs are more abstract and diffuse; and widespread (but erroneous) beliefs that market failures usually exceed government failures.

Figure 1: Quarterly growth (per cent) in real GDP per person (smoothed)

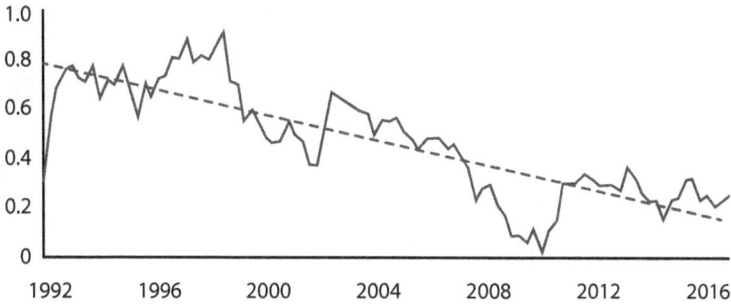

Source: See Footnote 3. The solid line is quarterly smoothed growth (3 year centred moving average); the dotted line is the linear trend for the period shown.

A focus of this chapter is on the fiscal incentives faced by state governments and how these incentives cause regulatory problems. This suggests reforms to the federation—worthwhile for many reasons—will also assist in cutting back Australia's red tape burden. These reforms should be combined with a range of changes to regulatory processes, to stem the flow of regulation and reduce the existing stock of regulation.

Evidence of the malaise

The clearest evidence for a deterioration in Australia's performance is provided by GDP per person. This is shown in Figure 1, with a downward trend also shown. The period from 2008 to 2017 is easily the longest sustained period on record for low growth in GDP per person—9 years of (smoothed) growth below 0.4 per cent per quarter. This is much longer than any other period since records started in 1973, including recessions.[3]

Unsurprisingly, the federal government, and many other commentators, do not focus on these figures—instead arguing Australia is having a record-breaking period of headline GDP growth.[4] For example, headline growth in Australia in 2016 was stronger than in any G8 country.[5] However, this apparent strength in recent years is an artifact of our strong population growth rates.[6] High levels of immigration are effectively papering over underlying weaknesses in the economy. We sometimes hear that Australia has had 26 years without a recession; but using the better GDP per person measure there were recessions in 2000 and 2006.[7]

Using the GDP per person measure, Australia's performance relative to the OECD was strong before the Global Financial Crisis (GFC), growing by more than the OECD weighted average between 1995 and about 2008; as shown in Figure 2. This was during the so-called golden period of economic reform.

While Australia had a slowdown during the GFC, Figure 2 shows it was remarkably milder than the OECD average. The reasons for this performance are not the subject of this chapter, but the outperformance is likely to be related to foreign demand for mining commodities, the floating exchange rate and monetary policy and not with fiscal or other government policies.[9] This view is consistent with a paper published by the RBA estimating the mining boom provided a significant boost to Australia's GDP.[10] However, since the end of the GFC recovery, Australia's performance has been at or around the OECD average—likely below average since about 2013. This lacklustre performance can't be explained as being due to the

Figure 2: Real GDP growth per person in Australia and OECD (smoothed)

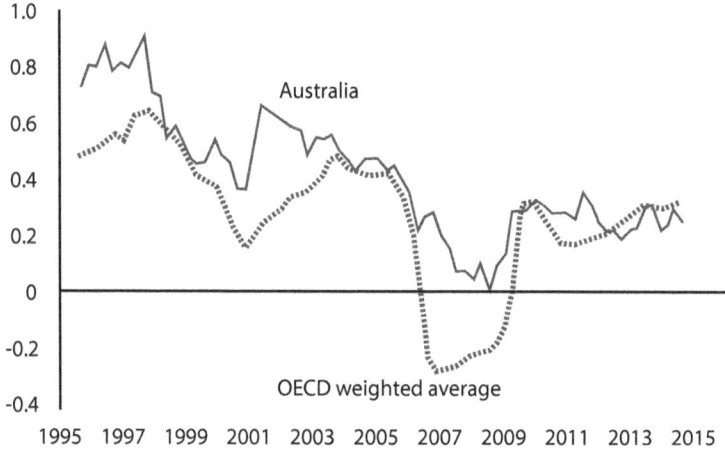

Source: OECD.Stat, code HVPVOBARSA. Figures are for real quarterly growth, seasonally adjusted and smoothed by taking a three year centred moving average.[8]

end of the mining boom—estimates published by the RBA suggest the end of the boom would cut GDP only slightly compared to the earlier positive effect.[11] Other evidence suggests GDP growth should in fact be higher, not lower, after the end of the mining boom.[12]

Income and wages affect Australian households more directly than GDP, and the stagnation is even clearer on these figures. Nominal wages are growing at a record low rate and real wages have been flatlining for some time.[13] Real income per person has barely increased for almost 10 years, as shown in Figure 3.

While employment growth has recently been strong, this is more than offset by the weakness in wages growth;

Figure 3: Real net national disposable income per person (thousands of dollars)

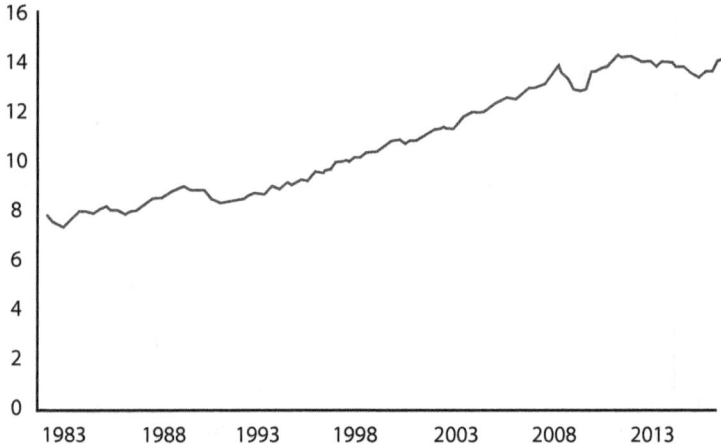

Source: ABS, Australian National Accounts: National Income, Expenditure and Product, September 2017, Cat No 5206, Table 1.[14]

as a result total compensation of employees, a measure that combines the effect of both wages and employment, has been growing at a historically slow pace.[15] These income, wage and compensation measures are additional evidence of Australia's recent economic weakness.

However, the end of the mining boom affected national incomes and wages much more than GDP, so the current flatlining of these measures could just be a result of the end of the boom rather than a symptom of underlying economic problems.[16] In addition, weakness in wage growth is occurring in other developed countries, with Australia's recent performance not noticeably worse.[17] As a consequence, sluggish wage and income growth does not provide clear cut evidence of an economic malaise.

Figure 4: New private business investment as % of GDP

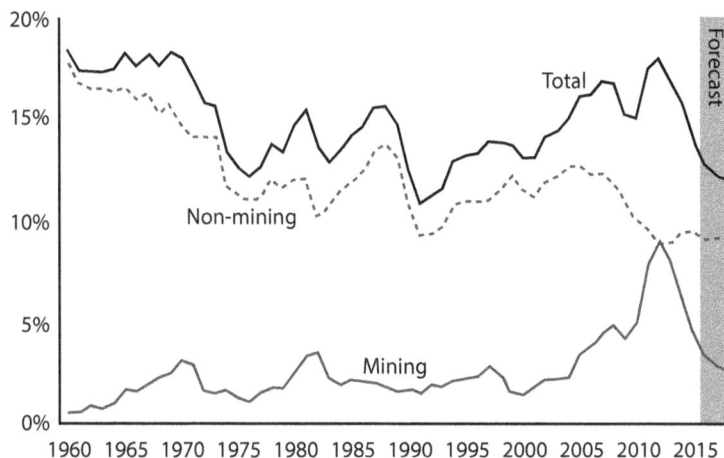

Sources: ABS for history, Commonwealth Treasury for forecasts.[16]

Nevertheless, poor performance on wage and income measures is partly caused by red tape and regulation. This is because government rules are driving up the cost of living, which in turn reduces real incomes and wages. There have been steep increases in prices in sectors that are heavily regulated by the government, such as childcare, health, education and utilities while prices in less regulated sectors, such as food and clothing have barely grown at all.[18]

Australia is also performing weakly on business investment, with the Productivity Commission in 2017 arguing 'The investment slump is particularly concerning'.[19] Figure 4 shows business investment from 1960 to 2018 as a share of the economy, using Treasury forecasts. The decline in mining investment since the end of the boom is unsurprising; what is surprising is the failure of non-mining investment to rebound to previous levels. This means total investment is forecast to flatline at very low levels as a share of GDP; these levels have only previously been seen in the middle of the 1990s recession. Investment was stronger in the middle of the 1970s and 1980s recessions than it is today.

As investment is one of the main drivers of future economic growth and wellbeing, this does not bode well for Australia being able to recover from the malaise outlined earlier.

There are global problems with private investment, as identified by several experts.[20] However, Australia's investment performance is sliding relative to other developed countries. Based on the IMF's World Economic Outlook, Australia's total investment to GDP ratio is ranked as ninth in the OECD in 2017, around the historical average, but is forecast to fall to twentieth by 2022, the lowest ranking on record. Similarly, Australia's investment to GDP ratio is set to decline relative to the OECD average over the same period.[21] Australia's historical advantages in investment will be lost if nothing is done.[22]

Australia has also had a marked decline in our ranking against other countries on various competitiveness measures, as shown in Table 1. The figures show Australia's economic performance is declining relative to other developed countries and compared to our past performance.

There are a number of other measures of economic wellbeing, but they are not the focus of this article as the outcomes on these measures are less clear cut:

- Overall productivity has stagnated for more than a decade, with the level of multifactor productivity (MFP) in 2017 about the same as the level in 2004.[24] In other words,

Table 1: Australia's declining competitiveness

Index	Ranking		Change
	2010	*Current*	
World Economic Forum Global Competitiveness	15	22	Down 7 places
World Bank Ease of Doing Business	9	15	Down 6 places
Heritage Foundation Index of Economic Freedom	3	5	Down 2 places
IMD Competitiveness Yearbook	5	21	Down 16 places
Fraser Institute Economic Freedom of the World index	5	9 (in 2015)	Down 4 places

Current ranking is for 2017 unless specified. Sources: World Economic Forum, Global Competitiveness Report, various years; World Bank, Ease of Doing Business Index, various years.[23]

MFP growth over that period has essentially been zero. Conversely, labour productivity growth has been stronger over this period, driven by large capital investment.[25] However, both these productivity figures have been heavily affected by the mining boom and the post-mining boom figures are not yet clear.[26]

• Inequality and the labour share of income are frequently used to criticise Australia's economic performance, but it is not clear that either measure has deteriorated in recent years.[27] More importantly, inequality and the labour share are poor indicators of economic performance. A highly innovative economy is good, but this is likely to result in a gain in incomes at the top, which will cause an increase in inequality. Substantial capital deepening in an economy is also likely to be good, but will probably cause a reduction in the labour share of income.[28]

- There have also been large increases in household wealth, largely driven by increases in house prices.[29] However this is not an indicator of good economic performance because a major driver of house prices is burdensome planning and development regulations—that is, excessive red tape.[30]

Causes of the malaise

The decline in Australia's relative performance is likely caused by several factors.[31] A significant factor is the growing tax burden; in particular, bracket creep and fiscal drag more broadly are adding to the tax burden by about 0.3 percentage points per year cumulatively.[32] In 2016, Treasury estimated that bracket creep over four years to 2020–21 would reduce GDP by 0.35 per cent.[33] The economic cost of tax increases would be larger for a longer period of bracket creep. The ongoing declines in the competitiveness of Australia's taxes on capital are another factor.[34] As argued earlier, the mining boom cannot provide a substantial explanation of Australia's underperformance since the GFC recovery.[35]

However, most relevant to this chapter, another contributor to Australia's lacklustre performance is the excessive red tape burden on the economy. Some examples of the economic cost of red tape include:

- Rules imposed by the government have been estimated to cost the economy $94 billion per year, and rules imposed by businesses themselves, probably as an indirect result of government regulation, cost $155 billion per year for a total cost of $249 billion per year.[36] There has also been a growing share of employment in compliance work, from 6 per cent in 1996 to 9 per cent in 2014.[37]

- National Australia Bank indicated its annual cost of complying with regulation was $265 million in 2014, a figure that had tripled over the previous three years.[38] The increase in regulation since 2014 would mean this figure is an underestimate.

- Annual tax compliance costs for individuals was estimated at 0.3 per cent of GDP in 1995, a figure that doubled to 0.6 per cent in 2014.[39]

- One estimate is that the overall cost of excessive regulation to the Australian economy (in terms of lost GDP) is $176 billion per year.[40] This is the estimated cost caused by regulation being more burdensome than the minimal effective level of regulation.

These costs of red tape cause substantial reductions in GDP and the other economic measures which have been weak since the GFC as noted at the start of this chapter.

Most governments at state and federal levels have an agenda for deregulation and regulation review, but significant concerns can be raised that these agendas are not succeeding in reducing either the stock or flow of regulation. A 2009 review argued many regulations that should not be seen as adequate were subject to regulatory review and were found to be adequate—even best practice.[41] A 2012 Productivity Commission review found there were considerable gaps between agreed regulatory review principles and practice; and the primary benefits of regulation review have been forfeited through a lack of ministerial and agency commitment.[42]

Flaws with the current federal government's deregulation agenda include, for example:

- A number of important federal government regulations implemented in 2015–16 were not required to have a Regulation Impact Statement (RIS) because the policies were subject to 'independent review'. This included three of the most significant policy announcements in that period: the setting of Australia's greenhouse emissions target after 2020; the government's response to the Competition Policy Review (the Harper Review); and the government's response to the Financial Systems Inquiry (the Murray Inquiry).[43] These were major areas of regulation and they have not been assessed as to whether they are in fact 'best practice'.

- The federal government's Major Bank Levy was assessed by the Office of Best Practice Regulation (OBPR) as being compliant with the government's requirements.[44] This is despite the Levy having major flaws.[45] The Levy is poorly designed, does not align with international experience, and will largely or completely be passed on to consumers. It is estimated to reduce GDP by $1.7 billion per year, more than the forecast annual revenue from the levy of $1.5-1.6 billion, has a potential to increase the risk of the financial system as a whole and the process for developing the levy breaches numerous regulation requirements, even though the federal government absurdly asserted that the Major Bank Levy was best practice regulation.[46]

- The regular red tape repeal days have stopped and the deregulation reports appear to be defunct, with no additions to the relevant website relating to 2016 or 2017.[47]

Problems with the incentives for reform

If poor regulation is harmful to the economy, why do governments persist in implementing bad regulation and fail to remove or reform existing poor regulations? In general terms, this damaging outcome occurs because governments face disincentives for regulatory reform, and conversely face perverse incentives to implement excessive or badly designed regulation. Some of these harmful incentives include:[48]

- the benefits of regulatory reform are abstract and diffuse while the costs are identifiable and concentrated;
- a widespread view that the government can fix all problems;
- policy makers (and the general community) overstate market failure and understate government failure;
- excessive risk aversion of policy makers;
- a failure to understand that business costs are largely passed on to consumers;
- a desire by governments to appear to be 'doing something'; and
- policy asymmetry—regulation faces low hurdles while deregulation faces high hurdles.

This chapter focuses on an additional perverse incentive: the fiscal incentives faced by state governments—particularly from the system for distributing the GST to the states.[49]

For the federal Budget, 87 per cent of tax revenue in 2017–18 is expected to come from taxes related to income, while 13 per cent is forecast to come from consumption-related taxes, when the GST is excluded, as shown in Table 2 (the GST is included in state government analysis later).[50] Regulatory reform, broadly speaking, will result in increased economic activity, leading to growth in income and consumption, and causing increases in the revenue from all the taxes connected

Table 2: Federal government tax revenue excluding GST, 2016–17

Tax	% of total revenue (excl GST)	Impact of regulatory reform on tax revenue
Personal & related taxes	63%	Positive
Company & related taxes	24%	Positive
Total income taxes	87%	Positive
Excise	7%	Positive
Other indirect, excl. GST	7%	Positive
Indirect taxes, excl. GST	13%	Positive

Source: 2017–18 Budget. Numbers may not add due to rounding.[49]

with income and consumption. Therefore regulatory reform will likely increase all the major federal government revenue sources and the federal government has financial incentives to implement higher-quality regulation, and to reform existing regulations.

By contrast, many of the financial incentives for state governments are neutral to harmful regulations because many regulatory reforms do not improve state government revenues.

Land tax revenue is reduced by reforms to planning laws. This is because planning reforms are likely to result in lower property prices.[51] Planning reforms are likely to increase housing turnover so the net effect on stamp duty revenue is less clear, but some analysis suggests the impact of price movements on stamp duty outweigh the movements in turnover.[52] Therefore it is likely that planning reforms will have a neutral or negative impact on overall revenue from taxes on land.

The other major tax that causes perverse regulatory incentives is the GST. As the GST is fully passed on to the states, all the incentives caused by this tax affect the states alone. It might appear that the GST provides the right incentives for regulatory reform, because deregulation will grow the size of the economy and hence GST revenue. However, this superficial analysis ignores two redistributions of GST revenue that severely mute, or even negate, the incentives for reform.

First, any additional GST revenue generated in a particular state due to regulatory reform is distributed to all other states in proportion to population. New South Wales (NSW) was about 32 per cent of Australia's population in 2016, so NSW received 32 per cent of the GST revenue it generated in that year. By contrast, the Northern Territory (NT) was only 1 per cent of Australia's population, so received only about 1 per cent of GST revenue it generates. In other words, NT initially gets just 1 per cent of the revenue benefit of reform in the territory. Just this effect alone substantially mutes the revenue benefit of reform.

But the redistribution does not end there. There is further redistribution from richer states to poorer states through Horizontal Fiscal Equalisation (HFE).[53] This HFE redistribution further reduces the fiscal benefit of reform. A reforming state becomes richer, and the HFE formula redistributes the increased income in that state to other states, while a state that becomes poorer because of bad regulation is subsidised by richer states. Thus the combination of population redistribution and HFE redistribution severely mutes the incentives for regulatory reform, and in fact is likely to discourage reform.[54]

Table 3: State government total revenue including GST, 2015–16

Tax	% of total revenue (including GST)	Impact of regulatory reform on tax revenue
GST	42%	Negative/Zero
Land tax	8%	Negative
Stamp duty on land	15%	Negative/Zero
GST & taxes on land	65%	Negative
Payroll tax	17%	Positive
Other taxes, incl. gambling, insurance, motor vehicle	19%	Positive
All excl. GST & taxes on land	35%	Positive

Source: ABS.[52] Numbers may not add due to rounding.

So the analysis above indicates that land tax revenue is reduced by regulatory reform, while reform is likely to reduce GST and stamp duty revenue. In total, this is about 65 per cent of the revenue of all state governments in 2015-16, as shown in Table 3 where incentives are either neutral or negative.

By contrast, only about 35 per cent of state government revenue has positive incentives. Payroll tax revenue, for example, broadly grows with the state economy, so revenue from this tax provides positive incentives for state-level reform.[55]

The analysis above is of the revenue side of government budgets. The incentives on the spending side are less clear-cut: regulatory reforms can boost spending, as many spending items grow automatically with wages or GDP such as the Age Pension and defence spending. The growth caused by reform may reduce welfare spending, but on the other hand transitory unemployment can be caused in reformed sectors, potentially requiring structural adjustment packages such as occurred in the dairy, car manufacturing and irrigation industries.[56]

The federal Budget has analysis supporting this argument; finding faster GDP growth will tend to increase federal revenue as a share of GDP and reduce unemployment spending, while implying that other areas of federal spending are largely unaffected as a share of GDP.[57]

In summary, while there are many incentives discouraging regulatory reform at both the state and federal level, there is an additional disincentive for state government regulatory reform: the tax systems of state governments and the GST distribution formula create additional poor regulatory incentives.

Solutions

Along with tax reductions, a priority for addressing Australia's economic malaise should be reforming harmful regulation. This chapter does not focus on the reform of individual regulations, instead recommending government-wide framework reforms that will reduce both the stock and flow of regulation.

The analysis above suggests that reforms to the incentives facing state governments should be a priority. Such worthwhile reforms include the following:

- Moving towards a per capita distribution of GST revenue to the states. A complete move to per capita distribution is unlikely, but there are worthwhile reforms to move in that direction. For example, the Minerals Council has proposed that mining activity be partly excluded from the GST redistribution formula.[58] This should encourage increased mining development—or at least reduce the disincentives to development. The Productivity Commission has also suggested that the extent of GST redistribution could be reduced.[59] This would reduce the penalties imposed on states that reform and reduce the subsidies provided to states that fail to reform.

- Transfer some income taxing powers to the states. Each state could choose an income tax surcharge applying in that state, and would retain all the funds raised with no redistribution to other states. This tax increase would be offset by a reduction in federal government income taxes and a cut in funding from the Commonwealth to the states.[60] This reform will provide states with sharper incentives for reform—they will gain direct access to the revenue base that is most likely to grow with improved economic growth.

Another significant reform would be to reinstate reform incentive payments, based on the successes of the incentive payments that were used under National Competition Policy (NCP).

Under this approach, the Commonwealth provided states with substantial funding, but states that didn't reform, or were slow to reform, were penalised. The Productivity Commission in a major review of NCP found the payments:[61]

- played a critical role in keeping reforms on track;
- could help to leverage reforms which, in the face of

opposition from vested interests, might otherwise be put in the 'too hard basket';

- allowed states to share in the fiscal dividend of reform; and
- allowed states to address transition costs or any adverse distributional effects from reform.

The Productivity Commission also found that the threat of financial penalties locked in earlier regulatory reforms and discouraged reform 'backsliding'—the reversal of previous regulatory reforms.[62]

The NCP incentive payments ended in 2005–06, which was just before the period when Australia's economic malaise started (see Figure 1), suggesting the abolition of the payments could be part of the reason for the subsequent declining performance.[63]

The 2017–18 federal Budget proposed the substantial housing payments to the states be amended to include financial incentives for reform in this sector.[64] If designed well, this could provide the many benefits of incentive payments as outlined above.

However, there are risks with this approach. Incentive payments could be seen as contrary to proper federalism that would minimise federal government interference in states. There is also a risk that if the federal government starts down a path of regulation, this would be easy to turn into micro-management of states. This could then easily become a harmful, rather than beneficial system. For example, incentives payments for reducing planning red tape could turn into incentives for increasing green tape—mandating environmentally-friendly design, energy efficiency, water tanks and similar.

However, the NCP framework shows how to design incentive payments to avoid this trap—have a simple framework. For the NCP legislation review program, this was broadly that states had to systematically review regulations that restricted competition, and reform or remove those regulations that did not meet a public benefit test.[65] The simplicity of this approach made it hard for governments to convert the system from good incentives to bad incentives.

This framework should be used for future incentive payments—require review and removal of regulations that do not meet a public benefit test. This would make it harder for the system to transform into micromanagement.

There are a range of other useful framework solutions to reduce the burden of excessive regulation. These solutions are not new. Over-regulation is a recognised problem, and many have proposed significant reforms, including the Business Council of Australia and the Productivity Commission in recent reports.[66] The worthwhile reforms include the following:

- Establish an Inspector-General of Regulation, modelled on the existing Inspector-General of Taxation but monitoring regulatory burdens across government. This was proposed by the 2002 Uhrig Review, which recommended this new body would investigate the systems and procedures used by regulatory authorities in administering regulation.[67]
- Separate the OBPR (and state equivalents) from government departments and establish these bodies as independent statutory bodies to reduce political imperatives in decision making.[68]
- Make a regulation impact statement (RIS) a statutory

requirement for all substantial regulations, having only very limited exemptions, such as for issues of national security and emergency.[69] For emergency regulations that do not have a RIS, mandate speedy sunsetting of the regulation with a RIS required for replacement.[70] This could include a requirement that draft RISs be required to be published for early consultation in relation to more significant regulations.

- Ensure RIS requirements apply to subordinate or delegated regulation.[71]
- Require regulators to provide an annual statement on regulatory reform, to be approved by the proposed Inspector-General of Regulation.[72]
- Implement regulatory budgeting, which involves measuring the economic cost of regulation and placing caps on this cost. A government implementing a new regulation that imposes a cost on society will need to implement regulatory reform to reduce the costs of regulation elsewhere. This approach can make use of already established approaches to estimate the economic costs of regulation.[73]
- There are also other proposals/policies to mandate a 'one in, one out' approach to regulatory changes, requiring one regulation (or more) to be abolished for every new regulation.[74] This might be a worthwhile step in the process towards more sophisticated approaches involving regulatory budgeting.
- To reduce the stock of regulation, implement automatic sunsetting of most existing regulations, and require rigorous processes outlined in this section for the reintroduction of regulations that have sunsetted. This

could be done as a reinvigoration of previous rolling reviews of industries conducted by the Productivity Commission.[75] The proposed Inspector-General of Regulation could be involved in these reviews.

- Ensure the onus of proof is on those wishing to add regulation, and is not reversed.[76] When regulations are sunsetted, have the onus of proof on the retention of regulation not the removal—that is, those wishing to retain regulation have to satisfy the burden of proof.

There is a long way to go to reach best practice in regulatory reform, as has been made clear in many reviews, particularly by the Productivity Commission.[77] The changes proposed above should close this gap and help address Australia's poor economic performance. Doing nothing will risk a continuation of Australia's economic malaise—at significant cost to all.

CHAPTER FOUR

Some (micro)economics of red tape and regulation

SINCLAIR DAVIDSON

> As soon as we surrender the principle that the state should
> not interfere in any questions touching on the individual's
> mode of life, we end by regulating and restricting the latter
> down to the smallest detail.—*Ludwig von Mises*

This chapter sets out the microeconomics of regulation theory and argues that the standard economic approaches to
regulation are unsatisfactory.[1] Traditionally economists have argued that regulation exists to overcome market failure. This is a
popular theory. The problem being, however, that market failure
has a precise meaning in economics and in practice is somewhat
rare. There is simply too much regulation to be explained by actual market failure. At the same time the alternate public choice

type theory of regulation—that it exists to benefit industry incumbents—fails to explain why those economies where we observe very high levels of regulation also tend to be very wealthy.

Most of the chapter is dedicated to explaining, in abstract terms, the so-called enforcement theory of regulation or an institutional theory of regulation. This theory explains why we have regulation and what the costs of regulation are likely to be. A lack of regulation is likely to be associated with market failure type problems, while excessive regulation is likely to be associated with excessive government intervention and bureaucratisation in the economy. Interestingly the enforcement theory suggests that while we might always need some level of regulation, we might not always need regulators *per se*. In addition, the relationship between regulation and economic prosperity is also highlighted. Finally I examine the demand and supply of regulation. Why is it that we appear to have an excess supply of regulation and how does that persist over time? I argue that anti-market bias and nirvana economic theories interact to ensure that there will almost always be too much regulation.

The economics of regulation

The economic theory of regulation can be broken up into three strands. The 'public interest' theory suggests that governments intervene in order to correct for various market failures such as externality, information asymmetry, and monopoly. The implicit assumption being that the costs of government intervention are lower than the costs of market failure. The 'special interest' or 'capture theory' of regulation suggests that industry seeks out regulation in order to create barriers to entry for new rivals and to maintain profitability.

The public interest theory of regulation and the special interest theory of regulation are polar opposites on a regulatory continuum. Each provides valuable insight into the regulatory process, yet both are incomplete and unsatisfactory. Proponents of the public interest theory, for example, struggle to explain how and why markets actually fail in practice, as opposed to failing in theory. In short, there is too much regulation given the amount of actual market failure that is likely to occur. While the special interest theory of regulation cannot explain why developed economies are so much wealthier today, than say a mere 100 years ago, when the level of regulation has increased dramatically. This observation appears to be inconsistent with the argument that excessive regulation impedes economic progress and undermines corporate dynamism.[2] In essence, there is too much wealth given the apparent costs of excessive regulation.

In a series of papers Andrei Shleifer (and various co-authors) has developed an institutional theory of regulation (Shleifer refers to this as the 'enforcement theory' of regulation) that examines four broad governance strategies that 'society' can pursue in order to achieve some objective relative to the trade-offs associated with those strategies. These strategies are; 'market discipline', 'private litigation', 'public enforcement through regulation', and 'state ownership'. The societal trade-offs as being the costs of private disorder and the costs of government dictatorship. Disorder relates to the ability of private individuals to inflict harm on others, while dictatorship relates to the ability of government and its bureaucrats to inflict harm on others.

In this framework, market discipline should be considered as the regulatory default. Of course, that is not always possible and at this point the control strategy becomes private litigation. The state begins to play a role as the rules of contract and tort law are administered by courts of law staffed by bureaucrats and judges. Courts of law exist, at this level, to enforce private agreements and to adjudicate disputes between private parties.

Chicago school economists have argued that the combination of market discipline and courts of law should suffice for any regulatory framework. Andrei Shleifer, however, has argued that courts cannot always resolve disputes cheaply, predictably, or impartially.[3] This is especially the case when the parties to the dispute have vastly different resources that they can deploy to a legal dispute.

Regulation occurs when the state not only provides a dispute resolution mechanism but also writes the rules that govern economic behaviour and transactions. There is substantial variation in how government can enforce its regulations. It can, for example, allow bureaucrats to engage in a regime of inspection and verification with fines being issued for non-compliance. Alternatively, the state can provide a set of rules that are privately litigated, or publicly litigated. Public litigation can consist of either civil or criminal charges. Similarly the regulatory agency can initiate litigation itself for breeches of the regulations, or act once a complaint has been received. This notion has been extensively debated in the context of financial regulation.

Rafael La Porta, Florencio Lopez-de-Silanes and Andrei Shleifer investigate the impact of security laws on financial markets across 49 economies including Australia.[4] In particular they investigate how security laws operate to protect investors and whether regulators with public enforcement or rules with private enforcement lead to better outcomes. After exhaustive empirical analysis, they find that legal rules matter, but that *regulators* do not always matter. So long as rules can be enforced in courts investors do not need to be protected by regulators.

James Barth, Gerard Caprio Jr. and Ross Levine find an analogous result in their investigation of bank regulation and supervision across 107 countries including Australia.[5] They summarise their results as raising a cautionary flag against regulatory practices that involve direct oversight and restrictions on banks. Their conclusions are remarkably similar to the La Porta et al. results. Regulations involving prescriptive behaviour and powerful regulators using public enforcement mechanisms are not the better techniques to employ for the purpose of social control.

Private enforcement of public rules, however, does require explicit rules. Edward Glaeser and Andrei Shleifer trace the development of so-called 'bright line rules' in their comparison of the medieval English and French legal systems.[6] In their model bright line rules emerge as a mechanism to control judges. As Jonathan Klick points out, however, it isn't clear why regulators would be any different from judges in the Glaeser and Shleifer model.[7] Just as bright line rules could and should control judges, so too bright line rules should control regulators.

Shleifer and his various co-authors appear to have a preference for regulation over litigation. In one paper, for example, they argue that litigation and regulation are conceptually similar but regulation offers advantages over litigation.[8] It is not immediately clear that this type of argument is correct. Private litigation consists of disputes between actual individuals who have incurred a loss as consequence of the actions of the counterparty. Regulation and litigation arising from regulation involves disputes over abstract principles and involve no actual loss.

The major advantage regulation offers to litigation is that parties to a dispute may have very different legal resources. Yet Shleifer and his colleagues do not explain how to overcome the inequality of legal resources between private individuals and the regulator itself. The regulator is able to pursue legal action subject to a budget constraint underwritten by the taxation power of the state. In Shleifer's enforcement cost model of regulation this issue is itself a 'dictatorship cost', yet it is not clear they even recognise this issue as being a problem.

To be sure there are apparent advantages of regulators over judges. Shleifer and co-authors have set out the arguments in favour of regulation over court orders and private litigation. First public regulators are specialised in the area and are motivated to pursue the regulatory objective. Second, regulators can act pre-emptively to prevent disorder from arising. Third, subversion costs for regulators may be higher than those of judges.

Conversely, however, regulators are bureaucrats and suffer from all the problems that the public choice literature has identified with bureaucracy. These include over-enforcement of regulation, mission creep, size maximisation and perquisite maximisation and, occasionally, a quiet life. Then there is the issue of the independence of regulators. It is quite plausible to believe that regulators should operate at arms-length from the government to prevent political abuse of the regulatory agency. This abuse could either consist of political interference to prevent regulation of favoured constituents, or as a tool to harass political minorities. The cost of that independence, however, is to dilute or even remove democratic control over the regulator. It removes accountability from an important and growing component of government.

All up we are left with theoretical arguments that suggest a range of benefits and costs that favour either litigation or regulation by regulators to control disputes. On the other hand we have clear empirical evidence that supports bright line rules and private litigation as a mechanism to provide social control over business.

Finally, state ownership appears to be an efficient response to those situations where the disorder costs are likely to be very high. Shleifer gives the examples of prisons, police force, and military where this is likely to be the case. The costs of disorder resulting from private ownership here are potentially so large that government needs to maintain control over these institutions.

All up the Shleifer enforcement cost model provides a high level tool to evaluate regulation and government intervention generally. A group of scholars at RMIT University have applied that general model to several very specific instances. In work with Jason Potts we have applied the model to the institutions of innovation policy.[9] In work with Chris Berg we have investigated media regulation and free speech.[10] It is important to recognise that each industry or activity should be evaluated for the best or optimal regulation—there can be no one-size-fit-all regulation. Consider for example the case of financial regulation—we showed that a litigation model is likely to be the better approach. That approach, however, may not serve well in the case of, say, airline safety regulations which may be better suited to enforcement via a regime of inspection than after the fact litigation.

The demand and supply of regulation

The enforcement theory of regulation can be used to explain the general relationship between disorder costs, dictatorship costs and economic prosperity. The Davidson-Potts curve, shown in Figure 1, hypothesises an inverse u-shaped relationship between disorder costs and dictatorship costs and economic prosperity. Clearly those societies that have very high levels of disorder or very high levels of dictatorship are less likely to be prosperous than those that well manage the tension between the two sources of social cost. It also provides insight into the assumptions being made by those who advocate for no regulation, i.e. market anarchists who under-estimate disorder costs while over-estimating dictatorship costs. Similarly those who advocate more regulation over-estimate disorder costs while under-estimating dictatorship costs.

The Davidson-Potts curve clearly shows that having too much regulation is clearly as much of a problem for society as having too little. While the costs of excessive regulation may manifest itself somewhat differently than the costs of having too little regulation the net effect is much the same— lower economic prosperity. That in turn then raises the next important consideration—why is it that we live in a society characterised by having too much regulation?

In order for regulation to persist there must be both demand and supply considerations that support it. There must be a demand for regulation before it can be supplied. Similarly there must a supply of regulation available to

Figure 1: The Davidson-Potts curve

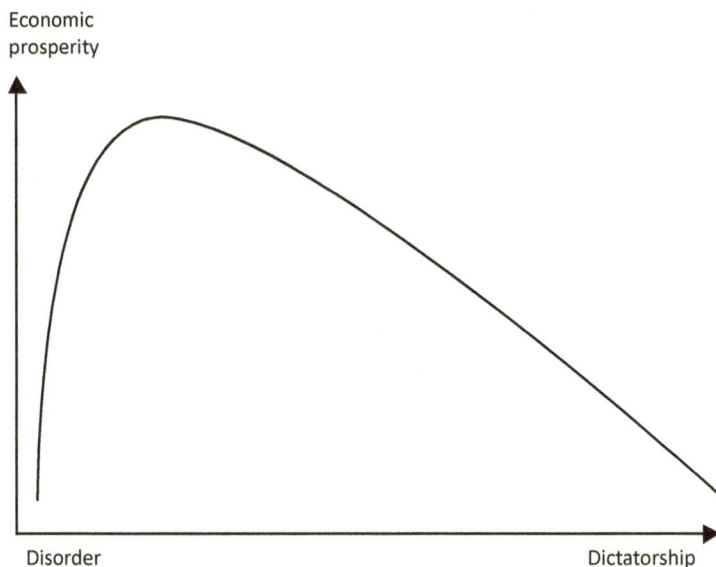

meet any demand for regulation. In the very first instance a supply of regulation can always be met in the first instance in the courts. Courts are the first government port of call to supply the demand for regulation. Then the tax system can be employed to regulate too. It is only after these two general purpose government technologies are deployed that we see the emergence of specialist regulators. Regulatory bodies, such as bureaucracies, can be expected to become self-perpetuating ensuring an over-supply of regulation.

The demand for regulation can be understood by reference to Bryan Caplan's model of voter bias.[11] Caplan develops a sophisticated argument attempting to explain why democracies appear to make basic economic policy errors.

His argument revolves around voters being irrational and also biased. While it is not clear that he succeeds in demonstrating that voters are irrational, his four-biases model is useful. In particular he argues that voters suffer from an anti-market bias, an anti-foreign bias, a make-work bias, and a pessimism bias. From our perspective the anti-market bias suggests that voters are likely to over-estimate disorder costs leading to an excess demand for regulation.

The nirvana economics fallacy outlined by Harold Demsetz largely explains the supply of regulation.[12] Demsetz argues that there are three fallacies that make up what he calls nirvana economics; the grass is greener on the other side, there can be a free lunch, and people could be different. In practice this means that people can imagine a perfect world, compare the real world to that perfect world and then imagine an intervention that will move our existing imperfect world close to their imagined ideal. This, of course, entails people having to under-estimate dictatorship costs.

So Bryan Caplan's model explains why disorder costs are over-estimated and Harold Demsetz explains why dictatorship costs are under-estimated. In combination this results in the situation where government and regulation is larger than the level that would maximise economic prosperity.

Conclusion

Australians have come to appreciate that they are over-regulated.[13] It is well known that over-regulation is likely to impose costs on the economy and society at large. The nature of that over-regulation, however, isn't well-understood. The consequence of de-regulation is also not generally well understood. For example, the consequence of reduced regulation is a lower level of dictatorship costs within the economy, not market anarchy. The approach set out in this chapter also indicates that a one-size-fits-all approach to regulation is likely to be misguided. Disorder costs vary from industry to industry and also over time and space. As such we should expect to observe very different regulatory bodies across industries and also different regulations across industries and time and space. In some industries, for example, we should see more private litigation rather than regulatory bodies doing the heavy regulatory work. That probably means that government should be looking at expanding the court system rather than, say, increasing the powers of the Australian Securities and Investments Commission or the Australian Prudential Regulation Authority or any one of the many financial regulators. Bear in mind, many politicians would prefer to create jobs for regulators than create jobs for lawyers (despite many regulators being lawyers by profession).

Overall, this chapter provides a theory that well explains the levels of regulation within the economy, explains why it persists, and also explains the various costs associated with that over-regulation.

Chapter Five

The politics of red tape

Georgina Downer

While the phrase red tape conjures up an image of bureaucrats churning out reams of Byzantine regulations,
the reality is red tape starts with politics. It's important, then,
to understand what drives our politicians to roll out red tape.
Given the amount of red tape in our society, one could query
whether politicians actually like red tape. The simple answer
is no, politicians do not like red tape, and this is the case irrespective of where a politician sits on the political spectrum.

In this chapter, red tape refers to regulation which goes beyond
what is necessary to address market failure. It is oppressive
or overly-complex regulation. The divergent outcomes in red
tape delivered by different sides of politics arise because of

ideological divides over what constitutes market failure and the most effective tools to address these failures.

Although it goes against their basic instincts to avoid being tangled in tape, politicians can be complicit in imposing new red tape or acquiescing to old tape tangles, due to a variety of external pressures, including the fear of inaction, decreased public appetite for risk, more effective activist campaigns enhanced by improved technology and funding, and the international regulatory environment arising from deeper global integration. These external pressures are growing in their power, scope and pace, posing a significant dilemma for politicians and the public when it comes to cutting red tape.

This essay proceeds as follows. The first section explores the proposition that neither the left nor the right of politics like red tape but what constitutes 'red tape' is a subjective and hotly contested political debate. The second section examines politicians' basic desire to limit red tape—the red tape reduction cycle—and the forces which eventually inhibit this. History shows that cutting red tape is good politics but hard to sustain. The subsequent sections examine the reasons why politicians impose new red tape.

Politicians do not like red tape, but disagree on what it is

Whether a person is campaigning for office or seeking to maintain it, no politician likes red tape for the sake of it. Rather, a politician's world view and political ideology will result in different attitudes about what is necessary regulation to correct market failures. The minimum necessary regulation to address a public policy problem in a left-wing politician's eyes may well be red tape for the politician from the small government centre-right. In this way, the politics of red tape is defined by how different politicians perceive minimum standards of regulation, rather than a general penchant for Byzantine regulation.

The default position in politics, irrespective of one's place on the political spectrum, is to decry red tape and only pursue what one considers to be 'essential' regulation. Consider the Greens. For the Greens, a core policy plank and public virtue is protection of the environment. Notably, in areas unrelated to the environment, the Greens claim to endorse or pursue policies which cut red tape. Take, for example:

- the Australian Greens' support for cuts to red tape associated with the GST compliance burden for small businesses;[1]
- the Australian Greens acknowledgment of the red tape burden for charities complying with the newly formed Australian Charities and Not for Profit Commission rules in 2016;[2]
- the Australian Greens opposition to the Coalition's imposition of 'red tape' on patients wishing to access medicinal cannabis;[3] and
- the Tasmanian Greens' support for amendments to building regulations cutting red tape for solar panels.[4]

The Greens appear to recognise the excessive and oppressive potential of regulations on businesses, the not-for-profit sector and ordinary Australians. Yet the Greens' rhetoric changes when it comes to environmental regulation. In that sphere, the Greens see heavy regulation as necessary to protect the environment, and prioritise the environment's interests above all else. The Greens do not see their environment regulations as red tape; rather, they see it as the minimum necessary regulation to achieve environmental virtue.

THE POLITICS OF RED TAPE

The Greens' policy on coal is a case in point. They completely reject coal-fired power as part of the nation's energy mix despite the devastating economic effects of a coal-free energy policy. Their solution is to regulate coal out of existence—they aspire to a 90 per cent RET by 2030 because they believe 'we cannot have the Great Barrier Reef and Coal'. They advocate for:

* no new coal or gas mines;
* the introduction of a $1 billion Clean Energy Transition Fund;
* the re-implementation of a carbon price;
* the cessation of tax-free fuel to miners;
* the imposition of a $3 per tonne thermal coal export levy;
* the introduction of the Renew Australia plan for 90 per cent renewable energy by 2030; and
* boosting funding for reef champions, high-tech water quality projects, the Great Barrier Reef Marine Park Authority and the Australian Institute for Marine Science.[5]

The Greens do not see these regulatory responses as economy-destroying red tape, but rather as necessary to 'protect' the Great Barrier Reef.

The Greens' grasp of the rhetoric of red tape illustrates how politicians of all political persuasions use the language of red tape and show a natural aversion to red tape as they perceive it. The political debate is over the existence of a problem, the prioritisation of winners and losers and then the quantum and nature of the regulatory fix.

The red tape reduction cycle

Anti-red tape campaigns have long been used by Australian politicians for electoral purposes and to drive reform agendas.

In 1976 Prime Minister Malcolm Fraser introduced red tape razor gangs, while Prime Minister Bob Hawke introduced the 'Minimum Effective Regulation' policy in 1986, requiring Regulatory Impact Statements. The Australian Labor Party under leader Kevin Rudd pledged in 2007 to wage a war on red tape, and appointed a Minister for Deregulation once elected to government. International experience is no different. In 1981, US President Ronald Reagan pledged to cut 'inefficient and burdensome' federal regulations, while in 2017 newly inaugurated President Donald Trump signed an executive order to cut two regulations for every one introduced.

Most recently the Abbott Government in 2013 was elected on a platform of cutting red tape. Its Regulatory Reform Agenda was driven in response to complaints from business that Australia was becoming less competitive due to excessive regulation. Australia had fallen in the World Economic Forum's Global Competitiveness rankings from 54th in the world in 2006-07 to 128th in 2013-14.[6] The Abbott Government proceeded to conduct four red tape 'Repeal Days' in 2014 and 2015 which saw a $4.8 billion reduction in red tape compliance costs.[7]

Nevertheless, there is a familiar cycle in red tape reduction efforts. Newly elected governments will start the process, which initially plays well for them politically. But, once the low hanging red tape fruit has been cut, what comes next is more difficult to sustain.

For example, after two years of cutting red tape, by 2015, the Turnbull Government moved onto the remaining red tape challenges which required cooperation with state governments and a deeper examination of systemic regulatory issues. In May 2017, as part of the Federal Budget, the

Federal Government announced $300 million in incentives for red tape reduction in the states through the National Partnership on Regulatory Reform.[8] The ongoing challenges of navigating Australia's federal system have so far stymied the Federal Government's attempts to cut red tape, however, with Queensland, South Australia and Victoria refusing to sign up to the partnership.

Australia's lacklustre experience of structural reform in recent years demonstrates how difficult it is for politicians to persuade the electorate of the need for this type of reform. This might be down to the cut and thrust of short term political debate and three-year political cycles, but also the declining persuasive talents of modern-day governments.

Politicians don't only have the electorate's waning interest and appetite for deregulation to contend with. Regulators themselves will mount campaigns against any curbing of their jurisdiction and regulatory reach, using their statutory powers to influence and conduct public policy, advocate for more powers and greater regulation, rather than leaving this to elected representatives.[9] This will often amount to reverse regulatory capture where the expertise of the regulator provides them with a solid platform from which to lobby legislators to increase the regulator's powers. No doubt from bitter experience, Robert Menzies famously said when referring to the insatiable growth of the bureaucratic state, '[o]ne thing about bureaucrats is that they'll never swallow their young. Leave them alone and you'll find them increasing every year.'

Further, special interest groups will often mount vociferous campaigns against deregulation to maintain red tape because of the benefits to incumbents of high costs of entry for newcomers. This has been the experience of the regulation of the digital economy by State Governments, for example in relation to Uber after strident lobbying from the taxi industry. Politicians and the politics of red tape are shaped by politicians' interactions with constituents, the media, activists and the bureaucracy to name a few. The pressure to capitulate and impose regulatory fixes and red tape stem from these interactions. The difficulty lies in withstanding them and, in the modern political age, the forces pushing for more tape appear to outnumber those seeking to dismantle it. The following sections survey the major political factors that encourage the imposition of red tape and the challenges faced by politicians in dealing with it.

The optics of action over inaction

For politicians, there is an existential and often irresistible urge to be seen to 'do something'. Every three years at a federal level, or four years at state level, politicians face the ballot box and receive the public's judgement on their performance. The political cycle incentivises action over inaction; it is difficult to withstand the allure of being the answer to someone's problems.

Red tape often arises as a response to societal ills—be it market failures, corporate collapses, environmental catastrophes, consumer or public health crises. Politicians will often identify problems through engagement with constituents, lobbyists, special interest groups or activists. While it is natural for a politician to want to help their constituents, the challenge is to maintain a balanced view about the overall impact of these problems on society when one's interactions are almost solely with the afflicted or the vocal activists and media class.

A regulatory fix is an easy and demonstrable way to respond to the appeals of one's electors or those who seek to influence them. Even for the most ardent believers of small government, it can be difficult to resist. A politician will make an assessment about whether there are votes to be won by doing something about the identified problem. Will those affected by the problem shift their vote because of a regulatory fix? Who will be the winners and the losers? Often red tape will result from the creation of a small number of vocal winners, while the rest of the population loses from the undue burden, but in only a marginal way.

For example, community concern whipped up over misconduct in the banking industry, especially during the Global Financial Crisis, has led to consideration of tough regulatory responses. These include controls on bank executive salaries and bonuses, regulation of the 'suitability' of certain banking products, and the introduction of a $240 million supercharged industry-funded ombudsmen scheme to cover disputes in the financial system (usurping the role of the courts). This tape could have serious consequences for the competitiveness of the Australian banking industry, while doing little about the misconduct.[10]

At its most extreme, the political response to a major public catastrophe is to launch a public inquiry or Royal Commission. While systemic failures can be identified through these inquiries, the recommendations can often amount to punitive window-dressing rather than effective prevention of future catastrophes. For example, there is little evidence that the dramatic increase in corporate regulation that arose after the HIH Royal Commission has done much to prevent subsequent corporate collapses.[11]

Changing attitudes to risk

As economies develop and poverty is reduced, society's focus moves from survival to wealth creation and fine tuning the nuances of life. With economic development comes an ever-decreasing appetite for risks to our quality of life. Modern day first world societies are increasingly preoccupied with potential hazards, 'dependent on a growing body of regulation, and a corresponding array of unintended consequences.'[12]

Former British Prime Minister Tony Blair has cautioned against the developed world's decreasing appetite for risk:

> [I]n my view, we are in danger of having a wholly disproportionate attitude to the risks we should expect to see as a normal part of life. This is putting pressure on policymaking and regulatory bodies to act to eliminate risk in a way that is out of all proportion to the potential damage. The result is a plethora of rules, guidelines, responses to 'scandals' of one nature or another that ends up having utterly perverse consequences.

In the end, 'a regulator who fails to regulate a risk that materialises will be castigated. How many are rewarded when they refuse to regulate and take the risk?'[13]

The impact of the precautionary principle in environmental regulation in Australia is a case in point. The precautionary principle means that a 'lack of full scientific certainty should not be used as a reason for postponing a measure to prevent degradation of the environment where there are threats of serious or irreversible environmental damage.'[14] This has led to a proliferation of red tape in an effort to minimise or eradicate potential risk, rather than actual, provable risks.

Social licence

Increasingly, a lack of 'social licence' is being used by activists
and politicians to justify red tape and regulatory intervention
in an industry. A social licence to operate is where a project
has 'ongoing approval within the local community and other stakeholders, ongoing approval or broad social acceptance
and, most frequently, as ongoing acceptance.'[15]

Recently, we have seen the Turnbull Government use the
term 'social licence' to justify swift and dramatic regulatory
intervention into the Australian gas market. In March 2017,
Prime Minister Turnbull warned that 'gas companies risked
their "social licence" to operate without reservation quotas
if they fail to supply Australian domestic industry'. After
talks between the gas industry and the Government broke
down, Prime Minister Turnbull announced in April 2017
the establishment of an 'Australian domestic gas security
mechanism' to allow for export controls to be imposed on
companies when there is a gas supply shortfall.

Social licence can cut both ways. The furore over David
Blackmore's wagyu beef farm in Victoria is a case in point. A
change in Blackmore's farming practices resulted in increased
odour and noise from his property. After complaints from
neighbours, the local council refused to give Blackmore
a permit to continue farming in this way—he had lost his
social licence to operate. Blackmore started an online petition
which gathered 120,000 signatures and forced the Victorian
Planning Minister to overturn the Council's decision. Once
Blackmore was able to activate a majority of voices to his
cause, this put pressure on the government to change the
decision, reinstating Blackmore's 'social licence to operate'.

Globalisation

While globalisation and the range of bilateral and multilateral trading agreements which support international economic relations have brought a myriad of benefits to the globe, it can also impose excessive regulatory requirements. Politically and legally it can be difficult for governments to withstand the domestic and international pressure to sign onto and ratify these international agreements, despite the onerous compliance costs and often spurious benefits to society.

International environmental and human rights agreements and more recently global finance agreements often result in domestic red tape. For example, the Nagoya Protocol to the Convention on Biological Diversity is an international agreement which aims at sharing the benefits arising from the use of genetic resources in a 'fair and equitable way'.[16] Australia is a party to the Nagoya Protocol but has not ratified it. Some scientists have expressed concern that the Nagoya Protocol imposes excessive red tape which will hamper disease prevention and monitoring, making it harder for scientists to collaborate internationally.[17]

The Basel capital accords, while delivering a coordinated global approach to banking regulation, have, on some measures, amounted to excessive regulation. Basel III, which was agreed to in the aftermath of the Global Financial Crisis, imposes risk-based international capital standards even on local community banks which have no international exposure. This has held back domestic lending, in turn constraining economic growth.

Supranational governments like the European Union impose one size fits all regulations on member states and impose stifling costs on economies. These regulations are incredibly difficult to change or remove given member states relinquish their legislative competences in return for the so-called benefits of membership.

Empowered political activism

The growing sophistication and scale of political activism through technological developments and expanded funding models presents perhaps the most significant challenge for red tape reduction efforts. Technological improvements have empowered activist campaigning, making its influence much more effective at inciting a community response and spurring on regulatory action.

We've seen activist pressure balloon to a scale unimaginable 30 years ago due to improvements in mass communication such as free and fast email, text messages, and most recently social media innovations. These innovations give special interest and activist groups much greater capacity to build— or give an impression of building—public support and pressure politicians to respond to problems, real or perceived.

The proliferation of opinion polling on seemingly every issue of public discussion empowers activists and lobby groups to pressure politicians to impose more red tape. Polling is now much cheaper through technological advancements such as robocalling and internet-based platforms. Polls drive news headlines which can in turn drive public opinion. They also give the impression that the public is overwhelmingly in favour or against a cause, when the reality may be more nuanced (consider, for example, polls for the United Kingdom's Brexit referendum and the 2016 United States Presidential election).

Push polling (where the pollster's questions lead the respondent to form a particular point of view) and online petitions are particularly effective at giving campaigns a sense of momentum in order to pressure politicians to change policies and regulations.

In recent years, there has been a proliferation of politically active NGOs and activist groups, empowered through favourable tax treatment and innovations such as crowd-funding campaigns. Where, in the 1980s, the environmental movement was relatively small and populated by a few NGOs such as The Australian Conservative Foundation, Greenpeace, The Wilderness Society and Friends of the Earth, today there are more than 600 groups on the Australian Government's Register of Environmental Organisations that qualify for Deductible Gift Recipient (DGR) status.[18] Environmental activists have campaigned hard against any changes to the rules relating to their DGR status given it 'enables them to more easily fundraise for their environmental, climate and social justice campaigns'.[19] They are particularly concerned about proposed changes which would require environmental organisations to 'commit no less than 25 per cent of their annual expenditure from their public fund to environmental remediation, and perhaps up to 50 per cent'.[20] These changes would pose a real threat to their funding model and ongoing sustainability of environmental organisations whose activities are 100 per cent advocacy and campaigning.

For example, the Lock the Gate movement has used tax deductible donations to expand its aggressive form of activism and stop much of the development of coal seam gas (CSG) in Australia. Since its establishment in 2010, Lock the Gate has successfully advocated for the cancellation of millions of hectares of gas licence applications and the ongoing moratorium on CSG in Victoria and the quasi-moratorium in NSW. The Lock the Gate Alliance is listed on the Register of Environmental Organisations and as such has DGR status. None of Lock the Gate's activities involve environmental remediation activities. It is purely a campaign and activist organisation. In 2016, Lock the Gate received over $1 million in donations and an additional $1 million in grants to fund its activities.

Conclusion

The challenge for those invested in the deregulation agenda is twofold. Firstly, how to capture the public's imagination when it comes to the virtues of cutting red tape; and secondly, how to combat the instinct to use a regulatory fix to solve society's ills. Crafting persuasive arguments for the next generation of structural reform must form part of any future deregulation campaign. Using campaign technology and applying pressure on key influencers will also be key. In the end, the cycle of red tape reduction and creation does not occur in a vacuum. It is inherently political. Activating a critical mass of winners from red tape reduction and matching the aggressive activism and sophisticated campaigns of red tape proponents must form part of the solution.

Part Two

Red tape: history and culture

CHAPTER SIX
A regulatory culture?
MATTHEW LESH

Australians like to think of ourselves as larrikins—free spirited, rebellious, and embracing individuality. The reality of the way we govern ourselves, however, is quite different. This is often observed by visitors who arrive in Australia seeking freedom and sunshine but find something else. Canadian entrepreneur and magazine publisher Tyler Brûlé recently remarked during a visit that nanny state rules have put Australia on the cusp of becoming the 'world's dumbest nation'. 'There will be a collapse of common sense here if health and safety wins out on every single discussion,' Brûlé said, taking aim at Sydney's lockout laws, airport curfew, and dining regulations.[1]

Brûlé only scratched the surface of Australia's regulatory culture. We have, in many ways, a unique willingness to use the power of the state for a liberal democracy. Australia is one of the world's only countries that requires the wearing of helmets to ride bicycles, we led the world in the adoption of anti-tobacco policies such as plain packaging, compulsory seat belt laws, and random breath tests, and are one of very few democracies that require people to vote.[2] The Australian experience of federalism has delivered overlapping bureaucracies rather than decentralised governance.[3] As of September 2017, there are 1,232 Australian government organisations, including departments, committees and statutory bodies often known just by their acronyms—the ACCC, APRA, ASIC, and the RBA.[4] Meanwhile, showing our deference to bureaucracy, Australia pays top public servants more than any other OECD country.[5]

Australia is obsessed with government. It infiltrates every part of our lives and political debate. When there is a problem the instinctual response is to demand government intervention. This was succinctly summarised by historian Keith Hancock in 1930 who said 'Australians have come to look upon the state as a vast public utility, whose duty it is to provide the greatest happiness for the greatest number'.[6] This sentiment was echoed by Terry Moran upon appointment as head of the Commonwealth Public Service in 2008, who noted his life as a public servant—a term Australia invented—had 'not been about boring administration, but about improving things—the Benthamite concept that the role of government is to achieve the greatest good for the greatest number'.[7]

Moran's positive spin reveals an important element of this puzzle. Few explicitly advocate for more government *per se.*

There is, however, relentless advocacy for policy solutions to fix the near infinite list of human problems. These policies are justified in pursuit of a benevolent practical goal, 'greatest good for the greatest number'. Compulsory voting because we want to make sure people have their say. Industrial arbitration to reduce conflict between business and unions and to deliver high incomes. Compulsory superannuation to ensure savings for retirement. Compulsory bicycle helmets to prevent people hurting themselves. Lockout laws in response to late-night violence. The list goes on.

Every time action is taken, often with benign intentions, it expands the role of the state in a way that is difficult to undo. Every policy establishes 'path dependency,' that is, the policy implemented cannot easily be reversed because it creates an expectation that government has a role in that field, and creates supportive constituencies who depend on the policy's survival.[8] This dynamic—demand for policy to fix problem, a utilitarian policy, and difficulty of reversal—helps explain Australia's red tape problem. Independently, every new policy appears to be solving a problem, but cumulatively and collectively they have placed extraordinary burdens on our lives and businesses.

The never-ending expansion of the role of government has come with a cost. Firstly, to our liberty which is slowly chipped away with each new piece of interventionist action. Secondly, the expansion of government has damaged our economy and potential for human flourishing. The IPA has estimated that red tape is costing the Australian economy a whopping $176 billion a year, that is, $19,300 per Australian household.[9]

The purpose of this chapter is to explore the underlying ideology that drives Australia's regulatory culture: our disposition to see government as the solution to our problems, and the utilitarian belief that the costs and benefits of policies can be accurately assessed. Australia's red tape problem is analysed within the historical context of our political culture.

This chapter argues that Australia's regulatory state is built on Australia's Benthamite utilitarian political culture. Utilitarian political philosophy, as developed by British philosopher Jeremy Bentham, dominated nineteenth century thinking. It colours our view towards the role of the state and utilitarian logic has been a relentless justification for increased regulation, with limited consideration of guiding values, unintended consequences or the bigger picture.

This chapter proceeds as follows. Firstly, the 'political culture' concept is defined. Secondly, the development of Australia's political culture is outlined. Thirdly, this political culture is linked to Australia's red tape problem. Finally, a brief discussion of how to cut red tape within the constraints of Australia's political culture. To tackle Australia's red tape crisis reformers must make the practical, utilitarian case for why each specific piece of red tape and over-regulation is not maximising society's happiness.

What is political culture and why does it matter?
Culture, and specifically political culture, is an elusive concept. It can neither be precisely defined, nor should we expect culture to be stable. Culture is more of an ever-changing vibe than a scientific concept. Nevertheless, we know it when we see it. Over time groups of people develop customs that have implications for how we behave, what we eat, how we dress, and so much more. Cognitive scientist Dan Sperber defines culture as the spread of ideas and practices from one person to another.[10] Culture spreads because we are social, and want

approval contributing to conformity, and because of the informational element, it is beneficial to survival to learn best practice from each other.[11]

Political culture is the subgenre of a society's culture that relates to politics, such as the guiding political beliefs, the structure of the state, and the role of government. Political culture is the collective manifestation of psychology and history that have led to beliefs, values and attitudes amongst populations that differ by country.[12] It is a both the product of collective political history and the life histories of individuals.[13] Almond and Verba's *The Civic Culture* introduced the concept to political science through their attempt to systematically account for democratic development and stability across countries.[14] In the post-war period, they argued Britain and the US have a 'civic culture' that keeps destabilising elements in check, which Germany, Italy and Mexico did not.

Political culture is a useful concept to help understand the meta-political elements of society and the shared dispositions towards government. The underlying, generally unspoken, rules about how debate is undertaken and what problems are considered to require solutions. This is given expression and moulded by institutions, rules, and procedures, and, ultimately, policies. People are, to an extent, rational and will therefore respond to incentives. Political culture, like formal and informal institutions, help define behaviour in different political contexts.

The development of Australia's political culture
Political culture can only be separated from innate human tendencies through analysis of differences between countries—and therefore is best illustrated in comparative terms. Despite our shared Western heritage and colonial history,

Australia's political culture differs substantially from the United States of America for example. This is evident in institutional design, the disposition towards government, and public debate.

The US designed their constitution with the presumption of humankind as flawed, and therefore government by humans requires checks and balances, separation of powers, and an extensive bill of rights.[15] The Australian constitution is far more practical and expansive. It includes a long list of powers (that have been interpreted even more expansively), very few restrictions on government power, and limited checks and balances.[16]

The difference is further evidenced in the discourse of our politics.[17] Australia's politicians are not famed for grand rhetoric and vision. 'Australia is not a country of great political dialogue or intense searching after problems (or recognition of problems that exist),' Donald Horne accurately assessed in *The Lucky Country*.[18] In contrast, rights, liberty and freedom are constant themes on both sides of American politics—even if there is often limited agreement on the precise meanings of these ideas.[19]

These differences reflect Australia and the United States' differing histories.[20] The American disposition towards government is interwoven with their founding experience, a revolt for independence against the British. In contrast, Australia took gradual steps towards federation in collaboration and with support of the British.[21] The United States' coming of political age was the eighteenth century, the era in which radical thinking was dominated by the likes of John Locke. Australia's political coming of age was the nineteenth century, as Australia transformed from penal colony to free settlement culminating with democratisation and federation. This was the era when Jeremy Bentham and John Stuart Mill's utilitarianism was ascendant. In sum, America got Locke, Australia got Bentham. This gave Australia, as I shall argue in this section, a utilitarian political creed.

Utilitarian thinking is not and has never been the only line of thinking in Australian politics.[22] Political scientist Louis Hartz, in his comparative study of European colonies, argues that fragments of British society, as well as local environmental factors, explain the differences between Australian and American political culture. Australia, it is argued by Hartz's collaborator R. N. Rosecrance, took on a 'radical culture,' which, for the era, meant the radical demands of the Chartists. However, as Australian academic William Coleman has pointed out, this is an oversimplification: many traditions influenced early Australian colonists, and that continues to be the case today.[23]

For example, Chris Berg finds, from analysis of book sales and auctions in early nineteenth century Australia, a cross-section of early philosophical influences, including Adam Smith's *Wealth of Nations*, Edmund Burke's *Reflections on the Revolution in France*, and many more.[24] There were natural rights liberals in early Australia, such as Bruce Smith who wrote *Liberty and Liberalism* in 1887, and George Reid, Australia's fourth prime minister and leader of the Free Trade Party.[25] Today, there is a libertarian in parliament, the Liberal Democrat Party's David Leyonhjelm.

Nevertheless, these ideas have influenced but not dominated politics in Australia. Historian John Gascoigne finds 'natural rights' advocates did exist in early colonial Australia, however, in the counter-revolutionary atmosphere directly following the French and American revolutions, they were unable to take hold.[26] On the other side of politics, one can find socialist thinking and policies. However, an extreme socialist vision was never successful in Australia, as epitomised by the rejection of Prime Minister Ben Chifley's proposal to nationalise the banks at the 1949 election.

Hugh Collins influentially argued Australia has a utilitarian political culture.[27] 'In what is argued about, how these disputes are conducted, and upon what assumptions the debates proceed, the distinctiveness of Australia's politics is fully revealed', Collins writes.[28] Collins posits that Australia's mental universe is 'essentially Benthamite', referring to British philosopher and reformer Jeremy Bentham. Bentham's ideas 'endured as the dominant ideology in the twentieth century, shaping the nation's institutions, images, and ideas'.[29] Collins finds that, 'colonial political struggles of the nineteenth century were, consciously or unwittingly, bearers of' Bentham's ideas.[30]

Bentham was a prolific scholar on a range of topics from criminal justice reform to bureaucratic structure.[31] He is best known for his utilitarian political philosophy. The classical utilitarians, which include Bentham and John Stuart Mill, argue that all humans have equal moral worth, everyone should be treated equally by government, and public policy's role is to maximise the overall utility, that is, the 'greatest happiness for the greatest number'.[32] Every policy is therefore assessed on its ability to bring pleasure, and should be implemented if it brings more pleasure than pain, that is, if the benefits outweigh the costs. Utilitarianism provides strong arguments for political equality and the rule of law, important in an era dominated by hierarchies, limitations on voting to property owners, and birth family's importance for life outcomes.

The classical utilitarians were individualists: utility is judged at the individual level. They are typically classed as liberals, however liberty was largely justified on practical grounds—

that it achieved a positive outcome not as an end in itself. For example, liberty of the press is justified so that people can share information, and ensure the government knows their views, not because people have the right to express their views.[33] Bentham explicitly rejected the natural rights approach of Locke, which he described as 'rhetorical nonsense—nonsense upon stilts'.[34]

The moral claim that we are all equal, and therefore it is the state's role to provide practical solutions for the general happiness, is apparent throughout the attitudes of Australians and discourse of Australian politics. As Collins argues, Bentham's utilitarian notions suit Australia's 'conventional sense of identity'; 'practical, sporting, fair minded, and egalitarian,' and focus on 'common sense'.[35] Historian Keith Hancock puts it a bit differently, claiming Australia's reliance on the state was 'collectivism of means' to achieve individualist ends.[36] 'To the Australian, the State means collective power at the service of individualistic 'rights'. Therefore he sees no opposition between his individualism and his reliance upon Government'.[37]

In Australia, politicians are ever-searching for policies to help address issues, and rights are rarely discussed. There is no bill of rights in the Australian constitution.[38] In fact, the First Fleet departed England as the Americans were writing their constitution, in an atmosphere where the British establishment was particularly hostile to notions of rights.[39]

The foremost conduit for Benthamite utilitarian thinking in Australia is Chartism. The Chartists were a British political reform movement that advocated for the 1838 People's Charter: universal male suffrage, the secret ballot, no property qualification for parliament, pay for parliamentarians, equally sized constituencies, and annual parliamentary elections.[40] Two of the three authors of the People's Charter were associates of Bentham, and the Chartists were aligned with Bentham's thinking on policy decisions reflecting the equal value of all humans.[41]

The British Chartists' ideas came to Australia with vengeance.[42] Australia, lacking the established power hierarchies of Britain, was fertile ground. Many Australian political reformers were themselves formally involved in the Chartist movement in Great Britain, including prominent agitators at the Eureka Stockade, and even 'Father of Federation' Henry Parkes who had participated in Chartist campaigning in Birmingham before emigrating.[43]

The Australian colonies were some of the first places in the world to introduce universal male suffrage. By 1859, all Australian colonies except Western Australia and Tasmania allowed all adult males to vote.[44] The same could not be said for Britain until 1918. 'Within ten years of the discovery of gold, practically the whole program of the Chartists is realised in the Australian colonies', historian Keith Hancock noted.[45]

David Llewellyn's PhD dissertation found extensive evidence of Benthamite influence on early Australian politicians and bureaucrats, the rum rebellion, Australian law and economics, the anti-transportation campaign, education, and the land system.[46] Bentham wrote three pamphlets on Australia, pertaining to transporting criminals and the role of the governor.[47] Bentham's view that the New South Wales governor had no legal power to make regulations for the civilian population likely influenced leading colonist John Macarthur who helped overthrow Governor Bligh in the Rum Rebellion in 1808.[48]

In addition to the Australian links with Bentham, there are other reasons Australian political culture became utilitarian. Greg Melleuish argues that in order to avoid conflict in a multidenominational society policymakers needed to keep religion separate from politics and focus instead on the 'practical' function of Australia: the delivery of agricultural produce for Europe.[49] Utilitarian political reasoning fitted well with a 'society devoted to economic development'.[50] Historian John Gascoigne similarly argues that the early Australian state needed extensive power to enable economic development, and therefore Bentham's idea of state power for the general good of society served the colonial administrators' purposes.[51]

The International Social Survey Programme found Australians have strong support for an expansive role for government in Australia. Ninety-eight per cent of Australians think it is the government's role to provide health-care for the sick, and 94 per cent think government should provide a decent living standard for the old, 85 per cent think government should help industry grow, and 80 per cent think government should provide decent housing.[52] Australian attitudes towards government are dominated by notions that the state exists for practical, utilitarian purposes.

A Benthamite regulatory system

Historian of the British utilitarians, Elie Halévy outlines three core characteristics to Bentham's moral and political philosophy: (1) the greatest happiness or utility principle; (2) universal egoism, that is, humans are motivated by pleasure and pain; and (3) the identification of one's interests with those of others.[53] It is the final element that is most problematic in policymaking. Bentham argued that legislators can identity, understand, and, if democratically elected, would want to and be able to maximise the general happiness. He thought that utility could be scientifically measured and maximized in public policy, and is even responsible for inventing economic vocabulary such as 'maximise' and 'minimise'.[54]

While the appeal of this approach is evident, there are a number of fundamental problems. Frederick Hayek identified the core economic challenge as the 'knowledge problem', the dispersion of information and knowledge of preferences.[55] Hayek argues that 'the knowledge of the circumstances of which we must make use [for planning] never exists in a concentrated or integrated form, but solely as the dispersed bits of incomplete and frequently contradictory knowledge which all the separate individuals possess.'[56] In addition, as Herbert Simon argued, humans suffer from 'bounded rationality', we lack the time and cognitive ability to address all potential problems.[57] Finally, politicians and bureaucrats have their own interests that are not necessarily aligned with the public.[58]

Bentham, particularly in his early writing, noted the futility of trying to support the economy through regulation.[59] 'Every statesman who thinks by regulation to increase the sum of trade, is the child whose eye is bigger than his belly,' Bentham wrote.[60] In practice, however, utilitarianism has been used to justify maximal technocratic government. The notion of a planner being able to maximise 'general happiness' has provided never-ending justification for government action. Bentham is father of the bureaucrat's favourite tool: the 'cost-benefit analysis,' the supposedly objective measuring of the costs and benefits of policy.[61]

It is impossible, however, to measure the subjective value that each individual receives from a particular policy. Policy makers lack the knowledge and cognitive ability to ever assess all the costs and benefits in the short and long term. The social world is complex and number of unforeseeable outcomes are infinite.

Furthermore, decision makers can and do manipulate a cost-benefit analysis to provide the beneficial answer when they are seeking to justify action.[62]

Halévy argues that Bentham did not think liberty was as high a priority as security in policymaking, therefore 'his philosophy is essentially a philosophy written for legislators and men engaged in government, that is to say for men whose profession it is to restrict liberty'.[63] Writing from an Australian perspective, L.J. Hume argues that utilitarianism, because it did not seek to limit government power and protect individual rights, is not a form of liberalism.[64]

Utilitarian logic, even to the extent that the classical utilitarians used it to justify liberty on consequentialist grounds, has come to be used to restrict liberty. British jurist A. V. Dicey identifies three causes of the rise of the 'authoritative side of Benthamite liberalism' in the late nineteenth century Britain. Firstly, the loss of faith in laissez-faire meant 'the principle of utility became an argument in favour, not of individual freedom, but of the absolutism of the State'.[65] Secondly, democratic reform which gave legislators, now representatives of all wage-earners, legitimacy for further intervention. Finally, the increasing role of the state in additional policy realms.

This experience is writ large in Australian history. Following the early success of democratic reform, which delivered elected legislators who were representatives of the people, utilitarian logic was used to increase the role of government and the regulatory state. In the hands of politicians and bureaucrats—who will forever claim their policies are in the public good—utilitarian logic was used to justify governmental intervention. This is a formula for maximal government intervention, red tape, and in the worst circumstances, despotic majoritarian dictatorship. Bentham's followers laid the foundations for the expansive modern state in Australia, because of the focus on the 'greatest happiness' rather than liberty.[66]

The flaws of utilitarianism help explain Australia's red tape problem. Each individual piece of regulation may have been justified as beneficial to society, taking away a little liberty to maximise the general happiness. In some situations, this was correct. A set of regulations is necessary for the functioning of society, establishing the core institutions and rules of the game.[67] However, this is not where regulation has stopped. Because the full impact of regulation is not acknowledged and not properly understood, and because the impact on individual activity cannot be fully foreseen due to limited knowledge, bureaucrats can claim a net benefit to society that does not in fact exist.

This leads to a continuous expansion of red tape for two reasons. Firstly, the existence of some regulation, once a precedent is established on practical grounds, provides a never-ending source of justification for more regulation. Secondly, the beneficiaries of the status quo, which, for example, place barriers to market entry, also form a coalition to protect the pre-existing regulation in perpetuity and develop further regulation to their benefit. In the classic public choice conundrum, the beneficiaries of deregulation are dispersed and unorganized and those who favour it are well organized and influential, presenting a strong coalition in favour of regulation.[68] This is particularly evident for regulation that restricts free trade, which benefits a small number of domestic producers at an overall cost to consumers.[69]

Bentham's ideas are also responsible for the modern regulatory state in other ways. The bulk of Bentham's writings were on perfecting government by replacing the common law with written codes.[70] This approach inevitably empowers the legislator to extend their reach into more areas of law in the process. Bentham also discussed the necessity of delegated legislative power, that is, regulations. He wanted the legislator to sketch out 'a sort of imperfect mandate' which was then left 'to subordinate power-holder to fill up.'[71] This is, again, a recipe for red tape as it empowers bureaucrats with limited knowledge of how society functions to control it.

Australia's political history is replete with regulation justified using utilitarian logic. The Australian Settlement, from shortly after federation till the 1980s, was in effect a series of heavy-handed regulations including White Australia, Industry Protection, Wage Arbitration, State Paternalism and Imperial Benevolence.[72] These policies were adopted for 'technical rather than principled' reasons.[73] The formal aims were to provide a decent standard of living, protectionism to secure the economy, industrial arbitration to minimise conflict and provide high wages, and close ties to Britain, and later the United States, for security.[74] The result was a loss of competiveness and ultimately economic downturn.

The criticism, and eventual dismantling, of the Australian Settlement was also put in utilitarian terms. The Hawke-Keating Government undertook reform to make the Australian economy more competitive amidst the faltering economic situation, and were certainly not ideological devotees to liberal economic reform. The floating of the dollar, privatisation, and trade liberalisation did not, however, mean the end of regulation in Australia. In fact, as diagnosed in the European literature, the Australian state has transformed from including 'positive state' elements such as public ownership to more of a 'regulatory state'.[75] Consumer, banking and corporate regulations have flourished, driven by the idea that the newly liberalised economy required regulation to keep it in check.[76] This, as Chris Berg explains, led to the establishment and expanding role of regulatory agencies, which further separated from democratic chains of accountability.[77]

Conclusion

'The ideas of economists and political philosophers, both when they are right and when they are wrong, are more powerful than is commonly understood. Indeed, the world is ruled by little else,' economist John Maynard Keynes remarked.[78] This has certainly been the Australian experience of Jeremy Bentham and utilitarianism. Whether or not Australian politicians and bureaucrats have ever heard of Bentham it is clear that in their manner of operation they are considerably influenced by his ideas.

Bentham's utilitarian ideas arrived in Australia through a number of conduits in the nineteenth century, particularly the Chartist movement, and has subsequently spread like wildfire into the way we think about government's role, partake in political debate, and establish institutions. W. H. Greenleaf notes Bentham's doctrine 'can be made (or can be seen) to bear both laizzez-faire and interventionist implications'.[79] In the Australian case it has tended to justify the latter.

Utilitarianism has been used to justify each piece of additional regulation, ignoring dispersion of knowledge, the natural limits of humankind, and the possibility that, even after democratic reforms, legislators and bureaucrats might have their own set of interests. This has led to the enormous expansion of red tape in Australia, which is damaging both our liberty and our prosperity. The red tape problem is interrelated to Australia's Benthamite utilitarian political culture.

Utilitarianism may be one of the core causes of the problem, but it is also potentially a solution to Australia's red tape issues. The classical utilitarians, particularly Mill, did have liberal instincts because liberty can be justified on utilitarian grounds.[80] People being free to pursue their own goals without unnecessary interference from government does maximise human happiness. Limiting the role of government can increase pleasure.

This was just the experience of advocates for the abolition of red tape in the case of the Road Safety Remuneration Tribunal. The Tribunal, established in 2012 by the Gillard Government at the behest of the Transport Workers Union, was justified to protect driver 'safety' however, in fact, was set to push up pay rates for independent truck drivers to unaffordable levels, potentially pushing 50,000 owner drivers out of work.[81] The legislation was ultimately abolished by the Turnbull Government in April 2016 following an extensive campaign by truckers and critics of red tape.[82]

The Road Safety Remuneration Tribunal provides an important case study in a successful deregulation campaign in Australia. The legislation, which was quietly passed under the 'safety' banner in 2012, went unnoticed until its practical impact was felt by a destructive pay decision, at which point it was abolished for utilitarian reasons. In order to secure Australia's future prosperity, reformers must make the practical case for red tape reduction that matches Australia's utilitarian political culture.

CHAPTER SEVEN

1901: Federation as bureaucratisation

WILLIAM COLEMAN

Historians find explaining the Federation of the six Australian states in 1901 a somewhat toilsome task. They have no big answers to ply with; it is widely allowed that no stern imperative drove Federation; no bright lure of gain animated the act; no tug of expedience yanked the event into realisation.

In truth, circumstances of the day encouraged inaction. In terms of international security, 1898 was not 1908. The United States' establishment of itself as a Pacific power that year (the annexation of Hawaii, Wake Island, the Philippines, Samoa) had enhanced Australian security. In terms of the economy, the economic crisis of 1892 had served only to sweep Federation from the political agenda.[1]

In terms of politics, the Federation episode is only with difficulty construed as an upshot of the struggle for power. Labor parties—the new force of the Federation decade—did not exist at the 1890 conclave of Premiers that launched the journey that would end in Federation. And the conflicted attitude towards Federation in the Labor parties that rapidly formed in the 90's surely bespeaks an uncertainty of the costs and benefits of Federation to those parties, and their adversaries.

An aura of gratuitousness, then, encircles Australia's Federation affair. One signal of this is Barton's impassioned plea to the Constitutional Convention to include 'posts and telegraphy' as one of the functions of the new Commonwealth, on the grounds that otherwise the new state would lack occupation.[2] Here we behold the spectacle of Federationists fervently labouring to erect a complex machine of federal government; and then casting around for things for it to do.

And yet every event has a cause, and, in the quest for an explanation of Federation, historians have resorted to invoking 'sentimental' forces. They are surely right. But there are other causes. Careerism surely figured. And there were doubtless sectional economic advantages. But this chapter posits another palpable cause.

Federation was a manifestation of the impulse in Australian life to bureaucratisation. Federation might even be deemed a culmination of a century of operation of this powerful impulse. Except that 'culmination' suggests an endpoint. And there was no end in the process; Federation was more like a critical moment in bureaucratisation of Australian life, a point of take-off.

Bureaucracy

In tracing Federation to 'bureaucracy' this chapter uses the term to denote more than simply government administration; it uses it to designate an entire sphere of life. This is a sphere born of the impulse to order; which operates through the collective and conscious pooling of information, with the crucial assistance of quantification, or at least categorization; which results in rules, systems, 'plans': where the disconnected is now connected, and arranged in serried ranks; brave new provinces of law and order established; and the wild successfully tamed.

In government administration the object of the impulse to order is human beings; and the vehicle of collective action is the 'committee'. A committee may be distinguished from other decision making bodies by the (supposed) unity of purpose of its members, and with a consequent tendency to make decisions by consensus. It contrasts with more 'democratic' decision making bodies where a conflict of purposes amongst members is freely accommodated, and decisions are commonly made by majority.

Bureaucracy as a 'sphere of life' extends beyond government administration to encompass science and technology. The impulse to predict and control; the reliance on a public intelligence (the 'conference' is allied to the 'committee'); the great 'bureaucracies of nomenclature', that science, doubtless rightly, prizes; the production of (natural) laws: all these gratify and arise from the impulse to order. Thus the applied scientific expert and their institutions—so prominent in Australian life—sits near the bureaucrat. 'He is no metaphysician, but that does not worry Australians; he is legal, that is to say expert, and therefore much admired in our homeland'.[3]

Which brings us to the law. Bureaucracy as a sphere of life also encompasses certain modes of law. Granted, customary law is well beyond it. The growth of the 'general principles' of the common law is weakly cognate; but it lacks the certitude that 'good things are designed' which animate the strongest impulses to order. However, the codification of laws and the construction legal codes is very much within the bureaucratic sphere. The legal officer prescribing some code—the Commissioner, that is to say, 'the bureau judge'—is a familiar figure in Australian life and highly kindred to Bureaucracy.

Bureaucracy has been powerful in Australia from its genesis, for at least three reasons.

Australia began as a piece of administration. 'The most enduring feature of any colonial regime,' it has been said, 'one of the first to appear and the last to leave, is the administrator, the colonial bureaucrat, high, middle and low.'[4] The apex of the management of colonial Australia was itself a bureaucracy; the Colonial Office, which in the key mid-century period was presided over by James Stephen, a 'strict legalist' with a 'passion for system and uniformity'.[5] Beneath it acted the governors, who, too, were public servants, in as much that they were accountable to the Colonial Secretary.

Bureaucracy, broadly understood, may also have had a utility in Australia's circumstances. In the face of a completely incomprehended natural resources base, scientific technology offered some salvation; along with considerable employment for surveyors, geologists, agronomists, hydrologists, pharmacists, meteorologists, etc. Australia is also an unusually urbanised nation, and the ordering of urban life has smaller costs, and larger benefits, than a rural existence.

Thirdly, the weakness of other spheres of life in Australia gave room to bureaucracy. The country's tatterdemalion social structure spelt a paucity of the gentleman figure that the parent society relied on, and bureaucrats were substituted to fill the gap. Thus a head of the Department of Public Instruction could be born in a workhouse (William Wilkins), but as a tested public servant, their like were trusted to perform as a substitute gentleman to neutralise the restless, raging egos of a raw frontier society. Beyond the haphazardness of its social structure, bureaucracy also benefitted from the fact that the market sphere was weak, from at least the 1890s. To adapt the thinking of Patrick Morgan, the approximate centenary of European settlement saw the fading of the impulse of self-transformation that had been so essentially characterising of the settlement until then (see the likes of John Barker, Walter Padbury, and James 'Philosopher' Smith)—and was so obviously animating of the market sphere.[6] One consequence of this recess of the market sphere was the emergence of the ethic of 'mateship'. This proved, in the event, to be something of a humanising counterweight to bureaucracy. But the recess of the market sphere around 1890 also plainly cleared a path for the bureaucracy's advance.

The officialdom fathers

So much for the thesis. What is the case for interpreting Federation as a culmination of the bureaucratic impulse?

The first strain of evidence is 'circumstantial'; it is that several persons so closely involved in federation pushes were bureaucrats. Ask: who is the first person known to have mooted the creation in Australia of federal body? Was it a patriot and would-be statesmen, W.C. Wentworth? Was it the visionary Rev J.D Lang?

Was it, possibly, a young Henry Parkes, the 'Father of Federation'? It is widely acknowledged that the first person known to have proposed a 'central authority' in Australia superior to the separate state governments was Sir Edward Deas Thomson. In his thirty years of 'intimate connexion' with the government of NSW, Thomson was from 1828-1856, the principal public servant of NSW; the chief advisor of all governors, the son-in-law of one, and the 'channel through which all the governor's correspondence flowed'.

Historians concur that it was Thomson who in 1846 advised Governor Fitzroy to recommend to the Colonial Office that it create 'a superior functionary' in Australia to review and possibly veto the Acts being produced by the separate legislatures in Sydney, Hobart, Adelaide. Here, we see in a single phrase—'superior functionary'—the travesty of present day Australian 'federalism'; which is conceived as a bureaucratic structure in which the 'head office' in Canberra exercises oversight of state 'branches'.[8]

A few years later Thomson publicly championed the 'General Assembly of Australia', that been devised by the under-secretary of the Colonial Office, James Stephen, and in which Australia's 'provinces': 'may have continued to exist on paper, but would never have developed much functional or political importance'.[9]

Thomson's advocacy of the establishment of some kind of central Australia-wide power, then, preceded both J. D. Lang's 1850 proposal for 'a great Federation' under the style and title of 'The United Provinces of Australia',[10] and Wentworth's 1850s conversion to a 'federal assembly'. In 1848 Wentworth had stormed against the proposals of Stephen, conceding no more than a 'congress from various colonial legislature ...

might be got together for short periods at certain intervals'.[11]

In the second push to federation, that came in the 1890s, we again see an eminent public servant at the very centre. Ask once more: 'Who was the Federation figure whose career most exclusively identified with Federation? Who was the Federation figure whose career in federal government was the most enduring, successful and fulfilling?' Opinions will differ. But this chapter ventures that the person was not a politician. For almost all political figures of the Federation movement, Federation proved a disappointing second act.[12] It can be cogently argued that the person most exclusively and most successfully identified with Federation was Sir Robert Garran (1867-1957), the longest serving 'permanent head' the Commonwealth has (so far) had.

The year the Federation episode began, 1889, was the year Garran completed an MA on 'federalism'. The new graduate 'pushed aside his anticipated career as an equity barrister for zealous involvement in the federation movement throughout the next decade'.[13] The clever, practical and equable young man was soon private secretary to George Reid, and, with just a short pause, secretary to the drafting committee of the Constitutional Convention, where he found his verbal formulations 'wedging themselves into the bill'. So ubiquitous was Garran at these deliberations he was often assumed to be a 'delegate' to the Conventions. Similarly, 'false memory' recalls him in attendance at the critical private meeting in Melbourne of Premiers in 29 January 1899, when in truth he was hundreds of kilometres distant. Not purely an eminence grise, Garran was also an ardent public advocate of Federation, his *Coming Commonwealth* of 1898 being read by 'everybody' and 'soon sold out'.[14] When the Commonwealth came, the new polity was christened by his co-authoring the 1008 pages of *The Annotated Constitution of the Australian Commonwealth*, which for 70 years remained the bible of constitutional lawyers.

In 1901, feeling like 'as a junior barrister suddenly promoted to the final court of appeal', Garran was appointed by Alfred Deakin the first public servant of the new Federal government, as Secretary to the Attorney-General department. Also Parliamentary Draftsmen, and later Solicitor General, he was for 32 years a permanent head. In this capacity he was an advocate of the establishment of Canberra in the 1920s, and saw 'no reason why Canberra should not become the centre and focus of artistic life in Australia'. After retirement he remained an active advocate of Federation. He was the first (published) historian of the federation movement (in *The Cambridge History of the British Empire*).[15] He co-authored *The Case for Union*, published in 1934 to combat secession in Western Australia. He championed the establishment of Canberra University College in the 1930s, and in the 1940s the ANU, and appropriately was the awardee of its first degree. Fittingly, the title he gave to his autobiography, completed in the last weeks of his life, is *Prosper the Commonwealth*.

Unity in uniformity

But a skeptic will be indifferent to the particulars marshalled above: the fact that in the two key pushes to Federation the most eminent civil servants of the day were zealous Federationists may seem to be no more than guilt by association.

A stronger case for this chapter's thesis would rest on some correspondence between the nature of Federation as conceived by the 'fathers', and the nature of bureaucracy. And there was a correspondence. For the key colouring presumption of all Federationists was that Federation would be a federation of uniformity. 'Unity in uniformity' was, in effect, their watch word, and it may be contrasted with the alternative of 'unity in liberty'.

The trade in goods illustrates the distinction. As is well known, the states imposed tariffs on each other's goods. These barriers violated the tenets of Free Traders, and offended the sensibilities of many more. But there is more than one solution. One is a Customs Union, where no state has a tariff on imports from within Australia, and every state has the same tariff on imports from outside of Australia: unity in uniformity. And this was a key element of the Federation. But another solution is a Free Trade Area. This would prohibit any state from imposing tariffs on goods imported from other states, but allow each state to impose tariffs on imports from other countries as it pleased. A Free Trade Area equally serves the overthrow of barriers between the states just as much as Customs Union. But from its beginning, the federation movement never countenanced that possibility. From the beginning it was assumed dogmatically that NSW must have the same tariff on imports from other countries as Victoria, which must have the same tariff as on imports from other countries as Queensland etc.

The vexed question of naturalisation also illustrates the difference between 'unity in uniformity' and 'unity in liberty'. Prior to Federation, a person naturalised in one state remained an 'alien' within the boundaries of another. Federation vested naturalisation in the federal government; unity in uniformity.[16] An alternative would have been to leave naturalisation with the states—licensing different states to have different naturalisation requirements—but to establish the mutual recognition of each other's naturalisations.[17]

The relevance of 'unity in uniformity' to the thesis of this chapter is plain: uniformity is acutely cognate with law-likeness, and thus the ordering impulse of bureaucracy. Bureaucracy cherishes uniformity, and Federation, as construed by the 'Fathers' was a means to that uniformity.

One time zone to bind them all

A clinching illustration of the triangular nexus—uniformity/ bureaucratisation/federation—is found in the history of telegraphy. In the generation before Federation 'intercolonial conferences' of the six ministers of Postal and Telegraphs were frequent; some 14 by 1898. Although conducted at a 'ministerial level', 'senior technical bureaucrats ... readily took the initiative in tendering advice and drafting submissions to politicians and wielded enormous influence over ministers, especially in the 1860s and 1870s when ... critical decisions were made'.[18] The most senior of these senior technical bureaucrats was Charles Todd, hero of the overland telegraph to Darwin, expert on all things electrical, and Post -Master General of South Australia from 1870 to 1905.

In 1893 there took place in Brisbane another 'Postal and Telegraph' conference that, among other tasks, sought to settle the issue of time zones. Todd held no ministerial position, but nevertheless bore the title of Post-Master General, and was South Australia's representative at the conference. Remarkably, he persuaded that Conference to resolve to establish a single time zone for the entirety of Australia. 'One Nation, One Time Zone', evidently. So at the summer solstice the sun would rise in Perth at 8.14am, and in the winter solstice at 9.17 am. This eccentric proposal was 'strongly urged' by Todd, and adopted without dissent. It was Thomas McIlwraith, the Premier of Queensland, who pressed the recision of this unreal decision; and it was reversed in the subsequent Conference of 1894, never to be heard again.[19] McIlwraith 'favoured only a limited form of Federation and in 1900 advised Queensland ... to abstain';[20] and he was obviously one the 'provincialists' so bemoaned by Federationists and later historians of their cause.

Equality and hierarchy

If Federation was a means to gratify the bureaucratic value of uniformity, there was corollary, as John Nethercote has argued.[21] Uniformity spells equality does it not? Federation becomes a means for equalisation, and so we have levelling, bureaucratic behemoths such as the Commonwealth Grants Commission.

But one may additionally argue that Federation amounted to a means of accommodating another bureaucratic value that, on the face of it, is hostile to equality: hierarchy. Hierarchy is another way of creating order, especially when uniformity is either unobtainable, or not useful. If everything can't be made equal, the compulsion to order requires any given thing be classed unambiguously superior to, or inferior to, or 'corresponding to', every other thing; the end point of this ordering by ramification is the familiar branching hierarchy, with a single summit or fount, and might be contrasted with less hierarchical orderings such as 'the network'. Australian Federation, in the caricature that prevails in the country today, is obviously a branching hierarchy, with Canberra at the summit.

The pudding's proof

The most concrete proof of the interpretation of Federation as Bureaucratisation presumably lies in the consequences of Federation. And Federation plainly accentuated the pre-existing bureaucratising tendency in Australia. A key illustration is the White Australia policy. The various colonies had long passed Anti-Chinese Acts (typically taxing Chinese immigrants), and a few years before Federation NSW and WA extended the scope of these beyond Chinese. Western Australia went furthest in its Act of 1897 that 'prohibited'

> Any person who, on being asked to do so by an officer appointed under this Act, shall fail to himself write out, in the presence of such officer, in the characters of any language of Europe, a passage in English of fifty words in length taken by such officer from a British author, and to append his name thereto in his own language; Western Australia Immigration Restriction Act 1897.

The new Commonwealth on its creation acted promptly to reduce the heterogeneity of the acts of the six states into a tidy, unbending and comprehensive formula. It adopted a dictation test quite unknown in four of the six, and decisively more stringent that Western Australia's. The *Immigration Restriction Act 1901* prohibited any person who, 'fails to write out at dictation and sign in the presence of the officer a passage of fifty words in length in an European language directed by the officer'.

Despite the apparent rigour of this clause, its efficacy did rely on 'the officer' using the test in ways that would secure its intended but unstated purpose. And the new Commonwealth was concerned that her officers were not always doing so. In

1909 the permanent secretary of the Department of External affairs was dispatched to Western Australia to investigate apparent laxity there in the implementation of the test.[22] The secretary had cause for concern. In that year Leoncio de Garra, a Philippine who had worked for six years in the state's pearling industry, was subjected to the test in English, and passed. Procedure required that in this untoward situation a test in a second European language be applied. But the officer knew only English. So he asked de Garra to paint a water colour with the words 'Advance Australia', and de Garra succeeded in meeting this undemanding challenge.[23] Here we see the humanising counterweight that mateship could constitute to the cruelty of bureaucracy. But de Garra was the last 'coloured' person ever to pass the dictation test in Australia. Bureaucracy had won.[24]

Beyond government, Federation, misconceived as a bureaucracy in three layers, served as the template for the bureaucratisation of Australian civil society at large in the century subsequent.[25] But to blame Federation for Australia's bureaucratisation is to make Federation overly culpable, because, as this chapter has argued, Federation was in large part the result of bureaucratisation. Bureaucracy will find devices other than Federation to pursue its values of uniformity and hierarchy; 'international treaty obligations' are an obvious one. And Bureaucracy did find other devices before it found the Commonwealth: Intercolonial Conferences;[26] Premiers' Conferences; and the Federal Council of Australasia.[27] All these constituted a 'federation before Federation', and all amounted to attempts to rule Australia by committee. The Constitutional Conventions of the 1890s, though formally parliamentary in procedure, had a strong flavour of the committee about their conduct. And these institutions only amounted to the most prominent manifestations of a vogue—if not a mania—for Australians in the last decades of the nineteenth century, to assemble themselves into hierarchical Australia-wide structures; ranging from the religious (Primitive Methodists, Congregationalism, YMCA, Presbyterian Churches of Australasia) to the prosaically economic (trade unionists, Protectionists, Free Trade, Fruitgrowers); not to mention Australian Natives, Australasian librarians, and the Australasian Association of the Advancement of Society, at the opening congress of which, in 1888, Forrest, predictably, appealed for Federation.

In some ways Australian society has been revolutionised since 1901. But more than a century later Australians remained encumbered by the posterity of their grandparents' grandparents' passion for contriving order.

CHAPTER EIGHT

Red tape: Tethering Australia to the world

GREGORY MELLEUISH

By the 1930s the nature of red tape was well understood in
Australia and its qualities appreciated. In one of Lennie
Lower's grandfather stories, 'Red Tape In The Sunset':

> Life at home is now hellish. As we're all living on Grand-
> father's superannuation, he has taken over the manage-
> ment of the house. He spends most of the housekeeping
> money on forms. If I want a drink of water, I have to fill
> in form XB7, and then he rings up the Water Board and
> inquires how things are at the reservoir, and after that he
> gets onto the Weather Bureau and wants to know about
> the prospects for rain and if they will kindly furnish him

with statistics of the rainfall as from 1890 up to the year
ending June 30, 1935. Then I go next door and get a drink
of water.[1]

So, what is the source of red tape and the desire to create
ever more complex rules and regulations? There are perhaps
three answers to this question. First, it is an aspect of human nature to endlessly elaborate on cultural products so
that over time things which were quite simple become very
complex. Second, it is a feature of what has been termed the
'cultural patterning' of the West to produce complex forms
of culture which favours the creation of ever more red tape
and regulation.[2] In part, this is because one of the defining
cultural characteristics of the West is the corporation as a legally defined entity. Finally, red tape and regulation is largely
the product of what might be termed modernity as the type
of society which encourages the propensity to engage in the
activity of developing complex rules to direct and control human activity.

In fact there may be aspects of all three factors in the
development of red tape and regulation in the West and
Australia. Michael Cook, for example, cites the example of
kinship arrangements amongst Australian Aborigines.[3] It is
clear, however, that the amount of cultural elaboration which
can occur in an illiterate society is limited. It is only with
the development of writing that bureaucracy and elaborate
systems of law become really possible. In fact, it can be
argued it is writing which makes bureaucracy possible, along
with a written code of laws. Human beings, generally, have
a tendency to elaborate on their cultural practices so that
they become more and more complicated. But a society

restricted to oral transmission of its beliefs and practices is restricted in terms of the degree of elaboration it can achieve. The invention of writing, especially the alphabet, allowed for much greater possibilities.

This codification, and subsequent elaboration, of law can be seen both in Judaism and Islam. In the West, it can be argued that a key moment in this development was the codification of Roman law carried out by Justinian in the 530s. That was a defining moment for the West. It helped to create a new sort of bureaucratic order. And, as anyone who has read the Anecdota of Procopius knows, Justinian was believed by many to be a demon in human form.[4]

Roman law helped to set the pattern for Western development in the eleventh century which was when the Gregorian reforms within the Western Church made it legalistic and bureaucratic in nature.[5] The Western Church came to be defined by its laws and its various written documents which have undergone considerable elaboration over the centuries.

Documents and bureaucracy seem to go together in the West as part of our cultural patterning. For example, Molly Greene compares the Venetian regime in Crete in the seventeenth century with the Ottoman one which succeeded it. The Venetian regime is much better documented and works within a framework of written law and written commercial agreements, including such things as insurance documents. Documents of this type, along with legal, ecclesiastical and political documents have been lovingly preserved in the archives of all Western countries. The Ottoman regime, on the other hand, relied far more on oral arrangements although the Kadi court did record its judgements in writing.[6] Even its commerce relied on oral contracts.

Another good example of elaboration can be seen in the literary genre of commentary, whereby texts are commented on, elaborated and developed over an extended period of time.[7] This was a particular feature of medieval and early modern European thought. I think that it is still a major feature of the way in which that peculiar medieval survival, the academic culture of universities, works. Scholars are inculcated into a practice which involves knowing what has been said on a particular topic, providing a commentary on that knowledge, and then indicating how they have advanced it. They are most certainly not encouraged to develop innovative and imaginative ideas outside of the existing framework. That is one reason why universities are so prone to 'groupthink'.

An oral society has limitations in what it can do in the way of elaboration, although the members of such societies have much better memories than those of literate societies. But a society with writing opens up endless possibilities. It has written records stretching over centuries, commentary on those records and elaboration of ideas over time.

In this regard, technology matters. Print opened up new possibilities as subsequently did the typewriter, the computer and most recently digital modes of textual reproduction. It is worth noting that Islamic civilisation long resisted printing and that printing of Islamic works did not really take off until the nineteenth century. As with the case of the coming of literacy; technology matters when it comes to the growth of red tape and regulatory practices. Put another way, there are limits to what a state can do and it largely depends on capacity. To do a lot requires that the state possess a considerable amount of what Michael Mann terms infrastructural power.[8]

Most pre-modern states lacked this capacity. To give an example, even though Ming China possessed a bureaucracy of professionals chosen by examination, its capacity to do much was limited by the relatively small numbers of such mandarins. The capacity of China to extract the taxes to support a bureaucracy was limited. In fact, Chinese officials rigged the census data for their regions so they would not be forced to collect more tax.[9] Hence one needs to be careful; the will to dominate may be there but the capacity to make that will a reality may be lacking.

In the case of Australia, the simple and easy answer to the origins of Australian red tape is that it all goes back to the convict origins and the need to have a lot of rules to run a prison. Except ...

With the coming of responsible government Charles Cowper dismantled much of the old structure of the old 'Official' order in New South Wales, preferring to employ cheap clerks in preference to an expensive public sector full of senior administrators.[10] In the second half of the nineteenth century the 'state' in colonial Australia did not have the capability to do a lot. Of course, colonial parliaments kept lovely records of their proceedings in leather bound volumes of Hansard, but they did not involve themselves in much legislation.

Nor could they necessarily create elaborate bureaucracies. The colonial state lacked the capacity to do an awful lot. Their major role was the creation of infrastructure, especially railways and primary schools, and then later dams; these were major undertakings and left little time for meddling in the lives of ordinary people.

Moreover, the public services remained 'patronage bureaucracies' until the 1880s and 1890s.[11] In New South

Wales, there was a strong belief that politicians should control those servants of the public who were meant to implement the will of the people as expressed through their representatives.

In part because they lacked independence from politicians, colonial public services did not have 'policy directorates' devoted to dreaming up useless new things for governments to do. They did not employ graduates, largely because the colonial universities produced only a few of these, most of whom became lawyers. In fact, the Commonwealth public service resisted employing generalist graduates until the mid-1930s.[12]

The first two big bureaucracies in Australia were the railways and the Education departments, both of which date from the 1870s and 1880s. The Education departments of the various colonies became bureaucratic monsters over time as the number of schools and teachers under their control grew.

However, the times were changing and the technology necessary to support a bureaucratic culture was becoming available. The typewriter came into general use in the 1880s and the telephone in the 1880s and 1890s. The day of copperplate handwriting was dying.

Nevertheless, as one reads C.E.W. Bean *On the Wool Track*, published in 1910, one gets a sense of a social order in the outback which is dynamic and energetic and which is not bound by red tape. While the capacity of the politicians and the bureaucrats to exercise an enormous power over the large rural areas of their colonies was limited this meant that there was considerable scope for local initiative.

Bean described the 'genius of Australia' as a 'quality of

Australians' to 'make something out of nothing'. He attributed 'that extraordinary versatility, the capacity to do anything' to the English origins of Australia, arguing that it required bush life to bring it out, a life in which an excessive specialisation is not possible, 'countrymen will remain beyond comparison the most capable men in the nation'.[13]

The men of the bush were dynamic and very capable of doing what needed to be done, improvising and solving problems without having to resort to an occupational health and safety manual. Such capability to engage in innovation was born of necessity but also of freedom.

But even by Bean's day things were changing. The bush was slowly, but surely, being tied to the governments of their capital cities as technologies of communication made such control possible. Henry Lawson understood that process:

Ah, then our hearts were bolder,
And if Dame Fortune frowned
Our swags we'd lightly shoulder
And tramp to other ground.
But golden days are vanished,
And altered is the scene;
The diggings are deserted,
The camping-grounds are green;
The flaunting flag of progress
Is in the West unfurled,
The mighty bush with iron rails
Is tethered to the world.[14]

The late nineteenth, and early twentieth, centuries saw the growth of bureaucracy and its attendant red tape and regulation across the western world.[15] The size of government grew as governments attempted to involve themselves in the lives of their peoples, beginning with education. As the bush was tethered to the world by railways so Australia was bound to the cultural patterns of the Western world and increasingly tied up in red tape. The frontier was being closed.

By the 1890s the new model public services based on merit and controlled by a public service board came into being. Interestingly, in New South Wales, it was George Reid, a genuine Free Trade liberal who led the way in such reforms. In the early twentieth century, the cult of efficiency, largely the product of the university educated, especially in areas such as medicine and engineering, was being advocated, one example being the desire to collect statistics about as much as possible. Such activity is exemplified by the first Commonwealth statistician Sir George Knibbs.[16] Quantification, efficiency and regulation go hand in hand.

The mental framework for a world which would tether and bind Australia was being created. Efficiency required data; rules and control rather than the capacity of individuals to be innovative was now the key to solving problems. The old ways of the outback were being overridden by the new ways of the professional city slicker:

> I am sitting in my dingy little office, where a stingy
> Ray of sunlight struggles feebly down between the houses tall,
> And the foetid air and gritty of the dusty, dirty city
> Through the open window floating, spreads it's foulness over all.
>
> And in place of lowing cattle, I can hear the fiendish rattle
> Of the tramways and the buses making hurry down the street,
> And the language uninviting of the gutter children fighting,
> Comes fitfully and faintly through the ceaseless tramp of feet

And the hurrying people daunt me, and their pallid faces haunt me
As they shoulder one another in their rush and nervous haste,
With their eager eyes and greedy, and their stunted forms
    and weedy,
For townsfolk have no time to grow, they have no time to waste.

And I somehow rather fancy that I'd like to trade with Clancy,
Like to take a turn at droving where the seasons come and go,
While he faced the round eternal of the cashbook and the journal-
But I doubt he'd suit the office, Clancy, of 'The Overflow'.[17]

The late nineteenth century was the time when the world was divided up into different time zones, when time was standardised.[18] It was the period when 'time and motion' studies were commenced as work was broken down into its various components and put back together again, all in the name of measurement. This was the world of modernity.

The great statement of this new way of 'being in the world' was the characterisation of bureaucracy by the Prussian Max Weber. Order and regulation combined with efficiency created a much more powerful, and potentially despotic, state. It also created a new type of human personality who could be fashioned so as to be an efficient cog in well-oiled bureaucratic machine. It is interesting that Weber suffered a nervous breakdown.[19]

The most tangible expression of the desire for creating a new type of culture in Australia, one based on rules and regulations, and the supposed efficiency they bring, rather than on individual initiative, was the development of the arbitration commission and its wonderful workings. This was, of course, fuelled by a desire to create what H. B.

Higgins termed a 'new province for law and order' and it was a clear example of the way in which the new cult of efficiency worked.[20] Reason would provide the 'order' which would replace the supposed 'anarchy' which was believed to be the necessary consequence of individual initiative. It would also, of course, radically increase the power of those, generally with a university education, who became the regulators.

Consider the way in which the basic wage was calculated based on (very dodgy) statistics, the ways in which wages were broken down into their components by the Court and then adjusted accordingly. The 'new province' was founded on the idea that it was possible to create harmony in the workplace through the imposition of a set of rules and regulations created by a judge. The way forward, supposedly to 'justice', was a world bound together by red tape and regulation. It was a world which only recognised certain types of issues, those which could be reduced to an amount of money, as being important in the workplace and treating all workplace problems as if they could be treated in those terms. It was so very mechanical as the real world of individuals interacting with each other and solving problems accordingly was superseded by a set of rules and regulations bound by the need to express everything in numerical terms. Red tape and regulation went hand in hand with what is best termed the numerical imperative. Whereas Victor Trumper had been a great batsman who was renowned for his batting style, Don Bradman is defined by his batting average.

While the Australian colonies were expanding and developing it was possible to keep a 'red tape' culture at bay. The state could only do so much under these circumstances and those in the outback were largely left to their own devices. Nineteenth century liberalism in its Australian manifestation was voluntarist and the governments of those days had neither the capacity nor the will to impose red tape regulations on their citizens. It was an age of exuberance and enthusiasm in Australia. Nevertheless, the cultural patterning which leads to a red tape society was present. Like it or not, the potential for red tape lies deep within all of us.

The potential for a social order which had as its model an efficient machine, a machine which, its adherents believed, would produce a much more ordered and harmonious society, had been expressed before the Great War. However, it was the war which helped to make a regulated and red tape society much more of a reality.

Future Prime Minister Billy Hughes had written the following before the war:

> (The state) ought not to interfere ... in pursuance of some plan to make people happy in some particular way. The individual ought to be permitted to be happy in his own way ... To compel people to wear a particular kind of dress, live in a certain kind of house, eat certain foods, and drink, or abstain from drinking, certain liquids, are all interferences with liberty, justifiable only when the freedom, happiness and welfare of the general community cannot be secured without it.[21]

The irony is that it was Hughes, invoking 'the freedom, happiness and welfare of the general community' during World War I who helped to advance the regulatory state which today is very much concerned about what individuals eat and drink, and even about what they wear (think 'covering up').

Sir Robert Menzies was very aware of the way in which the invocation of the Defence power of the Commonwealth

Constitution had increased the central power of the Commonwealth and given it the taste for regulating the lives of ordinary people. Menzies appreciated that the Acts put in place in both wars were temporary but also understood the longer term cultural impact which this war time regulatory culture had had on the Australian people. Discussing the aftermath of World War II, Menzies put it this way:

> The compulsion to 'go the Commonwealth' during the war and immediate post-war period has tended to breed new habits of thought. Organisations and people have developed the habit of 'going to the Commonwealth' for the satisfaction of a great variety of needs or demands, even though the problems involved may clearly be within the normal jurisdiction of the States and not within the peacetime jurisdiction of the Commonwealth.[22]

The terrible years between 1914 and 1945 did indeed 'breed new habits of thought' and Menzies understood that those new habits needed to be resisted as far as possible. Unfortunately, the developments of those years also provided the new intellectuals, and their cult of efficiency, the opportunity to create new, and increasingly powerful, state structures, particularly at the Commonwealth level. The times seemed to indicate the need for regulation, the state and the intellectuals jumped at the opportunity, and despite Menzies' best attempts to reverse what had been essentially temporary measures, it has proven, in the longer term, extremely difficult to do so.

PART THREE

Case studies

CHAPTER NINE

Environmental regulation and red tape

DANIEL WILD

Excessive environmental regulation is one of the single biggest impediments to business investment, job creation, and economic growth in Australia. Environmental law has expanded rapidly at the state and federal level since the 1970s. This chapter presents three case studies which highlight this growth. The first two case studies involve matters within the *Environment Protection and Biodiversity Conservation (EPBC) Act 1999*: Section 487, which allows environmental groups to challenge ministerial approvals of projects, such a coal mines, in court, and the 'water trigger' which extended the range of potential projects that require approval by the federal environment minister. The third case study is of state-based native vegetation laws.

The chapter then argues government intervention to increase environmental conservation has been based on highly flawed grounds. In particular, the chapter argues that the claim that environmental conservation is a public good is misplaced; that environmental policymaking suffers from information aggregation deficiencies; and that the public choice school of economics presents serious challenges to the efficacy of environmental policy making.

The growth of environmental law in Australia

Environmental regulation has expanded rapidly in Australia since the 1970s. One approach to demonstrate this growth is to count the number of pages of environmental law passed each year. This is a crude approach with a number of drawbacks: it doesn't account for the relative significance of the laws being passed, nor does it control for the possibility that some of the additional pages passed could be in reference to laws being repealed. However, it is a simple approach that enables easy comparisons through time and is sufficiently accurate to track broad changes.

The first federal government department partly devoted to environmental matters was introduced in 1971 by the McMahon government with the Department of Environment, Aborigines and the Arts. According to Morgan Begg, in 1971 the Commonwealth government administered just 71 pages of environmental legislation. As Figure 1 shows, by 2016 the federal Department of Environment and Energy administered 4,669 pages of environmental legislation, an 80-fold increase from just 35 years earlier.[1]

One of the most significant additions to federal environmental law was the introduction of the Environment

Figure 1: Pages of Commonwealth environmental law

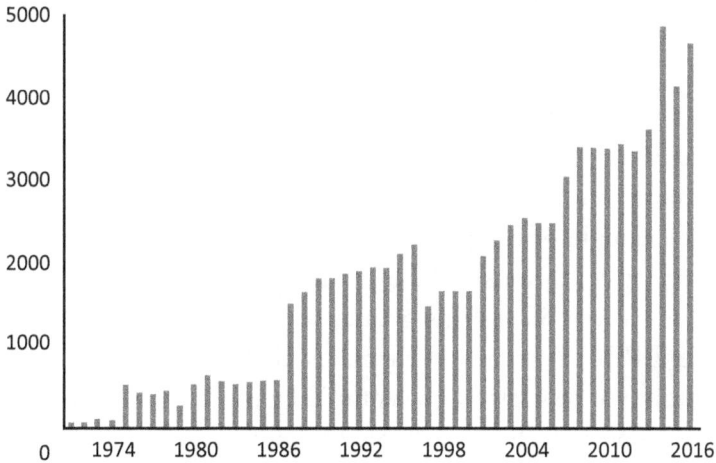

Source: *Institute of Public Affairs*

Protection and Biodiversity Conservation (EPBC) Act by the Howard government in 1999. The EPBC Act is the largest and most significant piece of federal environmental law, currently spanning two volumes and 1,117 pages—a quarter of all federal environmental law by page count.

The EPBC Act provides the federal government with substantial control over economic activity. Specifically, the EPBC Act requires that a project proponent receive approval from the federal environment minister in cases where that project could have a 'significant impact' on a matter of national environmental significance (MNES). Examples of affected projects include coal mines, gas projects, or dams. There are currently nine MNES including world heritage properties, national heritage places, wetlands of international importance, and nationally threatened species and ecological communities.

There are a range of public policy issues with the
EPBC Act. The need for project approval from the federal
government results in projects being routinely delayed. And
when projects are eventually approved, that approval is
provided on the basis that the project proponent meets an
extensive set of conditions. In a 2014 report on the major
project approvals process, the Productivity Commission gave
the example of the project which was required to meet 800
primary conditions and 1,500 sub-conditions.[2]

However, of perhaps greater concern is that built within
the EPBC Act are mechanisms that allow an increasing
number of projects to be captured by the approvals processes
over time, as well as mechanisms that allow project approvals
process for a given project to be drawn out. The remainder of
this section provides two case studies to demonstrate these
issues.

Environmental 'lawfare'

Section 487 of the EPBC Act provides environmental groups
such as Greenpeace with the legal standing to challenge the
ministerial approval of projects. This means even after project
proponents have completed the extensive environmental approvals process, they can still be—and frequently are—subject to legal challenges which delay project implementation.

Parties are typically provided with legal standing where
they can demonstrate the direct negative consequences of a
policy decision. For an individual this requires demonstrating
that their interests—such as a property right—would be
negatively affected should a particular decision proceed,
such as a farmer whose crops would be damaged by a
nearby mine. Section 487 automatically extended legal

standing to environmental groups, irrespective of their having a direct interest in a given project. Specifically, under section 487 an individual can claim legal standing where the individual is a citizen or resident of Australia and has 'engaged in a series of activities in Australia or an external Territory for protection or conservation of, or research into, the environment' within two years of the relevant decision. Similarly, an organisation can claim legal standing where the aforementioned conditions are met and 'the objects or purposes of the organisation or association included protection or conservation of, or research into, the environment.'[3]

Environmental groups have not used this legal privilege in the way it was originally intended—to provide an interested third-party with the incentive to verify the legality of Ministerial decisions. Rather, environmental groups have explicitly used this legal standing to slow down economic development. Cases brought to court under section 487 have a high failure rate. Just four out of 32 cases (13 per cent) which have proceeded to judgement have been successful. And only one out of those four successful cases resulted in a substantial change to the minister's original decision.[4]

Environmental groups have explicitly detailed how they would use legal means to achieve their broader ideological agenda of disrupting Australia's coal industry. This was outlined in the Greenpeace authored activist document *Stopping the Australian Coal Export Boom*.[5] The key strategy outlined is to 'disrupt and delay' key projects, while gradually eroding public and political support for the industry. To do this, the document states that green groups will 'get in front of the critical projects to slow them down in the approval process' by undertaking 'significant investment in legal capacity' in order to engage in sustained legal battles.

The fundamental policy problem with section 487 is it provides environmental groups with asymmetric influence over policy decisions. At most environmental groups are obligated to compensate project proponents for court costs in the event the case is dismissed. However, court costs are only a fraction of the total economic costs. Research by the Institute of Public Affairs found that project proponents had spent a cumulative 7,500 days, or 20 years in court at a cost of up to $1.2 billion.[6] Conversely, others in society who would be negatively affected should a project not proceed—prospective employees, for example—do not have access to equivalent legal recourse. This results in the law providing disproportionate influence to environmental groups vis-a-vis project proponents and other potential beneficiaries of project development.

The 'water trigger'

The second case study analyses the addition to the EPBC Act of the so-called 'water trigger' to the list of MNES by the Gillard Government in 2013. The 'water trigger' requires all large coal and coal seam gas projects which may affect a water resource to receive approval from the federal environment minister. The notional motivator for the introduction of the trigger was to address perceived public concerns over the effects large projects could have on water resources. Then environment minister Tony Burke said in the second reading of the bill:

> The challenge we have had until now is that people quite reasonably expect the minister for the environment and

water to take into account, by law, the impacts of coal seam
gas and large coal mining on water resources.[7]

There is no obvious public policy rationale for the introduction of the water trigger. 'Community concern' is a nebulous
concept which could be used to justify all types of government interventions. It is, in and of itself, an insufficient basis
on which to form public policy. Regardless, if there were genuine concerns over the effect of projects on water resources,
it would seem natural to not limit the provision to only coal
and coal seam gas projects. The coal sector is a small water
user, representing around 0.8 per cent of national water consumption. By comparison, the agricultural sector consumes
62 per cent of national water resources, yet is not affected by
the provision. Indeed, industry was not consulted until after
the bill was introduced into Parliament, nor was a Regulation Impact Statement or cost-benefit analysis completed.

The absence of a bona-fide public policy rational has
led some to suggest that the introduction of the water
trigger was a politically motivated move on behalf of the
Gillard Government to continue to secure the support of
independent MP Tony Windsor. The former CEO of the
Minerals Council of Australia, Mitch Hooke, described the
water trigger as 'a political agenda that has no environmental
dividend.'[8] The Australian Petroleum Production and
Exploration Association argued that the water trigger was
a political fix by the Gillard government to secure Tony
Windsor's vote in 2013.[9]

The water trigger is an example of the ways in which
poorly designed pieces of public policy can be expanded
to regulate an ever increasing array of activities. Many on

the political left seek to expand the EPBC Act to include more 'triggers'. Both the Labor party and the Greens support expanding the water trigger to include shale and tight seam gas developments.[10]

More worryingly, it has been suggested that the list of MNES even be expanded to include greenhouse gas emissions. According to the 2008 *Independent Review of Environment Protection and Biodiversity Conservation Act 1999*, the greenhouse gas trigger could operate by setting a threshold of emissions released over a certain period—or over the life cycle of the project; projects which produce above that threshold will need to undergo assessment and approval under the EPBC Act.[11] Such an addition would result in virtually all significant projects coming under control of the federal government—precisely the outcome the anti-development lobby seeks.

Native vegetation regulations

State level regulation has also proven to be a substantial deterrent to business investment, particularly in the agricultural sector. Native vegetation is a natural resource which is indigenous to a given area. Native vegetation is considered to enhance the biodiversity of a given ecosystem, which can improve water quality, provide habitats for wildlife, and reduce salinity levels. Native vegetation can also provide benefits to farmland productivity by improving soil fertility and preventing soil erosion. This means farmers have a natural incentive to conserve native vegetation insofar as it confers a net benefit to them. Hence, some level of native vegetation would be retained even without government regulation.

The central public policy issue arises where the amount of

native vegetation the government deems desirable is greater than what private land-owners are willing to provide. In this case regulation is frequently used to force landowners to provide, or retain, extra native vegetation. However, the provision of additional native vegetation comes at a large expense to private landowners. The main cost being the opportunity cost of land which can no longer be used for commercial purposes. This reduces the amount of land that can be used for productive purposes, which causes property values to decline.

Native vegetation regulations also lead to flow-on consequences. Because regulations are changed frequently, and often in a retrospective manner, the future income stream attached to a property becomes less certain. This increases the risk premium for investment, which raises the costs of loans and reduces the demand for investment. Over time this leads to less investment in the agriculture sector which spills over into other areas of the economy. For example, it is likely that lower investment will result in fewer hectares being used for farming purposes, which reduces competition and output and raises food prices.

However, while farm values are usually diminished by native vegetation regulations, historically, compensation for loss of property value has not been forthcoming. According to the Productivity Commission, compensation has been the 'exception rather than the rule.'[12]

The absence of compensation is a clear violation of landowners' property rights. In Australia, the basic right to property is stated in Section 51 (xxxi) of the Constitution, which stipulates that the Commonwealth must provide compensation 'on just terms' to property it acquires.[13] While

S51 (xxxi) only refers to compensation for the acquisition of property (rather than loss of value resulting from regulation), it enunciates the centrality of private property to Australia.

Some have argued that compensation should not be provided for depreciated property values because the law recognises regulation to be separate from acquisition. For example, the Australian Network of Environmental Defenders Office (ANEDO) has argued that:

> [i]t has long been accepted under the common law and through High Court decisions that Government regulation of activities that can occur on private property (such as whether land may be cleared or not) does not constitute an acquisition of property and therefore no right to compensation is activated.[14]

It is true that regulation which prevents certain uses of land is not legally recognised as a 'taking' or 'acquisition' because the title of the land remains with the landowner rather than being transferred to the government. However, from the landowners' perspective, the difference between acquisition and regulation is a distinction without a moral, economic, or practical difference. Indeed, acquisition can be conceived of as an extreme form of property right erosion through regulation. Otherwise stated, government regulation can render private property effectively public through regulation to the point where the property owner has no real freedom to use their land in their own preferred way.

The reality is that the property which had been originally acquired by the landowner, following regulatory changes, becomes a completely different property and should be understood as such.

Environmental laws are based on poor public policy

Environmental regulation in Australia has been based on poor public policy rationales and is beset by a number of challenges. In particular, the claim that environmental conservation is a public good is highly contestable; environmental conservation is subject to an information aggregation problem; and the 'public choice' school of economic thought presents challenges to the incentives governments face when introducing environmental regulation.

The public good challenge

A typical justification provided for government intervention into environmental matters is that environmental conservation is a public good. It has long been recognised by economists that public goods are a form of market failure in which optimal decision making at the individual or firm level leads to inefficient outcomes at the society-wide level. In particular, it is held that individuals are able to free-ride on the provision of environmental amenity such that private organisations are unable to recuperate the full marginal cost of the provision of that environmental amenity. As such, environmental amenity goes underprovided and government intervention is required to ensure the optimal amount of amenity is provided. For example, the Explanatory Memorandum for the Environment Protection and Biodiversity Conservation Bill 1998 argued that 'many of the benefits provided by the environment are used free of charge, and often access cannot be denied. Without government involvement, free access and use can result in adverse effects on the environment.'[15]

The problem, however, is that in the development of public policy the term 'public good' is often used incorrectly.

Proponents of environment regulation often claim that native vegetation retention, for example, is a public good because people other than the private land owner benefit from native vegetation retention. Even the Commonwealth Treasury has stated that 'a particular natural resource policy challenge is public good conservation, which refers to conservation activities undertaken on private land, which may benefit local communities or society in general.'[16]

However, such a broad definition would capture any private action which conferred an uncompensated benefit to a third-party. Indeed, one could apply the same logic to a suburban house with nice frontage that others benefit from when they walk past. Under the definition set forward above this would be defined as a public good because people other than the private land owner benefit from the frontage. Consequently, following the logic of native vegetation laws, the homeowner should be forced to maintain the frontage against their will because otherwise others walking past would miss out on something they value.

However, the conditions under which government intervention can reliably deliver net benefits are vanishingly small. The text-book definition of a public good is a good which is defined as both non-rivalrous and non-excludable. A good is non-rivalrous where one person's consumption of a good doesn't affect the ability of another person to enjoy consumption of the same good. While a good is non-excludable where someone cannot be excluded from consuming a good or service, such as via an admission price.

Environmental conservation can be considered non-rivalrous, but only to a degree. For example, one individual can visit a nature park without affecting the ability of other individuals to visit and enjoy the nature park. However, as more people enter the nature park becomes crowded and, after a certain point, the capacity of an additional entrant to enjoy the nature park to the same extent as the previous entrant is diminished. As noted by the OECD, 'the property of non-rivalry is lost when the good is so heavily consumed that congestion or over-use begin to reduce its availability to others.'[17] Free-to-air television is an example of a truly non-rivalrous good: no matter how many people turn on their TVs, an additional person will not affect the others enjoyment.

Environmental conservation also fails to take on the properties of excludability. Individuals and organisations are able to purchase land, dedicate that land for environmental conservation purposes, and exclude people from entering the land unless they pay for admission.

The information problem

However, even if the conditions of a public good were satisfied, the decentralised nature of information would inhibit the ability of governments to provide the optimal amount of environmental conservation.

Indeed, one of the key drawbacks of environmental conservation laws is that they are based on top-down administration by government officials. However, the preferences of politicians and government officials rarely reflect the diverse preferences of individuals throughout society. Some individuals place a higher value on certain types of conservation than others, while some are willing to pay more or less for such conservation. But because regulations are one-size-fits-all, these diverse preferences are not sufficiently taken into account, nor could they be.

Friedrich Hayek recognised the basic information problem of public policy when he wrote that:

> *if* we possess all the relevant information, *if* we start out from a given system of preferences and *if* we command complete knowledge of available means, the problem which remains is purely one of logic [emphasis in original].[18]

But, Hayek continues, these ifs cannot be taken as given because 'the "data" from which the economic calculus starts are never for the whole society "given" to a single mind which could work out the implications, and can never be so given.'[19]

This inability for governments to aggregate information that reflects the preferences and wishes of individuals across societies is a classic problem with central planning, be it economic or environmental. This makes it difficult, if not impossible, for governments ensure the provision of environmental amenity results in a net benefit. In the absence of market mechanisms, central planners are unable to know what type of environmental conservation should take place, and in what quantity to supply it. This lack of knowledge results in, for example, governments being unable to optimise the trade-off between sacrificing agricultural output with environmental amenity.

The public choice problem

A final challenge to environmental conservation is provided by the public choice school of economics. This school argues that the assumptions used by economists to analyse private behaviour should also be applied to government decision-making.[20] Rather than acting to forward the interests of individuals in society, the public choice school holds that political actors design public policy so as to forward their own goals and ambitions. Political parties seek election or re-election, while bureaucrats seek to expand their institutional power, progress their careers, and set up potential job opportunities outside of the public sector.

The public choice school, therefore, challenges the notion that environmental conservation is primarily directed toward overcoming the public good market failure problem, or that policy is designed to achieve an optimal balance between environmental conservation and economic activity.

An example of how this transpires in Australian environmental policy can be seen with policies that mandate renewable energy generation. The most prominent policy of which is the Renewable Energy Target (RET), which requires energy retailers to purchase a certain amount of energy from renewable sources rather than coal or gas. Notionally, the policy is aimed at reducing Australia's greenhouse gas emissions, in an effort to make a contribution toward reducing global climate change.

However, an impartial public policy assessment of renewable energy promotion would involve: assessing the extent to which human activity contributes to global warming or climate changes; assessing the extent to which renewable energy subsidisation will reduce that human contribution; and evaluating those claimed benefits against the economic costs of renewable subsidisation. It is evident that, based on such an evaluation, government subsidisation of renewables is not a net benefit. Specifically, human activity accounts for just 3 per cent of total greenhouse gas emissions. And, of that 3 per cent, the RET reduced global emissions by just 0.0005 per cent per year on average since its inception in 2001.[21] This means the RET makes no noticeable difference to the global temperature or climate.

However, the RET has imposed significant economic costs. Deloitte estimated that real GDP would be $29 billion larger in 2030 if the RET were to be abolished.[22] While ACIL Allen estimated that total energy prices for end-users would be approximately $30 billion higher over 2014-30 as a result of the RET.[23] Hence, normal cost-benefit analysis shows renewable energy subsidisation is not in Australia's national interest.

However, viewed through the public lens, the motivating reasons for renewable energy subsidisation becomes more apparent. Firstly, there has been a substantial bureaucratic apparatus established to oversee, advise on, and implement renewable energy programs. The benefits following from this apparatus—mostly to highly-paid and sometimes influential and powerful bureaucrats—would be jeopardised should renewables programs be abolished, and hence pressure is placed on maintaining the status quo. Secondly, politicians can derive electoral benefit through appearing to be acting to improve environmental outcomes. And, thirdly, renewable energy firms clearly receive commercial benefits from renewable energy programs, and so have an interest in exerting political pressure to maintain those programs.

Conclusion

Environmental regulation in Australia has grown rapidly since the early 1970s and is now one of the single biggest impediments to business investment, job creation, and economic growth. Environmental 'lawfare' through the use of section 487 of the EPBC Act, along with the introduction of the water trigger, has expanded the reach of the federal government and environmental activists over economic development. Additionally, state-based native vegetation laws have eroded private landowners' property rights, on unjust terms and typically without compensation.

Moreover, this expansion of environmental regulation has been poorly justified. In particular, the claim that environmental conservation is a public good is highly contestable, environmental conservation is subject to an information aggregation problem, and the public choice school of economic thought presents challenges to the incentives governments face when introducing environmental regulation.

Rather than continuing with the status quo, governments should seek to reduce environmental regulation: devolving responsibility for environment protection to state governments, and introducing market-based approaches as opposed to direct top-down government regulation.

CHAPTER TEN

Housing affordability and red tape

ASHTON DE SILVA

Since the early 1990s housing, and in particular housing affordability, has been a major focus of successive governments as well as the general populous. According to Nicole Gurran and Peter Phibbs, ten government initiated inquiries and/or policy processes were implemented between the years 2003 and 2015.[1] Public engagement in the housing debate has been substantial, for example the inquiry into Housing Affordability in 2013 formally acknowledged over 200 submissions.[2]

Housing, and the notion of 'home' more specifically, has long been recognised as a cornerstone of our society. Politically and socially, as reflected in the words of Sir Robert Menzies, it is a fundamental determination of our (collective) wellbeing:

the real life of this nation is to be found ... in the homes
of people who are nameless and unadvertised. ... The home
is the foundation of sanity and sobriety; it is the indis-
pensable condition of continuity; its health determines the
health of society as a whole.[3]

In the context of the individual it also matters. Notably Abraham Maslow identified it as a second-order requirement of
each person's psychological health—specifically the need for
a safe and secure shelter (that is, a home).[4]

These statements identify that access to quality housing is
important socially for all Australians. In more recent times,
its (macro)economic prominence has grown substantially.[5]
This is arguably due, in part, to households perceiving
housing (home) ownership as a fundamental requirement of
(financial) security.

Not surprisingly therefore demand for, and in particular
ownership of, housing also known as the 'great Australian
dream' continues to grow. The alternative, renting, is often
regarded as an inferior option for many. This demand-side
consideration however is not the only factor characterising
housing affordability debates. Supply-side factors are
numerous and are accepted by some to be the major
contributor to the housing affordability issue. Understanding
how these supply factors interact with demand is extremely
challenging. This challenge is compounded by the fact that
the influence of various factors change across time and space
thus impeding the effectiveness of policy measures. [6]

The purpose of this chapter is to illuminate a fundamental
area of reform that is necessary if the consequences of housing
affordability are to be minimised: the planning system.

In the next section an outline of the demand and supply-side influences are presented. It is argued that the central authorities cannot confidently influence demand-side features of the market. Rather, the most effective course of action for any government is to focus on what it is actually responsible for—planning processes and regulations. Complementing this discussion are observations based on three focus groups. Although not the primary objective of the focus groups, the findings clearly point to several inefficiencies—inefficiencies where the government can and should effect changes in policy and practice.

Mortgage finance

A key feature of Australia's housing market is mortgage finance. Over the last 25 years this industry has evolved to be one of the most innovative in the world. Reflecting this, it is notable that in recent decades owner-occupiers-with-mortgages have generally made up one half of owner-occupiers (noting there has been a slight increase in the last ten years).[7]

Mortgage servicing costs (in particular interest rates) have declined dramatically in recent times. Nearly thirty years ago, in 1990, the official cash rate (the rate lending institutions use as a benchmark) was at a peak of 17.5 per cent—it is now below 2 per cent. Coupled with this (interest) cost of credit decrease typical mortgage durations have increased (30 years from 25 years) enabling borrowers to service higher loan amounts. New loan products have also emerged reflecting in part the changing labour market dynamics (for example, low doc loans) and thus expanding the set of potential borrowers beyond their historical type.[8]

Determining the net effect of reduced servicing costs on housing affordability can be a difficult issue. For example, interest rate decreases during the early 2000s could be considered as a good thing—enabling households to overcome price gains (not directly resulting from decreases in the cost of borrowing) at comfortable levels of serviceability. In more recent times, lower interest rates could be considered as a major contributor to the affordability problem inflating demand.

In short, understanding how the financial market interacts with housing markets (and therefore affordability) is fundamentally important. A discussion on the successful (or not) use of financial levers to address housing affordability however is beyond the scope of this chapter.

The demand and supply side

Debates ensue as to whether demand or supply-side factors are (most) responsible for the housing affordability crisis. In Table 1 major factors categorised as demand, supply or intra are listed based on the Productivity Commission report into First Home Buyers.[9] Five demand side influences are iden-tified and four supply side conditions are stated. Taxes and concessions are identified as being 'intra demand—supply'.

In our free and democratic society engineering household types (demographics) and mandating consumption flows (preferences) are beyond the gambit of central authorities.[10] Importantly, they do not have any means to lift each household's economic circumstance. This leaves two possibilities; investor demand and rental markets.

Reducing investor demand, a policy often touted, has significant downside risks. Ceritus paribus, reducing

Table 1: Housing market factors

Demand	Intra demand and supply	Supply
Demographics (number and types of households)	Taxes and concessions	Construction costs
		Infrastructure costs
Household economic circumstances		Land availability
		Land release and development processes including fees and regulation
Investor demand		
Consumer Preference		
Rental prices and availability		

Source: Based on Figure 1.1 page 39, Productivity Commission (2004)[11]

investor demand is likely to reduce the supply of rental accommodation. This could have significant consequences for local economies—especially those characterised by (relatively) high transient populations reflecting industry specialisation such as education (one of Australia's most important export sectors). Further, rental accommodation can provide greater access to job opportunities for those in low paid industries. A reduction in rental properties could also increase demand for housing welfare solutions. This could also hinder productivity resulting from less efficient employee-employer matches. In addition, socially it may result in communities being less diverse.

Previous attempts to target housing affordability through taxes and subsidies have been arguably ineffective. For example,

in relation to the first home buyer grants, various experts have
observed:

> However, the grant will typically bring forward the pur-
> chase decisions of these first time buyers, and grants will
> then have a limited impact in raising the equilibrium rate
> of home ownership.[12]

Another expert noted 'subsidies, such as the untargeted first
home owners grant (FHOG) to first homebuyers are unlikely to be effective.'[13] Although more nuanced, a government
panel formally stated:

> In the short term, where supply of housing is constrained,
> the FHOG can increase house prices ... such increases
> are not as large as the grants themselves ... The original
> FHOG had a lower impact on real house prices over time,
> largely because supply becomes more elastic over a longer
> time period.[14]

In summary, the ability of authorities to effectively moderate demand-side forces is questionable—this is an important
empirical and political principle albeit a controversial one.

Governments (and authorities) significantly influence
supply-side factors (costs). For example there is a National
Construction Code that: 'provides the minimum necessary
requirements for safety, health, amenity and sustainability
in the design and construction of new buildings (and new
building work in existing buildings) throughout Australia.'[15]
Other ways in which authorities may influence supply is
through production costs, namely:

• Construction costs (that is, labour market regulation).
• Infrastructure charges—these are charges often incurred

by developers. It is notable they have been and continue to be a source of concern for developers, as demonstrated in the next section.

- Supply of land—through (re)zoning. It is interesting to note that many have argued that house price growth is primarily a reflection of land cost increases—rather than construction costs.

- Development process costs can escalate if there are regulatory hurdles and appeals to negotiate.

Poignantly, John Stuart Mill once observed: 'A person may cause evil to others not only by his actions but by his inaction.'[16] Substituting 'person' for 'central authority' describes the challenge for governments—in particular, knowing when and when not to (dis)incentivise housing market actors is the critical feature of effective governance. Unfortunately, many government failures occur from incorrectly assuming the extent to which they can effectively influence consumer activities. The thesis of this chapter is that the government will have most success in constructively tackling housing affordability if it focuses on the planning process.

This is corroborated by the 'simpler planning with faster processes' recommendation featured in a recent submission by the Property Council:

> A major component of the cost of producing new housing is the sheer complexity of the system. Unnecessary complexity means unnecessary costs in designing projects, complying with rules which deliver little value, working through rezoning processes in outdated planning controls, and spending money on unneeded consultant reports. Approval processes which are slow, complex, politicised or

span multiple levels of government also add considerably to the cost of producing housing. Planning reform is required to make planning frameworks simpler and approval processes less complex.[17]

In addition, in their 2012 report COAG concluded:

The Working Party's examination of the housing supply chain identified multiple instances where developers and builders faced significant delay, uncertain time frames and unpredictable regulatory frameworks in bringing new land and dwellings to market. Such delay and uncertainty increased the cost of housing by increasing developers' holding costs and by adding to the risk that businesses face in the development process.[18]

The analysis of focus group transcripts in the next section shows there is a tremendous amount of good that governments can action—if they choose to do so.

Stories from the coalface

In 2016 three focus groups were conducted as part of a funded inquiry into housing policies, labour force participation and economic growth.[19] Participants were selected using a snowball recruitment process through an initial key industry contact. There were approximately eight participants per focus group. The main aim of the focus groups was to test a framework which attempted to map (conceptually) how market actors' decisions and perceptions of housing policy instruments influence the economic effects on housing supply.[20]

The focus groups involved a mix of participants in the land development and housing industry as well as regulators. The conceptual framework identified three spatial scales: inner-city, middle suburban and outer/peri-urban. Each focus group was asked to discuss the influence of macro-prudential regulation; foreign investment laws; urban growth boundary strategic planning; and local government development controls. Importantly, the focus groups:

> revealed a general understanding of key housing policy instruments, but this understanding was based on very practical understandings of the policy instruments. Direct tangible constraints on development, such as planning regulations around building design, were appreciated more sharply by those involved in housing supply than mechanisms that operated in a less embodied sense and via other actors, such as the availability or cost of capital as provided by the major lending banks.[21]

The sharper appreciation for tangible constraints such as planning regulations around building design provides a rich source of data for the issue addressed in this chapter. As this short review of focus groups transcripts reveals the regulatory system is failing households. Several themes emerged that could be examined. In this chapter two key themes are discussed: Ignorance of economic principles and inefficient disruptions.

Each of these themes corroborates the satirical observation of James H. Boren: 'Bureaucracy is the epoxy that greases the wheels of progress.'[22] The stickiness of bureaucracy is multidimensional. As the discussion below highlights, it can be in the number of regulations as well as the processes that encompass them.

Theme 1: Ignorance of economic principles

In more than one focus group it was noted that there is a significant lack of appreciation of market principles. In relation to being required to increase the number of lots per hectare one participant stated: 'The market determines whether you can sell it.' Suggesting that, at times, requirements can be out of touch with consumer demands. This view is supported by the comment: '… and I've actually heard a councillor articulate it once … nobody cares about the developer's profit.'

This lack of appreciation of stakeholder incentives seems to reflect a greater concern shared—that is, a lack of understanding of basic economic principles. Whereas the previous quote points to a concern about the lack of knowledge of the 'Theory of the Firm' and in particular how profits are directly linked to meeting consumer needs and wants, the next statement seems to point to a lack of understanding of supply side nuances.

In particular a greater number of smaller dwellings do not necessarily correspond to economies of scale. Space limitations forbid a deeper discussion, however a clear frustration voiced by developers was the additional costs such as 'party walls' and 'light requirements'. One participant explicitly stated:

> See that's something the Government doesn't understand. You want to elevate the yield out of a hectare but you don't understand the added cost of the creation of that product.

Notably, one participant articulated the consequences of this lack of understanding:

> … don't have a clue about land economics, therefore they make these decisions, a multistorey in … Rezoning, put all these imposts, does it have a positive value? We don't know. We don't care. This is what we want. So therefore

nothing happens for 10 years. Why? Because the land's got negative land value. Dumb stuff.

Concerns regarding delay were also noted in terms of the number and types of 'hoops' such as:

> There's many different ways, but it does seem for simple developments there are a lot of hoops to jump through and that those kind of hoops could be made a bit easier and free up land for our development and get things moving.

In addition, one participant shared their perception of how local regulators operate: 'Oh, we've got all these problems we've got to solve'. Adding the consequence to be: 'and then they're pushing down the regulation, not really understanding that every reaction they have causes a problem somewhere else.' In short, the significance of costs in terms of money as well as time seems to be unappreciated. This undermines confidence in the system as indicated by the following statement: '… is trained to spot what's wrong with it. What they don't like about it. We'll tell you what our problem is, but it's not our job to tell you how to fix it.'

Confidence is a fundamental feature of a well-functioning market. Stakeholder views indicate a lack of confidence in the current system. This is likely to be stifling innovation, creativity and supply.

Theme 2: Inefficient disruptions

The consequence of not understanding stakeholder incentives is accompanied by a concern about how processes can be disrupted. In particular, one participant noted the lack of accountability:

One of the other, a recent local government issue that's come before us is… delaying rezoning processes, … delays simply over the council election processes, so things like that where, "Oh, we're not going to even consider this site; we're going to get through the election, we'll look at it maybe in about, well then there's Christmas coming, so maybe in about February next year we might look at it." So I guess the delays come into it, and I know you would hear this from every source, but there's *no real adherence to statutory timeframes*; that seems to be secondary in everyone's mind all the time, and I'm never really sure why that is, because the timeframes are set there. (emphasis added)

As noted by one participant, disruptions can be absolute, noting a particular council had (in recent history) taken the attitude: 'We're not going to have any more development.' Further, the following statement regarding Design and Development Overlays (DDOs) Councils utilising legislation, achieves what seems to be politically motivated aims:

There's 26 different DDOs for the same zone, about height, setbacks, and multiply that across 26 councils and it's just gone, like it's become a paper explosion. And the whole purpose of the new zones was really to identify growth opportunities for housing, and the councils have just turned it around and used it as an opportunity to say, "No growth for housing in all these areas." And then exploded the paper trail as well, and that's only recent, that's only three years old.

This view is complemented by:

And that meddling, as you put it, creates a whole lot of cost. There's already a whole lot of cost associated with compliance and regulation, and the meddling puts a whole bunch of other cost in. And just the fact, you were talking about Plan Melbourne before that was supposed to provide certainty about, well that word's used a lot too, but about how, when and where, and what we can do. *But every municipality meddles with that, so there actually is no certainty.* (emphasis added)

The lack of certainty has the means to curb supply and therefore prolong/introduce housing stress. Councils evidently play a critical role, however they also face acute challenges given incumbent constituents can (and often do) exercise significant pressure on local members. Typically, there are two active cohorts; Not In My Back Yard (NIMBYs) and Yes In My Back Yard (YIMBYs). NIMBYs seem to have a greater influence in many areas. One participant postulated:

> Well it is because the council hasn't divorced themselves from the planning process, which should happen in all councils. But it hasn't and it, because they see it, they see the planning process as being intertwined with votes, and it shouldn't be.

Importantly, councils, whilst often bearing the brunt of criticisms, is not the only level of government disrupting processes. State governments are also at times seemingly unhelpful in addressing issues of housing supply. In particular, the role of state government in prescribing public infrastructure was identified as an area for concern: 'they don't know where the money goes, goes off into some coffer and sits in the government.' As an example the following comments were made in relation to Precinct Structure Planning (PSPs):

The money [pause] because we get the PSPs and the government said 'Right, school, school, school, public, private', ... and then the developer goes to the Department of Education, 'Well okay, when are you going to buy my land?' and they say 'Well there's no money. We can't buy it'. Whereas if they put an outer Melbourne ring road through your land or a railway station, a freight line, they have to buy it from you.

Compounding the burden of inefficient local and state government interventions is their interaction, as noted by the following statement:

The one frustration I continually have is that, and it's not just councils, it's the Minister, the state department, and even at the federal level, the environmental department saying, 'No, we want to preserve a whole lot of grassland ...' But every one of those controls or overlays or interventions has some impact on what I call affordability, the economics of being able to deliver a dwelling for a price. And even though most of the council and state government policies talk about affordability, when you're in the heat of the discussion about saying, 'No, that's not a good outcome because it's going to take away from the number of dwellings we can get on the site,' or something else, no one actually ever comes back and stands up for the affordability argument. *So no one in council or government is really responsible for taking ownership of the desire to deliver a certain number of dwellings in a certain timeframe for a certain price band.* (emphasis added)

Federal government intervention was also discussed—albeit briefly. Interestingly, views expressed corroborated observations by experts (quoted in the previous section of this chapter) that the effects of buyer grants were observed to be negligible in some areas. One participant stated:

> Well I can take you to a couple of corridors in Melbourne where a number of companies … when Kevin 07 gave every buyer $36,000.00 … and that just went straight on to the list price. Didn't go to the first home buyer …

In summary, the views expressed suggest that inefficient systems and processes are disrupting affordable supply.

Conclusion

Housing policy discussions are necessarily complex—spanning economics, politics, psychology and social wellbeing. This explains (in part) the strong and yet conflicting views of various advocates.[23] In the first part of this chapter a clear argument for advocating supply side reform was stated. In particular:

- The market is complex and how factors interact can change across time and space.
- Some demand side factors are out of policy scope.
- Focusing on other demand side factors may have negative consequences.
- Supply side factors are an obvious and natural focus for governments.

In the second part of the chapter, focus group transcripts from a study conducted in 2016 were briefly discussed.[24] Inefficiencies due to the number of regulations and their associated processes were two important themes emerging from these focus groups. Key market participants indicated supply of housing is inhibited. This suggests improvements to housing affordability can be achieved by streamlining the number of regulations and improving the processes that surround them.

CHAPTER ELEVEN

Over-criminalisation as red tape

ANDREW BUSHNELL

Traditionally, the criminal law governed obvious moral wrongs. What distinguished it from the civil law was that it expressed moral opprobrium on behalf of society. But since the industrialisation of the economy, the criminal law has expanded into the governance of the economy. The aim of these laws is not necessarily, at least in the first place, the condemnation of moral wrongs, but rather the attainment of ends that the state deems desirable.[1]

The breadth of the criminal law is now such that finding coherence between the descriptive reality of the law and a theoretical normative basis for it is difficult. Moreover, the normative basis of the criminal law is contested, and some people do not agree with the characterisation of the traditional criminal law as essentially about the enforcement of common morality through retribution.[2] It is beyond the scope of this chapter to resolve this debate. Instead, this chapter will focus on a particular subset of the criminal law, which I will refer to as the regulatory criminal law. The regulatory criminal law is the criminal law that:

- Aims to regulate economic activity; and
- The primary justification of which is utilitarian.

Prominent examples of the regulatory criminal law include the *Corporations Act 2001 (Cth)*, which imposes criminal liability on corporate directors and upon corporations themselves, and the *Environment Protection and Biodiversity Conservation (EPBC) Act 1999 (Cth)*, which imposes criminal liability upon individuals who take certain actions that affect the environment, imposing costs on the agriculture and mining industries among others. There are many other such laws at the Commonwealth and state level.

Because the regulatory criminal law governs the economy, and is often justified by reference to its economic utility rather than by reference to a supervening deontological moral principle (i.e. a right), it can be assessed in economic terms. Just as the normative basis of the criminal law is contested, so too is the proper extent of the criminal law. But in utilitarian terms, over-criminalisation is understood as those regulatory criminal laws that do not, in fact, contribute to the health of the economy.

In this chapter, I will apply this idea of over-criminalisation to Australia's regulatory criminal law, and I will argue that there is reason to believe that much of that law is inefficient, and thus a form of red tape. At the end of the chapter, I will return to the question of the normative basis of the regulatory criminal law to discuss whether, given its inefficiency, Australia's regulatory criminal law is better understood as a form of retribution rather than regulation.

Conceptualising over-criminalisation as red tape

The law and economics approach applies microeconomic principles to crime. It holds that an inefficient criminal law is one that costs more to enforce than it saves by its enforcement. This standard of inefficiency is also the economic definition of over-criminalisation. The economic theory of crime is that criminals make choices based on their own subjective assessments of the costs and benefits of available options.[3] The goal of an efficient criminal justice system is to deploy only those resources necessary for enforcing the law and to shape the behaviour of would-be criminals away from crime. As Gary Becker puts it:

> The optimal amount of enforcement is shown to depend on, among other things, the cost of catching and convicting offenders, the nature of the punishments ... and the responses of offenders to changes in enforcement.[4]

In this model, the criminal law works by deterring people from choosing crime. It supports a theory of general deterrence where individual criminals' punishments should include the social benefit of sending a signal to other potential criminals. The value of general deterrence is one of the main benefits against which the cost of a criminal law is measured.

The efficiency of general deterrence depends on the willingness or desire of rational actors to commit crime, otherwise known as the demand for offences. Where this demand is elastic, meaning that potential criminals' assessment of cost and benefit responds to external factors, enforcement expenditure should reduce crime. But the less elastic the demand, the less efficient are enforcement costs.[5] A criminal law can become inefficient not only through its direct costs in terms of enforcement but in its effects on people's behaviour. It is possible to over-deter: people might forego productive activity to avoid the risk (and potentially very high costs) of being enforced against.

An inefficient regulatory criminal law can be conceptualised as red tape: in its regulation of the economy, it goes beyond the minimum effective regulation, sustaining higher costs than necessary to achieve the aim of the regulation.

The primary inefficiency in Australia's regulatory criminal law is, theoretically, over-deterrence. However, much of the claimed deterrent effect of the regulatory criminal law is questionable. As such, one of the main questions to consider when thinking about the regulatory criminal law is whether civil enforcement would be more efficient. Australia's regulatory criminal law has three main features that give cause to question its efficiency: the use of strict liability, the use and threat of harsh punishment, and the use of criminal stigmatisation.

Strict liability

Strict liability removes the requirement of mental fault or mens rea. It punishes economic actors for proscribed outcomes, no matter the intention behind them.[6] Traditionally, the requirement of mens rea was one of the distinguishing features of the criminal law, consistent with its basis in the just punishment of moral wrongs.[7] In the Australian regulatory criminal law, there are a number of offences that apply this standard.

For example, the *Corporations Act 2001 (Cth)* and the *Environment Protection and Biodiversity Conservation (EPBC) Act 1999 (Cth)* both have a number of strict liability provisions. One prominent example is s 588G of the former act that imposes strict liability upon company directors for trading while insolvent.[8]

It has been argued that this is efficient because it saves enforcement resources by eliminating regulators' need to prove culpability.[9] On the other hand, though, the economist George Stigler argues that: 'In the area of economic regulation, guilt is often an inappropriate notion, and when it is inappropriate all costs of compliance must be reckoned into the social costs of enforcement'.[10] His point is that if a law is not morally required, then the costs of complying with that law are part of the overall cost of having that law. Since the law is morally optional, it is a social choice to impose the cost of complying with it upon businesses (and really, their shareholders, employees, and customers), and this cost must be compared with the social benefit that comes from businesses abstaining from the proscribed conduct. Therefore, the requirement of mens rea will be efficient where it prevents businesses from committing more resources to compliance than are saved by the criminal justice system through speedier enforcement.

In this vein, the Australian Institute of Company Directors told the Australian Law Reform Commission's inquiry into encroachments by Commonwealth laws on Australians' traditional rights and freedoms that strict liability offences increase risk aversion within companies, leading to reduced productivity and innovation.[11] In short, strict liability may over-deter by encouraging too much caution among businesses and their employees, and where it does, it contributes to over-criminalisation as a form of red tape.

Incarceration and other criminal penalties

One of the main reasons cited for the use of the criminal law to regulate economic activity is that it enables incarceration and other harsh punishments, which is said to increase the general deterrent effect of the law. The evidence of the Commonwealth Director of Public Prosecutions to the Senate inquiry into penalties for white collar crime is salutary in this respect: 'Arguably, nothing deters would-be white collar criminals more than a realistic prospect of imprisonment'.[12]

In Australia, a range of regulatory criminal laws carry prison sentences. For example, it is possible to be sentenced to five years in prison for breaching the director's duty to prevent insolvent trading, and to be sentenced to up to seven years in prison for damaging a protected wetland.[13] Typically, regulatory criminal provisions also permit courts to impose fines and professional disqualification, among other orders. Australia also imposes criminal liability on corporations, which can be punished with fines and other orders.

However, there is very good reason to believe that criminals do not respond to the severity of the punishments they face in prospect. Studies have shown that criminals react more to the chance of being caught than they do to the severity of the punishments that they face if caught.[14] Mirko Bagaric of Deakin University told the same Senate inquiry that 'Ninety-three percent of criminologists around the world know that there is no correlation between the severity of the penalty and a reduction in crime'.[15] If this is the case, the regulatory criminal law may be inefficient because it devotes resources to criminal enforcement needlessly.[16]

Whether this is accepted or not, the perception that general deterrence is true does have a real effect on the behaviour of honest businesses and individuals, which may change their behaviour is response to how they perceive risk. The threat of harsh criminal punishment makes businesses invest in more compliance officers. It also makes hiring people for positions exposed to criminal liability costlier.

For example, in late 2016, the Commonwealth Government announced new criminal penalties for bank employees found to have 'rigged' the benchmark rates at which banks trade with each other. This was met with concern that it would reduce trade and make attracting employees into positions that handled trades affecting those rates more difficult, and thus more expensive.[17] Earlier reports from the United States revealed that compliance officers in that country are now able to demand 'danger money' such is their exposure to criminal liability.[18] A 2014 report by Deloitte estimated that one in every eleven Australian workers was employed in the compliance sector.[19]

To the extent that the purpose of the regulatory criminal law is to make more stringent penalties available for malevolent economic actors, it is inefficient. There is no evidence that the severity of the available penalties meaningfully shapes the behaviour of potential criminals. Even allowing that it has an effect, this is purchased at the cost of greater diversion of private resources into compliance and at the cost of increased inefficiency in the justice system.

Stigmatisation

The other major reason often given for the need for regulatory criminal law is that being branded as a criminal is a special stigma, the threat of which increases the general deterrent effect of regulation. Stigma is a form of reputational damage. For economic actors, reputation can be expressed in economic terms: reputation affects the price that may be charged for goods and services and the ability to attract investment and staff.[20] The risk of sustaining this damage encourages businesses and individuals to comply with the law. If this is the case, then the costs of the regulatory criminal law identified in the previous section might be offset by the deterrent value of criminal stigmatisation.

Importantly, the special stigma of being branded 'criminal' is the main reason that in Australia and many other countries, corporations carry criminal liability.[21] Corporate criminal liability has long been controversial, with many commentators and jurisdictions believing it to be needless or even incoherent, since corporations cannot be morally blameworthy.[22] While retribution may not apply to corporations, it is possible to deter them from undesirable actions. As John T Byam writes

> A corporation run by rational profit maximizers will decide whether to commit an offense depending on the difference between the expected benefits of the offense to the corporation from the offense and the expected costs of the offense … The cost of punishment comprises the severity of corporate fines … and any damage from criminal stigma.[23]

To achieve general deterrence based on stigmatisation, regulators target high profile cases and publicise them. For example, in August 2017, the Commonwealth Director of Public Prosecutions (CDPP), on behalf of the Australian Competition and Consumer Commission (ACCC), completed its first successful prosecution of criminal cartel conduct, against Japanese shipping company NYK, which was ordered to pay a fine of $25 million. The fine would have been greater, the Federal Court noted, had NYK not cooperated with the ACCC and CDPP. In a media release following the judgement, ACCC Chairman Rod Sims said 'The sentence imposed on NYK by the Federal Court today sends a strong warning to the industry and the business community at large'.[24]

As with the use of criminal penalties, there are a number of problems with stigmatisation as a utilitarian justification for the regulatory criminal law. Stigmatisation presents a calculation problem for regulators and for businesses. Just as it is impossible for a central authority to set market prices, because it does not have the relevant information about the needs and wants of consumers, there is no way for anyone to know in advance the damage that an adverse finding will do to a business's reputation. This uncertainty increases costs for regulators and businesses:

- Regulators may expend resources trying to calculate this damage.[25] A related cost is the expense regulators incur in publicising adverse findings in order to achieve the reputational damage and supposed general deterrent effect.
- For businesses, the costs are that, given the above, regulators may impose greater damage than is warranted. In response, businesses may devote more than an efficient amount of resources to protecting their reputations.

Consider the collapse of the consultancy Arthur Andersen. In 2001, Texas energy company Enron was discovered to have committed massive accounting fraud. Its auditor, Arthur Andersen, was convicted of shredding documents related to the scandal. The conviction was later reversed, but by then the damage had been done. As a business that traded in large part on its reputation, Arthur Andersen was devastated by its implication in the scandal. The business collapsed, with most of its 28,000 employees losing their jobs.[26] The Arthur Andersen case reveals how the effects of an adverse judgement can be far beyond what would be a proportionate punishment, and thus far beyond the requirements of efficiency.[27]

The eventual reversal of Arthur Andersen's conviction also counts against stigmatisation as an efficient punishment. It has been argued that one of the benefits of reputational damage as part of general deterrence is that it is imposed early on in criminal proceedings. The damage may begin with the announcement of charges, well before conviction, and this places pressure on businesses and individuals to deal with regulators and seek an early resolution of the matters in question. This is efficient in that it reduces enforcement costs.[28] But the Arthur Andersen case illustrates that this efficiency can be illusory where, at the end of the process, guilt is not established. The destruction of value in the economy may not be vindicated by the result of the proceedings.

Another potential inefficiency is that it is possible that, despite the efforts of regulators to publicise their work, customers are not aware of an adverse finding, and as such there is no reputational damage, reducing the benefit of making a criminal case at all. In 2011, oil company BP pleaded guilty to 14 criminal charges, including 11 charges of manslaughter, stemming from the Deepwater Horizon disaster in the Gulf of Mexico.[29] The disaster began on 20 April 2010, and as its effects became apparent, by 9 June 2010 the market capitalisation of BP had been halved. But in the days following the settlement of the criminal case, the share price did not move.[30] In perhaps the highest-profile corporate crime case in history, the reputation of the guilty party was not measurably affected.[31]

For individuals, it is possible that reputation is not reducible to economic concerns. White collar crime laws, for example, seem to speak to moral opprobrium more than economic utility.[32] If this is the case, it is an example of a defendant being 'judgement-proof'—unable to pay the costs of the judgement. As Becker notes, for particularly heinous crimes, no amount of money can compensate for the harm, and so non-monetary penalties must be levied.[33] While this is a sound point in relation to the criminal law generally, it poses a problem for the regulatory criminal law, which is largely intended to affect economic ends. In the final section of this chapter, I will briefly consider the implications of the regulatory criminal law's non-economic effects.

The social costs of the regulatory criminal law

The expansion of the criminal law into regulation has caused a conceptual confusion in Australia's criminal law. At the outset of this chapter, we stipulated that the regulatory criminal law, being about the regulation of the economy, could be assessed in economic utilitarian terms. But it is possible that despite the inefficiency of general deterrence, the regulatory criminal law is justified by supervening moral concerns. That is, the distinction that we drew between the traditional criminal law and the regulatory criminal law may not be viable in every case: over-criminalisation may not be about over-deterrence, but over-retribution—seeking retribution when it is not warranted.

And in fact there is some reason to believe that much of the regulatory criminal law expresses a retributive theory of criminal law. In particular:

- Commonwealth statutory drafting advice suggests limiting the use of strict liability to certain circumstances and in conjunction with non-carceral, minor penalties.[34] This indicates a concern to preserve moral culpability as the heart of the criminal law.

- Much of the time, the criminal penalties are only threats, with regulators preferring to use a mix of persuasion and education.[35] This selective approach to enforcement of the full extent of the law is a tacit admission that the moral standing for doing so is dubious and thus the harshest penalties should be reserved for deserving cases.

- The creation of 'corporate culture' standards in corporate criminal liability similarly speaks to a desire to maintain normative coherence in the criminal law. Unlike most other countries, Australian law holds corporations criminally liable for acts the court deems it should have prevented through its internal governance structures. Commentary contemporaneous with the introduction of this law indicates that it was an attempt to resolve the problem of attributing moral blameworthiness to fictional entities.[36]

In writing the regulatory criminal law, Australian legislators have attempted to have it both ways, by writing laws for a utilitarian purpose that retain a moral character in practice. The conceptual incoherence that this introduces into the law is itself a social cost that should be part of the economic analysis. The regulatory criminal law trades on the inherent respectability of the criminal law but does nothing to support it. This can be seen clearly in the case of stigmatisation: stigma is a moral judgement, but in purporting to govern economic, rather than moral, concerns, the regulatory criminal law diminishes the connection between criminality and moral opprobrium. The stigma is subject to the law of diminishing returns: as more actions are denoted as 'criminal', the weaker is the moral judgement inherent in that designation.

However, this may be moot if we abandon the schema we established at the start of the chapter. If the regulatory criminal law is not really assessable in economic terms—that is, it is not primarily regulation—then this has an uncomfortable implication for Australia's regulatory environment. If indeed there is a consistent link between the regulatory criminal law and moral judgement, then in a certain sense Australia's legislators and regulators are advancing the proposition that acts like damaging a wetland or failing to obtain a business licence are akin to murder and assault. Which is to say, they deny that imposing these criminal penalties is over-criminalisation at all. From the perspective of economic liberty, this is much worse than inefficiency, as it speaks to an underlying suspicion of commercial enterprise. It is possible that rather than being bad regulation dressed up as criminal law, regulatory criminal law is bad criminal law dressed up as regulation.

Conclusion
Assessed on economic terms, the regulatory criminal law is inefficient. Its reliance on the theory of general deterrence leads to the forced and unnecessary expenditure of resources on enforcement and imposes costs on business and individ-

uals. But if Australia's regulatory criminal law is really about moral opprobrium, then free market advocates have a much larger problem to confront.

In its expansion of the criminal law into economic regulation, government has undermined the criminal law's conceptual coherence, which carries the social cost of decreasing confidence in the criminal legal system, reducing the deterrent effect of criminal stigmatisation, and signalling to entrepreneurs and investors that Australia values technocratic tinkering more than innovation and freedom. In this way, over-criminalisation, meaning inefficient regulatory criminal law, is a contributor to Australia's red tape crisis, and worse, that crisis has made a victim of the law itself.

CHAPTER TWELVE

Over-regulation in public services

AARON M. LANE

There is a popular perception that a culture of bureaucracy in the public sector is pervasive. Public servants have a reputation for being too preoccupied with following a strict interpretation of the rules to worry about satisfying the consumers that rely on their services. Many would consider the concept of public sector innovation to be an oxymoron.[1] As Ludwig von Mises observed, 'nobody calls himself a bureaucrat or his own methods of management bureaucratic.'[2] Rather these are pejorative terms, pointing criticism at those tasked with carrying out rigid policies and procedures—and at the system itself. But although nobody sets out to be a bureaucrat, there is a measure of truth in these stereotypes. There are in-built incentives in the public sector that make service delivery tightly regulated, and cause these constraints to grow in number and complexity over time.

Over-regulation in the public sector is a problem because of Australia's heavy reliance on the services that the sector provides. Australians' standard of living will be negatively impacted where over-regulation constrains improvements in those services. Another reason that the public sector is important to analyse from a regulatory perspective is that it makes up a substantial part of the Australian economy—in terms of both the magnitude of the budgets allocated to these services, and the proportion as a percentage of gross domestic product (GDP). Accordingly, red tape and over-regulation that drive up costs in the public sector will be an inefficient use of taxpayers' funds. Data from the recent Productivity Commission's Report on Government Services outlines the scale of government expenditure on public services. That report encompasses childcare, education and training, justice, emergency management, health, community services, and housing and homelessness services, and estimated that federal, state and territory governments' recurrent expenditure totalled $205 billion.[3] The report notes that this equates to around 69 per cent of total government recurrent expenditure and about 12.3 percent of Australia's GDP.[4]

There is an incredible breadth in the services provided by the public sector. This chapter will limit its focus to education—but the conclusions that are drawn have wider relevance for other areas of centralised service delivery. The education sector provides a reasonable sample size, as the Productivity Commission found that combined annual recurrent expenditure on government schools by the states and territories amounted to $34.9 billion, accounting for 86.6 per cent of government schools funding; a further $5.4 billion, equating to 13.4 per cent, was contributed by the Federal government.[5] However, this chapter seeks to move away from the current debates about how much additional public funding schools should receive and move the discussion towards the value of structural reforms. First, the connection between expenditure and regulation will be explored. Next, the observable increase in regulatory complexity over time is detailed. Finally, recent school autonomy initiatives are considered before offering some suggestions for future directions for reform.

Expenditure and regulation in education

Public sector regulation is inherently linked to the justification for government expenditure. This is because the government decides to undertake expenditure decisions and these decisions require formalisation that has the power of law. This section considers the main reasons that have been advanced for the public provision of education services that seem to have the most application to the Australian experience.

The first contention for the state provision of schooling is that education is necessary for the working of any free society.[6] Citizens need to be capable of reading, writing and comprehending material to make informed choices, to be productive, and to be able to govern themselves. Although the primary responsibility for children's education rests with parents, society will bear the burden of failure. Accordingly, there will be a legitimate role for the government to provide schools for children whose parents cannot provide for them, and where charitable efforts are not sufficient.

This was certainly the colonial Australian experience, where government expenditure for educational purposes was based on averting the social and moral problems of a new colony where a sizable proportion of the population were convicts. Writing in 1800, New South Wales Governor Philip King noted a need to 'save the youth of this colony from the destructive examples of their abandoned parents, and others who they unavoidably associate with'.[7] That year, King established an orphan school in Sydney using funds raised from import duties—an idea he had trialled six years earlier as Lieutenant-Governor of Norfolk Island.[8] The concept continued to be the primary rationale for other early public schools such as Sydney's Public Charity School for the education of poor children in 1810.[9]

Modern governments rely on this as a justification for compulsory schooling regulations, expressing it in the economic language of the principal-agent problem. For example, in 2017 the Victorian Department of Education and Training stated that:

> Parents have strong incentives to ensure their child receives a high quality education. However, there may be cases when the best interest of a child (as principal) in pursuing education is not fully reflected in decision making by their parent (as agent) where the parent is unable or incapable of promoting education for their child. If uncorrected, the principal–agent problem could result in children receiving suboptimal levels of education at critical early stages of learning, which can be costly to remedy.[10]

But, as Hayek observes: 'it is true that historically, compulsory education was usually preceded by the governments' increasing opportunities by providing state schools'.[11] This is confirmed by the early Australian account where by the 1830s the government had begun to expand into rural areas where the churches had not yet established schools—around 40 years prior to compulsory attendance laws.[12] There is an equity argument behind this expansion, in that people living in remote areas should not be disadvantaged by not receiving a minimum level of education because the establishment costs of privately providing education are prohibitive. Although there was also an economies of scale argument in the minds of legislators at the time. It was argued that a single government school would be more efficient than establishing several schools to cater for each denomination. In 1844, a committee of the New South Wales Legislative Council described the problem with the denominational system in these terms:

> Wherever one school is founded, two or three others will arise, not because they are wanted, but because it is feared that proselytes will be made; and thus a superfluous activity is produced in one place, and a total stagnation in another. It is a system impossible to be carried out in a thinly populated country.[13]

Of course, it is difficult to tell any early Australian story without reference to sectarian concerns. But these denominational systems were in competition with each other, and this system had received public assistance from the earliest beginnings of education in Australia in the form of land grants and direct funding contributions.[14] Here, there is evidence that the government's role in education extended beyond acting as a provider of last resort. Although it is difficult to distil the stated justification for this expenditure, one possibility for this is a response to positive externalities or the neighbourhood effect. Viewed this way, the benefits of education to society are greater than its private benefits— and society would not produce enough education without some kind of government intervention. Milton Friedman, among others, puts forward this argument and suggests that the 'most obvious' way to address the neighbourhood effect 'is to require that each child receive a minimum amount of education of a specified kind', and providing a subsidy for this minimum.[15] Of course, Friedman's key underlying point was that governments could finance education without directly managing schools.[16] But acceptance of the externality or neighbourhood effect is important because it suggests that there is an economic case for the role of the state in the provision of all general education.

This is not to say that there are not any flaws in the above justifications. Indeed, some argue that public provision is unnecessary and private ordering will always be preferable.[17] On the contrary, others claim that only a government-run system will maintain integrity in education.[18] In any case, the fundamental point to be made here is that in the early Australian experience there was a case made for a level of public expenditure that would provide children with a minimum level of education in the form of government run schools for those most in need and for rural areas, and for public support for the denominational system.

Those people making the decisions about public expenditure were not the same people as those tasked with implementing it. Accordingly, the system required a regulatory framework. There is an inherent link, therefore, between the rationale establishing a system of public education and the regulatory framework that is established. The implication is that the more extensive the scope of the system, the more complex we can expect the regulatory structure to be to cater for more interests.

In general, public expenditure will be approved by the Parliament in the form of an Appropriation Bill. Additionally, there will be a regulatory structure put in place to govern how those funds are used. Of course, this may be a constitutional requirement.[19] But even in the absence of this there will be a strong incentive for the Legislature (through legislation) or the Executive (through other forms of regulation) to control how funds are used to provide accountability, certainty, and enforceability. The politicians will not be able to be able to directly supervise the expenditure and day to day management of the services, so regulation functions as a mechanism of control—to ensure that the allocated budget is spent according to their wishes. Every condition or requirement put in place will necessarily limit the discretionary power of the public servants charged with implementing the services. Mises explains the intention:

> In order to avoid [arbitrariness] the king tries to limit the governor's powers by issuing directives and instructions. Codes, decrees, and statutes tell the governors of the provinces and their subordinates what to do if such or such a problem arises. Their free discretion is now limited; their first duty is now to comply with the regulations. It is true that their arbitrariness is now restricted in so far as the regulations must be applied. But at the same time the whole character of their management changes. They are no longer

eager to deal with each case to the best of their abilities; they are no longer anxious to find the most appropriate solution for every problem. Their main concern is to comply with the rules and regulations, no matter whether they are reasonable or contrary to what was intended. The first virtue of an administrator is to abide by the codes and decrees. He becomes a bureaucrat.[20]

It is in this way that Mises characterises bureaucracy as 'management bound to comply with detailed rules and regulations fixed by the authority of a superior body.'[21] From this point, the insights of public choice economics take us a step further in that bureaucratic agents will have their own incentives and act in their own self-interest. For instance, Tullock contends that bureaucrats have strong motives to increase their status and power within an organisation.[22]

Niskanen assumes that the bureaucracy tries to maximise its budget, and also argues that the bureaucracy will become the experts in the various programs that government delivers because they have greater information.[23] Stigler predicts that the bureaucracy could become captured by special interest groups.[24]

One consequence of this is that legislators may seek even tighter constraints over how the public service it to be provided under the guise of accountability and quality control. Another is that there will be a status quo bias and mission creep leading to an expanded role for government. These arguments tend towards the same direction—that over time there will be growth in regulatory complexity.

Increasing regulatory complexity

Eventually, colonial Australia's early system of public education became formalised in legislation. Firstly, Appropriation Acts authorised the expenditure of government funds for particular purposes—including education. Secondly, a regulatory framework was put in place for allocating those funds and determining how schools were to be managed. For instance, in New South Wales in 1848, a combination of legislation and executive orders established two boards—The National Board of Education, to provide funds for established government schools, and the Denominational School Board, to allocate state aid to church schools.[25] Similar institutional frameworks were put in place in the other Australian colonies. Curiously, while the system has undergone significant reform over time (such as the removal and eventual reinstatement of state aid to the private sector) it has not changed all that much in a broad institutional sense. In every Australian state and territory jurisdiction there is a system of government schools, and there are private schools with mechanisms for government funding.

Despite the relative simplicity of these institutional arrangements, there has been a measurable growth in regulatory complexity. Traditionally, page counts have been used as a proxy measure to observe the growth in this complexity.[26] On this measure, in New South Wales, the length of the *National Education Board Act 1848* was just two pages. Over the years the major reforms came in the form of the *Public Schools Act 1866* (5 pages), the *Public Instruction Act 1880* (6 pages), the *Education Act 1961* (15 pages), and the *Education Reform Act 1990* (79 pages). Today, the *NSW Education Act 1990* spans 97 pages.[27] Other state jurisdictions tell a similar story. For example, Victoria passed its first education Act in the form of the *Common Schools Act 1862* (4 pages), and early reforms and consolidations came with the passage of the *Education Act 1872* (6 pages), *Education Act 1890* (8 pages), *Education Act 1915* (35 pages), *Education Act 1928* (35 pages), *Education Act 1958* (44 pages). The 1958 Act was regularly amended in the years that followed. The earliest historical consolidation currently available shows that in 1997 the 1958 Act was 151 pages in length, and in 2005 measured 162 pages before it was repealed and replaced with the current regime—the *Education Training and Reform Act 2006*.[28]

Note that this is just the main legislation establishing the regulatory framework. These page counts do not include the multitude of other Acts regulating distinct aspects of the public education system. For example, prior to the repeal of Victoria's 1958 Act, these other pieces of legislation included the *Community Services (Attendance at School) Act 1970*, *Educational Grants Act 1973*; *Education (Special Developmental Schools) Act 1976*, *Teaching Service Act 1981*, *Victorian Curriculum and Assessment Authority Act 2000*, *Victorian Institute of Teaching Act 2001*, and the *Victorian Qualifications Authority Act 2000*. To give an indication of the additional regulatory burden that this legislation imposed, these Acts were consolidated into the *Education Training and Reform Act 2006*—along with other Acts governing post school training and education—and measured 450 pages as passed. Today, the 2006 Act has exploded to 755 pages.[29] Again, this is just the main legislative framework and does not include Regulations or Ministerial Orders made under the Act.

To be sure, the government's role in education has expanded throughout this time. Once a provider of last resort, today around two thirds of Australian primary and secondary school students are enrolled in government schools—providing both primary and secondary education.[30] But, as mentioned above, the broad institutional structures are not radically different. Here, there is a parallel with Bozeman's definition of red tape in that we can make a distinction between the legislation required to establish the institutional frameworks to govern a baseline level of service delivery, and red-tape which consists of those 'rules, regulations, and procedures that remain in force and entail a compliance burden but [do] not advance the legitimate purposes the rules were intended to serve'.[31]

Another complicating factor in the regulation of public sector services is Commonwealth involvement. Although states and territories have primary responsibility for regulating the provision of education, since the 1970s the Commonwealth government has been the major funder of the non-government sector. The *Australian Education Act 2013* (currently 152 pages) is the principal legislation passed following the 2011 Review of Funding for Schooling (known as the 'Gonski' review).[32] This legislation was further amended in 2017, and will impose 'requirements on States and Territories as conditions of this financial assistance, including requirements to comply with intergovernmental agreements on school education, and to implement nationally agreed policy initiatives on school education.'[33] Accordingly, Commonwealth involvement in the public provision of education adds an additional layer of regulatory complexity. The overlap in state and federal responsibilities adds direct costs to the system. The latest figures from the

Australian Public Service Commission show that at the end of December 2016, there were 1904 employees working for the Department of Education and Training.[34] None of these employees are involved in delivering front-line services.

However, that is not to say that Commonwealth involvement is all bad. A detailed study of Victoria's "Schools of the Future" (SOTF) reforms found that Commonwealths tied grants assisted the state government in pursuing this reform agenda.[35] Efforts to curb the regulatory burden within the education system will now be explored.

The recent reform agenda

Victoria was the first state to tackle a highly centralised approach to public service delivery. Within the education space, the flagship program of reform was the SOTF initiative instituted in the first term of the Kennett government (1992-1996). SOTF was designed to decentralise public education, providing greater autonomy and management responsibility to individual schools—and significantly reducing the size of the bureaucracy.[36] A major motivation for the SOTF reforms was fiscal. Former Education Minister Don Hayward explained that his department needed to make a contribution in eliminating the budgetary deficit, and public education was not being delivered efficiently.[37] For instance, the 1993 report of the Victorian Commission of Audit showed that Victoria spent 15 per cent more than required to provide school education services and expenditure was higher than New South Wales and Queensland on a per student basis.[38] Although not explicitly stated by Hayward, a major part of this cost was over-regulation as the size of the central bureaucracy was restructured and reduced from 2300 to 600.[39]

Hayward stated that he was keenly aware of the incentives of the bureaucrats, noting that restructures 'are often used as devices by bureaucrats to achieve their own agenda, and to place their cronies in key positions, with the ultimate objective of frustrating the Minister.'[40] With the restructuring of the bureaucracy came greater decentralisation of the education budget to the school level, local selection of teachers, and new measures for local accountability.

Reforms are continuing in this tradition, under the banner of 'Independent Public Schools' (IPS) programs. The leading developments have been in Western Australia and Queensland.

In 2010, Western Australia introduced its IPS initiative. This was a program specifically designed to reduce bureaucracy by devolving decision making power to the local level and 'cut unnecessary red tape that currently inhibits principals from being innovative'.[41] By 2016, 445 schools have commenced as an independent public school, covering 70 per cent of students and teaching staff.[42] According to the WA Department of Education, 'principals of Independent Public Schools have more freedom to make decisions about important matters that impact students' education such as student support, staff recruitment, financial management, governance and accountability.'[43] The Centre for Policy Evaluation's review of the IPS program in 2013 found that while the overall results have been positive, 'some schools have travelled further along the path to autonomy than others'.[44] One principal interviewed for this evaluation reported that the 'frustration with bureaucracy is far less'.[45] In another review in 2015, teachers reported that 'things happen much more quickly; things get fixed more quickly; things get approved more quickly; excursions are easier and less bureaucratic; red tape is less.'[46] However a key issue moving forward is the perception that the IPS program creates two tiers of government schools—those accepted into the IPS program and enjoying the benefits of autonomy, and those still subject to central control.[47]

In 2013, Queensland launched its own IPS program. Campbell Newman, then Queensland premier, claimed that the program would 'cut red tape, remove layers of management and give local communities a greater say in decision making.'[48] It did this through greater local autonomy by 'paving a smooth pathway through departmental processes', the 'freedom to directly recruit staff' rather than relying on the central system, more autonomy over partnerships and sponsorship with 'local businesses, industry and other community organisations', and 'increased flexibility to shape curriculum offerings.'[49] Like the other reforms, the intention was to give schools greater control to better meet the needs of its students. 250 government schools are now operating as an IPS. When the policy was announced by the Liberal National Party in the lead up to the 2012 state election, it was met with opposition from the incumbent Labor government—although they have continued with the program on returning to government in 2015. The Queensland Teachers' Union claimed that the IPS policy would lead to the 'ruination' of the public education system.[50] Of course, as Kevin Donnelly observes, teaching unions have been the constant opponents of school autonomy in Australia.[51] While government commissioned reviews of this program are yet to be released, early academic findings suggest that the program will yield positive results for innovation at the school level.[52]

In 2014, the Commonwealth government announced measures under an IPS banner.[53] The program essentially provides federal funding to support state and territory governments in their efforts towards greater flexibility and school autonomy.

A consistent theme with these state programs is they have been implemented administratively rather than through any legislative change. To put it another way, the executive arm of government has attempted to create a new institutional form—IPS schools, as distinct from centralised government schools—without undertaking regulatory reform. This means that many of the centralised regulatory barriers are still in place that limit the ability of schools to truly operate autonomously. As the 2015 review of the WA program notes, the term 'Independent Public Schools' 'actually describes schools with greater autonomy set firmly within system requirements and constraints'.[54] In this way, the school autonomy reforms appear to be more about limiting the central bureaucracy rather than tackling over-regulation—despite the language used.

The first consequence of not undertaking the underlying regulatory reform is that the administrative burden may simply shift from the department level to the school level. This chapter has identified a growing regulatory burden—without regulatory reform, there is a compliance burden that needs to be met somewhere within the system. For example, principals have observed an increase in the administrative burden under the WA IPS program.[55] As such, has over-regulation in the system actually been reduced, or has the burden simply been shifted from one location to another? Is this a case where of 're-regulation', where schools are given greater autonomy on one hand, but subject to new forms of control on the other?[56] The answers to these questions are important, because the school principal's role could change from being primarily about managing front-line service delivery to being concerned about complying with regulations previously managed by the central bureaucracy. It is for this reason that school autonomy programs have been described as 'simultaneous centralisation and decentralisation'.[57] Further research is needed on this front.

The second consequence is that the efficacy of school autonomy programs will continue to be limited by the prevailing legislative and regulatory structures. Take staffing flexibility for example, which is a key aspect of the IPS reforms. Research from the Institute of Public Affairs shows that government schools are subject to centralised employment regimes governed by state-wide awards or enterprise bargaining agreements.[58] Pay and conditions are standardised across the entire system, removing the ability for individual schools to use financial incentives to attract staff or to reward improved performance. The various awards or agreements also contain provisions that limit the ability of school principals to make changes in workplace practices by prescribing matters like school hours, the number of days in a school year, student-teacher ratios, and face-to-face-teacher hours. Fixing these matters surely limits the scope for innovation. For other matters, principals must comply with union consultation provisions which significantly increase the transaction costs of negotiating and implementing changes in work practices. A possible alternative would be to borrow from charter school laws in the United States, where public schools are established as separate legal entities. In this model, staff members are employees of individual schools rather than centralised government departments. This would make school councils and principals entirely responsible for recruiting and bargaining, shifting incentives to drive outcomes at the local level—and removing external interference.

The third consequence is that there is a risk that any action can be unwound by a future administration. To be sure, any legislative changes could be reversed as well—but there are higher transaction costs associated with this type of change. An example of this risk has been realised recently in WA. Shortly after the state election in 2017, the incoming Labor government announced that schools operating as an IPS will be required to consider hiring employees within the Department's pool of excess staff whenever they have a vacancy.[59] Although the government has stated its commitment to keeping the IPS program, these moves may be the first steps towards greater centralisation of service delivery.

The road ahead

School autonomy initiatives like SOTF and IPS have led to improvements in the delivery of public education in Australia. However, because these programs have been introduced without underlying regulatory reform, school autonomy has not addressed the problem of increasing regulatory complexity. Unless this problem is addressed, the provision of public education services may suffer under the weight of over-regulation—and will ultimately undermine the benefits of these autonomy programs.

This chapter proposes that the central role of regulation of public sector services is to provide a mechanism for elected representatives to control public expenditure and prevent arbitrary decision making. In this sense, public services will necessarily be regulated more heavily than private sector services. The beginning of the over-regulation problem is found in an expanded role for the state in service provision—once of provider of last resort, the state is now the majority provider of education services. There is a similar story across many areas of public service delivery. When the scale and scope of public provision increases, the regulatory burden will grow. This problem is aided by in-built incentives that foster regulatory complexity. The beneficiaries tend to be the bureaucrats and producers of services—not the consumers. However, deregulation of public sector services—by itself—will not necessarily be desirable as this would risk transferring power from the elected representatives to the bureaucracy. So any deregulation agenda must be coupled with introducing new mechanisms to promote user choice, giving consumers greater control over the way that services are delivered. User choice would function as a safeguard on an efficient use of public funds. A related safeguard is the threat of competition— under a deregulated system entrepreneurs must be empowered to develop not only new programs but also new methods, new sources of supply, new markets, and new ways of organising service delivery.[60]

There is no single model of competitive and deregulated approaches to education services, and there is a high degree of variation as to how school choice ideas like voucher programs and charter schools have actually been expressed in legislative and regulatory terms. A fruitful area of future research will be to assess these institutional structures drawing on the experiences of similar jurisdictions such as the United States, the United Kingdom, and New Zealand, which all have implemented some form of school choice.

The separation of public funding, management and delivery is possible for other areas of public service delivery as well, and this is beginning to take shape. For instance, the recent Harper Competition Policy Review recommended that Australian governments place 'user choice at the heart of service delivery.'[61] The Commonwealth government supported this recommendation in principle, but deferred a detailed consideration to the Productivity Commission.[62] That work commenced in 2016 and the Commission's first study report considered social housing, public hospital services, end-of-life care, public dental services, human services in remote Indigenous communities, and commissioning arrangements for family and community services as the key areas where competition, contestability and user choice reform could 'offer the greatest improvements in community wellbeing'.[63] These priority areas are in addition to the recent reforms to public disability services, with the introduction of the choice-based National Disability Insurance Scheme—providing an example of the value that structural reform can achieve.

This chapter begins to provide an account of the problem of overregulation on public sector services. As noted above, it is only a starting point but there is a clear agenda here for future research. This agenda lies in contrast to the dominant political debates—such as Gonski—that are preoccupied with the size of the public funding pool available and the formula used to allocate it. Another chapter in this volume focuses on the red tape reduction processes implemented around Australia. It is interesting to note that these efforts are generally focused on freeing the private sector from overregulation. Until now, very little attention has examined the problem or effect of overregulation on public sector services. The irony is that public services are perceived to be the most bureaucratic—and perhaps where there is the greatest scope for meaningful reform.

CHAPTER THIRTEEN

Red tape reduction: A new approach

DARCY ALLEN

Policymakers can approach Australia's over-regulation
and red tape problem along two complementary paths:
through identifying and targeting economic reform of particular sectors or regulations, or through measuring the regulatory
burden and placing institutional constraints on the regulatory
process itself. While this chapter is primarily concerned with
the latter, it is first useful to differentiate the two and examine
how the development of red tape reform policies and procedures, such as one-in-two-out constraints, can be interpreted
through the lens of economic theory. From here we can examine different ways to measure and cut the red tape burden,
review current best practice red tape reduction mechanisms,

and finally provide directions for future reform within an Australian context.

The first approach for policymakers to cut red tape is to identify and repeal specific regulations believed to sit above 'minimally effective regulation' (MER)—that is, to cut specific pieces of red tape. This reform approach is best characterised through the first of three phases of regulatory reform in Australia:

1. The Hawke-era reforms of the 1980s including liberalising trade barriers;

2. The move towards a general focus on intergovernmental regulation, including the National Competition Policy framework in the 1990s; and finally

3. The focus on regulatory procedures since the Howard Government in 2005, including the COAG national reform agenda.[1]

Each of these approaches to regulatory reform, however, faces distinct political economy incentives. The traditional path for policymakers is to target either specific sectors or bodies of regulation which are seen to go beyond what is minimally necessary to achieve a stated regulatory objective. This approach reasonably rests on the assumption that there have been some poor regulatory decisions in the past—that is, exceeding current MER—or that the optimum level of regulations may change through time as economic conditions change—such as the impact of technological change enabling self-regulation. This targeted approach involves subjective judgements over where to achieve regulatory reductions within political reality, while regulators simultaneously deal with current political matters. Targeted economic reform is fundamentally backward-looking—aimed at the stock of existing regulations.

There are several shortcomings of this traditional targeted economic reform approach, including the reliance on political will and appetite for reform, the need for subjectively-evaluated decisions by fallible policy makers, and the incentive problems of concentrated political benefits with dispersed regulatory costs leading to interest group formation.[2] Indeed, public choice theory and the economics of regulation have long taught us of these misaligned incentives of political actors and the public interest.[3] And, even despite these incentives, the cumulative effects of regulation—through layers of government and overlapping jurisdictional boundaries—are inherently unclear to boundedly rational political decision makers.[4] Put simply, for all of these reasons, regulation tends to accumulate.[5] Together, these shortcomings imply that the extent of Australia's red tape and over-regulation problem cannot be tackled through effective decision making alone—a successful red tape reduction strategy cannot rely solely on targeted economic reform from benevolent policymakers.

Partly in response to this, a new complementary approach to regulatory reform has emerged: red tape reduction policies and procedures. These institutionalised mechanisms include dedicated parliamentary sitting days to repeal legislation, the implementation of regulatory budgets, and 'one-in-n-out' policies. Unlike the approach described above, which relies on identifying and reforming specific regulations driven through political will, the development of institutionalised red tape policies and procedures seeks to force the cutting of the existing regulatory burden and preventing the future growth of the burden by constraining the actions of policymakers themselves. In this way red tape and over-regulation are seen as a result of incentive problems within the regulatory process itself, rather than being associated with past specific regulatory mistakes. As such, rules are implemented to reduce the stock of existing regulation and to constrain the flow of future regulation. This is achieved by shifting regulatory incentives—that is, changing the rules of the game within which regulators may regulate—and ultimately binding regulators to behave in certain ways.[6] In this way red tape policies and procedures can be understood as 'meta-level' or 'constitutional' rules that are implemented above the regulatory process.[7] Furthermore, from this perspective these policies and procedures are not only motivated by the weight of the accumulated regulatory burden, but can be seen as an acknowledgement by political actors of some of the shortcomings of the public interest theory of regulation as made by public choice theorists.[8] These rules can be considered a form of self-regulation regulating the regulators.[9] Red tape policies and procedures can be termed as 'enforced self-regulation' by regulators.[10]

While the creation of red tape reduction policies and procedures are only a few decades old, it is now timely to examine their evolution, which is the focus of the present chapter. A brief analysis of economic reform in Australia demonstrates that the approach to economic reform has shifted from targeted economic reform towards institutionalised policies and procedures. Alongside this shift, governments and think tanks have sought to measure and quantify the regulatory burden through a range of measures including pages of legislation, complex calculations of the cost impact of regulation, the time needed to comply with regulation, and the file size of regulation. This focus on quantification is unsurprising given red tape measurement is a necessary foundation on which an institutionalised reform agenda can be built, because it enables reform success or failure to be benchmarked. Finally, this chapter provides an overview of the latest attempts at red tape measurement—measuring the number of 'regulatory restrictions' or 'restrictiveness clauses'—which is a more nuanced and granulated approach to complement targeted reform in pursuing regulatory change.

Red tape policies and the need for benchmarking

In the early 1980s Australian economic reform was characterised by specific sectoral reforms such as the liberalisation of trade through removing trade barriers, the floating of the dollar, and the privatisation of various assets.[11] These reforms are widely lauded as a process of economic deregulation, and are associated with the consequent uptick in productivity and rise in incomes.[12] While this process must be understood within the claim of the rise of the regulatory state, this period of change can be understood as the first phase of modern Australian economic reform—which was a targeted approach to specific burdensome regulations.[13]

Then, in the late 1980s and early 1990s, Australian policymakers shifted away from emphasising specific areas of reform to a more generalised focus on the introduction and management of the regulatory process itself. For instance, the first Commonwealth regulatory assessments were introduced in 1986—which were the first form of what are now called Regulation Impact Statements (RIS). These are the first efforts to institutionalise red tape reform, attempting to step away from subjective identification by policymakers by measuring the burden of red tape and monitoring its impacts on individual Australians and businesses.[14] Deregulation and cutting red tape became political topics within themselves, rather than reform driven through specific policy measures.

With the Howard government in 2005 there was a further push for regulatory oversight and reform of ministerial portfolios. This push was in part due to the influence of business groups, culminating in the Banks Inquiry, which recommended over 100 specific reforms to existing regulation and proposed further areas for regulatory examination. Chapter 7 of the Inquiry also recommended more effective processes for regulatory reform, including a cost-benefit approach to regulation and the strengthening of RIS processes.[15] While institutionalised mechanisms of red tape reduction were not the central focus of this Inquiry, they were acknowledged as necessary due to inherent problems in the 'lifecycle' of regulation:

> The stock of regulation at any point in time is the end re-sult of a sequence of actions. A regulatory 'cycle' typically begins with a perceived economic or social 'problem' being identified for political action... This is followed by the crit-ical phases of deciding what government needs to do and implementing agreed courses of action... Finally, the cycle may eventually conclude with an assessment of how well the regulations are working and whether further actions are needed to improve or replace them.[16]

In line with this focus on the regulatory process governments have introduced various portfolios, ministers and depart-ments at the federal and state levels committed to cutting red tape. For instance, the responsibility of red tape reduction in Australia was originally with the Department of Industry, Technology and Commerce. Eventually an Office of Best Practice Regulation was created—which was moved from the Department of Finance in 2008 and to the Department of Prime Minister and Cabinet in 2013. The rise of specific offices of regulation, and the movement of those offices to different departments, signifies the increasing importance of red tape reduction within politics.

From 2014, with the Coalition Government's red tape reform agenda, there was a greater focus on measurement and quantification of the regulatory burden more broadly. This was following a trend across other countries, including the United States.[17] Indeed, the foreword to the first annual deregulation report in 2014 notes that the government aimed to 'reinvent the approach to regulation'.[18] This reinvention not only focused on making RIS mandatory for cabinet following various criticisms of it, but also quantifying the burden of existing regulations, with all portfolios estimating the dollar cost impact of government activities.[19] This created a $65 billion baseline measurement of regulatory burden, which is likely to be a significant underestimate of the entire cost of the regulatory burden.[20]

Once the regulatory burden had been estimated it was coupled with red tape reduction mechanisms (such as biannual red tape repeal days) and commitments to reduce red tape (cutting the cost of regulation by $1 billion annually). These red tape repeal days were modelled on an earlier Western Australian approach, but were later abandoned in 2016 because the success of the red tape repeal days made them 'redundant'.[21] Interestingly, part of this approach included linking policymaker remuneration to cutting red tape and 'changing the way regulators act and behave', further speaking to the misaligned incentives described above, and the recognition of the need for 'meta-regulation'. This red tape repeal push, while focusing more heavily on mechanisms of red tape reduction and claiming to have made decisions to cut red tape by over $4 billion, has since been criticised as only cutting the low hanging fruit of the regulatory burden.[22]

What is clear from this evolution of regulatory reform from the 1980s to present is a movement away from specific sectoral reform to the rise of institutionalised mechanisms to cut red tape. Furthermore, with this rise in institutionalised red tape reduction policies and procedures has come the need for measurement of the regulatory burden. To develop a system of accountability throughout the red tape reduction process a baseline of regulatory burden is necessary on which to measure success. The question, then, is how to measure red tape.

All measurements of regulatory burden, owing to the problem of subjective costs and an uncertain future, are necessarily proxy measures. Red tape costs are an indirect measure of the burden of regulation, and can never wholly take into account the entire opportunity costs of regulation.[23] Nevertheless, various government departments and other organisations such as think tanks have attempted to develop proxies for the regulatory burden.[24] Developing and deciding on a proxy of regulatory burden is considered the first step in the red tape reduction process because it precedes creating a baseline count.[25] As yet, the major focus of regulatory burden has been on creating dollar cost estimates of red tape burden through frameworks such as the Regulatory Burden Measurement Framework.[26] These dollar costs come from both bottom-up analyses—where departments are required to estimate the cost of individual regulations before those costs are aggregated—or top-down approaches—which attempts to estimate the cost using macroeconomic indicators such as foregone GDP.[27] Both of these approaches, however, suffer the problem of subjective costs and misaligned incentives of those measuring the costs.

Other proxies of regulatory burden include the number of pages of legislation, number of Acts passed, or the file sizes of regulatory instruments. Each of these measurements are useful for demonstrating the extent of the burden to the public, but face various shortcomings as a baseline measurement. For instance, a common proxy for regulatory burden is the number of pages of legislation. In Australia, the Commonwealth has over 100,000 pages of federal legislation, with 4094 pages of legislation passed through the federal parliament in 2016 alone, continuing on a persistent upward trajectory.[28] While the main benefit of the page count proxy is its simplicity—it is both easy to count and update, for public understanding, and its verifiability by third parties—not all pages of legislation are equal. One page that introduces a carbon tax may be much more burdensome than a page of redundant legislation with no effect. What's more, proxies of regulatory burden do not only suffer from the problem of imperfect measurement, but may also fail to adequately address the political problems of operationalising red tape reform efforts on them. For instance, developing a one-in-two-out approach of regulatory reform on the number of pages of legislation is insufficiently granulated to be effective.

These shortcomings of page counts have led to several other measures of regulatory burden such as the file size of legislation, which face similar criticisms of their actual impact on economic decision makers.[29] In the following section we introduce the recent focus on 'restrictiveness clauses' within legislation, providing a future for red tape reform in Australia.

The 'regulatory restrictiveness' approach

Recently, variations on a new type of baseline red tape measurement have emerged in Canada, the United States and briefly here in Queensland, Australia. Rather than counting the number of pages, dollar values, or file sizes of legislation, this new measurement involves counting the number of 'restrictive clauses' found in legislation. These are clauses that restrict, prohibit or compel individuals and businesses from or to certain actions, with words such as 'shall', 'must' and 'cannot'.

Given the success of this baseline measurement approach in British Columbia, this section briefly reviews this new textual analysis approach to regulatory reduction, with the intention of providing future direction for red tape policies and procedures in Australia.

A new measurement of red tape burden must complement existing measures in some way. Developing a baseline of restrictive clauses does overcome many of the shortcomings of other forms of red tape measurement for several reasons. Restrictive clauses may be more representative of the effect of regulatory burden because they are directly associated with the impact a rule has on human decision making. Further, restrictive clauses may be more nuanced for political operationalisation because they enable regulators to operate at a lower level of reform than repealing entire Acts or pages of legislation. Creating and updating a baseline of restrictiveness clauses can also be undertaken by third parties and at a relatively reasonable cost. Perhaps most importantly, however, a restrictiveness clauses approach to red tape reform has been demonstrably successful over the long term in British Columbia.

British Columbia's efforts at institutionalised red tape reform began in 2001 when a newly elected government aimed to reduce the regulatory burden by a third. One of the tasks of the appointed minister of state for deregulation, Kevin Falcon, was to develop a new measurement of red tape of which the government could determine its success. Falcon decided to use 'regulatory restrictions' as a way to measure and benchmark regulatory reform. This unique form of measurement was defined as 'Any action or step that a citizen, business, or government must take to access government services or programs, carry out business or pursue legislated privileges.'[30] Each ministry was required to count all of their regulatory requirements within their statutes, regulations and policies. This data was then fed into a database, and portfolios were given regulatory budgets of regulatory restrictions which they must cut.

These red tape reform efforts in British Columbia were remarkably successful. From 2001 to 2017 British Columbia reduced the number of regulatory restrictiveness clauses from 330,812 to 170,140, a 48 per cent reduction.[31] In approximately a decade, British Columbia went from being one of the worst performing provinces in Canada to one of the best.[32] Furthermore, this reform success in British Columbia has lasted across changes in government with policies such as one-in-two-out (which at one stage went up to one-in-five-out, but has since been decreased to one-in-one-out). Furthermore, the success of the red tape restrictiveness clauses in the province of British Columbia led to the Canadian government being the first country in the world to legislate a one-in-one-out policy in 2015, following the success of the policy from 2012 to 2014.[33] These successes led to a similar approach to red tape reduction in Queensland, Australia.

For a short time period, the Queensland government adopted a similar restrictiveness clauses approach. Its adoption followed a Queensland Competition Authority (QCA) issues paper and interim report in late 2012, which recommended the adoption of a British Columbia style approach to counting obligations.[34] The QCA saw the 'regulatory requirements' measure as supplementing existing red tape measures, such as page counts and in dollar terms, which would all be used together to reduce the regulatory burden.[35] The new count approach for Queensland, however, was directly modelled off the British Columbia approach—with the calculation of baseline count of 'regulatory requirements'.[36] The baseline count of 265,189 regulatory requirements in Queensland was first made on 23 March 2012. By 30 June 2013 that number has fallen by 4 per cent (9,404 fewer regulatory requirements). More broadly, the Queensland Government aimed to have a 20 per cent net reduction in regulatory burden over 6 years. While the now opposition government in Queensland maintains the aim of 20 per cent reduction in red tape, the regulatory restrictions count methodology has since been abandoned, rather focusing on the compliance costs of regulation.[37]

One of the critical features of a successful red tape reduction strategy is that it remains in place over changes in government. There are several potential ways to achieve this. As is the case in Canada, governments could legislate red tape reduction mechanisms rather than simply having a policy. In the absence of this, however, it is also useful to use measurements of red tape that can be effectively counted by third parties such as think tanks. The Mercatus Centre at George Mason University in the United States has recently automated a similar approach to counting regulatory restrictions called RegData 2.0.[38] A team of researchers has developed a panel of data of the restrictiveness of regulation through textual analysis of the Code of Federal Regulations (CFR) in the United States (a record of the entire corpus of federal law). This approach seeks to create a time series to map the number of regulatory restrictions within US legislation as well as measuring industry-level regulatory burden using machine learning, known as RegData 2.2. This nuanced measurement approach combined with creating industry specific training documents, has enabled within-industry and between-industry econometric analysis of the burden of regulation.[39]

Alongside researchers at RMIT University and the Institute of Public Affairs there are similar attempts to apply the RegData methodology to Australian regulation (applying this approach outside of the United States, however, requires a further step of first developing a database of existing Commonwealth legislation, given the lack of a CFR). The benefit of such an automation is not only to provide context to the broader challenges of red tape expansion—that is, by providing restrictiveness clauses (or similar) counts across a longer time frame—but also to introduce a level of accountability and measurement that is cost effective and can be calculated when political will for targeted economic reform is lacking.

The future of red tape reduction

With the increase in meta-regulation of the regulatory process through red tape policies and procedures there have
been many issues of measuring the regulatory burden. While
more effective measurement and red tape reduction policies
and procedures should not be seen as substitutes to targeted
economic reform, they are a complementary institutional approach to traditional economic reform and hold a clear place
in tackling Australia's red tape crisis. The new approach to
red tape measurement outlined in this chapter—through the
counting of restrictiveness clauses—presents a fruitful path
for future red tape reduction mechanisms as a more granulated approach to the political economy challenges of red
tape reduction.

Chapter Fourteen

Regulation and technological change

Darcy Allen and Chris Berg

B ecause new technologies expand the boundaries of what is possible—both by making us more productive and through the creation of institutions that extend the order of market and the space of mutually beneficial trade—innovation and the evolution of technology can be considered the fundamental source of human prosperity.

Indeed, while economists have consistently struggled to incorporate the impact of technological change within tractable mainstream mathematical models, there is now a growing consensus that the heart of a modern market economy is innovation.

This understanding of the importance of innovation and entrepreneurship, however, has an underappreciated significance for the analysis of regulation. As this book is being published, an array of technological advances are poised to dramatically change the way the economy functions and how we govern our interactions. These changes raise important questions on the relationship between red tape and technology. Indeed, governments must act in real time and in a dynamic world: governments impose regulation upon economies that are constantly shifting as businesses adapt to changing economic environments, consumer preferences, and technological developments.

In this chapter we explore the relationship between regulation and technological change in two directions: first, how technology impacts the burden of red tape, and second, the impact of red tape on technological change. We focus the former on the rise of RegTech—technologies that assist in compliance and enforcement of regulation—and emphasise the latter through the principle of 'permissionless innovation'—where entrepreneurial experimentation should be allowed by lawmakers by default. Our analysis of these connections provides a foundation on which to understand the political economy of technological change.

Using technology for regulatory compliance

RegTech—a contraction of 'regulation technology'—describes a wave of new technological applications that seek to make it easier to comply with complex regulation, monitor regulated businesses, and report compliance. While the RegTech field is diverse, RegTech applications usually focus on the regulation of financial services, applying technologies such as artificial intelligence (AI), machine learning, and distributed ledgers to make compliance with the complex array of regulatory controls as efficient and cheap as possible.

As financial services represent the first wave of RegTech applications, it is worth examining a case study of one such use in the highly regulated banking sector. Banks require a certain amount of capital in order to protect themselves against insolvency. Banks which fail to do so risk the funds of shareholders and depositors. While this creates an incentive for shareholders and depositors to impose discipline on the banks' lending, policymakers are concerned that those shareholders and depositors are unable to observe—and therefore prevent—reckless bank behaviour. Hence regulations to hold bank capital. Since the 1980s, these capital requirements have become vastly more complex. Under the first iteration of the Basel Capital Accords (an international regulatory standard that Australia has adopted) banks were required to hold capital weighted to the riskiness of their assets. In subsequent iterations (Basel II in 2004, Basel III in 2010) these risk weightings have become regulatory behemoths; byzantine regulations that dictate elaborate formulas and controls on capital (and now liquidity) holdings.

It's unclear whether these complex rules do anything to achieve their goal of institutional and systemic stability. Jeffrey Friedman and Wladimir Kraus convincingly argue that these Basel rules created perverse incentives to invest in the mortgage-backed securities that caused the global financial crisis in the first place.[1] To the extent market discipline fails to prevent banking recklessness, this is itself arguably a consequence of other government interventions into banking—such as deposit guarantees—that cushion bankers from the consequences of their actions.

Nevertheless Basel compliance is extremely costly. The National Australia Bank, for instance, spent $181 on credit risk management software to comply with Basel II in the mid-2000s.[2] One estimate suggests that global compliance costs in the financial services industry are expected to rise to up to 10 per cent of revenue by 2022.[3]

The demands of Basel II and III—and a host of similar financial services regulations, know-your-customer requirements and the European Union's Markets in Financial Instruments Directive—make regulatory compliance increasingly the domain not just of lawyers, but also of computer scientists and entrepreneurs.

RegTech not only allows compliance to be automated, but new technologies can be used to make compliance more efficient or effective. For example, machine learning can help identify anomalies in compliance data—either on the side of firms or regulators—to ensure that compliance data is high quality and correct and reduce regulatory uncertainty. AI can mine for opportunities to restructure business practices to make them more efficient within regulatory limits.

RegTech is not limited to financial services. Any regulatory requirement that has an information-gathering element is plausibly a candidate for RegTech innovation. For example, many resources firms are required to manage existing native vegetation around their projects, and are increasingly using drones to do so. Autonomous drones— already being used in mines in Western Australia—could be paired with artificial intelligence to identify vegetation loss or invasive species, removing human compliance managers.

RegTech offers both opportunities and risks for red tape reduction. At the outset it makes both compliance and enforcement with regulation more efficient. While often requiring significant upfront investment, RegTech can help firms not only adhere to existing regulations but some applications are designed to dynamically accommodate changes to regulatory frameworks as well. The rapidity of regulatory change is an often unappreciated part of the overall regulatory burden. Automated compliance reduces red tape costs on the firm side. Automated enforcement— auditing and surveillance of the firm—reduces red tape costs on the regulator's side.

We can also use RegTech to make more effective regulatory policy. Policymakers could adjust regulatory frameworks in a manner that targets more closely and proportionally the issues those frameworks are trying to address. The large amounts of data provided to regulators under frameworks such as Basel III can be analysed by artificial intelligence, ideally giving regulators and policymakers a deeper understanding of patterns of conduct in the regulated industry. Given the global focus on 'macro-prudential' regulation—which looks at the macroeconomic consequences of financial stability— RegTech can contribute towards an early warning system for financial crises. In these senses RegTech reduces the overall red tape burden, making both necessary and unnecessary regulation cheaper to enforce.

But RegTech is not unambiguously beneficial for red tape reduction. More efficient regulatory compliance does not necessarily mean that the overall burden of regulation will reduce. First, as a number of contributions to this volume have pointed out, compliance is only a small part of the red tape burden. Compliance is usually the most visible part of regulatory costs but is not the most burdensome. Less costly compliance can reduce pressure for general regulatory reduction. The cost of regulation is not necessarily paid by the firms on which that regulation is imposed. Indeed, lower compliance costs might make it easier for regulators to impose on firms more red tape or regulation that is burdensome to consumers, other third parties, or the economy as a whole.

An increasing importance of RegTech alongside a growing regulatory burden could also exacerbate differences between small and large firms. During the implementation of Basel II, large banks were able to take advantage of an internal-ratings based approach to capital adequacy in which they risk rated their own assets subject to costly accreditation by domestic regulators. This technologically complex procedure gave the major banks a funding advantage over smaller banks. The large investments necessary for RegTech implementations may also result in further competitive distortions.

It is also important to note that while the rise of RegTech is the result of competitive firms acting entrepreneurially in the face of a complex regulatory system, these efforts are a type of 'unproductive entrepreneurship'. The fact that RegTech exists and is expanding in importance is a manifestation of the idea that the incentive structures and institutions within an economy shift how entrepreneurs spend their time and resources.[4] The growth of the regulatory state as has been outlined throughout this book has shifted the incentives of private firms to invest their scarce resources into RegTech—and therefore ultimately away from more productive entrepreneurial activities. This cautions against the understanding that RegTech is a silver bullet for red tape reduction. Over the longer term, however, it is possible to see opportunities for RegTech to challenge the rationale for regulation by making it more efficient to achieve objectives through forms of private governance.[5]

For example, as we have noted, capital adequacy regulation is founded on the idea that shareholders and depositors cannot observe the risk-taking of the firm. But this will not always be true. Alex Tabarrok and Tyler Cowen have written of the end of 'asymmetric information', where new information technologies eliminate the disparities in knowledge between buyers and sellers.[6] Banks and other financial institutions might be able to place their accounts on trustless ledgers observable to the public, or keep them private but monitored by publicly observable algorithms that allow those stakeholders to monitor the solvency and performance of the firm. This sort of technological approach targets the rationale for capital adequacy regulation itself. In this way, advances in RegTech could make markets more efficient, reduce information disparities between buyers and sellers, and reduce not just the cost of regulation, but its necessity.

Permissionless innovation

It took many years to discover the useful applications for technologies such as the automobile, the laser and the internet.[7] Today, similar uncertainty surrounds blockchains, 3D printers and driverless cars. The uncertainty surrounding the very early stages of new technologies makes it important not only to examine the ways in which new technology can be used to reduce the existing regulatory burden, such as through RegTech, but similarly to explore how regulations impact the evolution and development of new technologies themselves. Therefore, in this section we ask: how does regulation impact how technological opportunities are discovered? The decisions of entrepreneurs to test and experiment with new technologies are influenced both by their personal capacity to make valuable judgements as well as the regulatory constraints on what they can and cannot do.[8] That is, on one hand entrepreneurs need to coordinate and share information with others, attain financing, and apply their own entrepreneurial skills to observe opportunities. These skills separate entrepreneurs from non-entrepreneurs. On the other hand, the ways that entrepreneurs can act on an opportunity once they perceive it—by, for instance, starting a firm or testing a new business model—comes up against regulatory constraints.

To be sure, by ensuring public safety and providing certainty, imposing regulations can theoretically aid the development of a new technology or industry. For instance, the argument can be made for regulations to provide standards that help entrepreneurs to coordinate the development of a technology in its early stages, thereby seeking to overcome collective action problems between entrepreneurs. The focus in this section, however, is on how regulations can impede entrepreneurs' ability to be entrepreneurial—including through the indirect opportunity costs that regulations impose—and to outline a principle of technology public policy, permissionless innovation, which can act as a guide to policymakers.

There are several ways which regulation impedes entrepreneurship and innovation, thereby slowing the discovery process and ultimately suppressing economic growth. Most directly and explicitly, regulations impair entrepreneurs' ability to perform certain actions and use technologies in particular ways. For instance, Australian policymakers are currently debating the safe use of drone technology and how this technology should be regulated in a Senate inquiry.[9] Directly prohibiting some actions with drones, such as flying beyond visual line of sight, clearly prevents a wide range of potentially revolutionary applications from being discovered.[10] Direct prohibitions like this one ignore the uncertainty surrounding the possible application of new technologies, thereby under-weighting the potential human prosperity that could come from such applications.

The hasty and heavy regulation of new technologies can also hinder entrepreneurial discovery in more indirect ways. The costs of complying with regulations—for instance, through expensive licenses and certification, or the costs in understanding the complexity of how regulations apply to various activities—distorts the growth new industries by inhibiting entrepreneurial entry. Indeed, as has been outlined elsewhere in this volume, business entry rates in Australia have been in precipitous decline. Similarly, an increasing compliance and regulatory burden has opportunity costs: shifting the productive activities of entrepreneurs and small firms away from customer-focused supply towards understanding and complying with regulations. It is this second driver that has contributed to the expansion of RegTech outlined in the previous section.

It is clear that over-regulation can impede the evolutionary process of technological change—through prohibition of activities, compliance costs and the shifting of resources towards unproductive activities—but before examining how policymakers can avoid these costs it is important to understand why they are implemented. One prominent driver of these regulatory costs is what has become known as the 'precautionary principle'. Here, new technologies and business practices are quickly regulated based on some hypothetical future harms that those may place on members of the public. In the recent Senate inquiry into the regulation of drones, for instance, public hearing participants discussed whether drones should be entirely banned for amateur users.

There are several interconnected explanations for hasty responses such as these, which can be broadly referred to as the 'precautionary principle'. One reason is simply that regulators often under-weight the potential benefits of using a new technology—particularly given that those uses are not yet known, by either entrepreneurs or policymakers.

At the same time the potential harms of new technologies are easily conceivable—loss of lives, declining privacy, job losses—and are often over-weighted in public policy decisions. These challenges are compounded by the lobbying efforts of disrupted industries, who contribute resources to lobby government for further regulation and privileges to protect their business models. These dynamics have been brought into clear view with the recent debates around the sharing economy and Uber.

Whatever the reasons for these tensions in the regulation of new technologies, however, the undeniable existence of a knowledge problem when regulating new technologies, and the huge potential costs in regulating too heavily, make is important to have a principled approach to regulating technological change.

This is part of the motivation for Adam Thierer, who developed the regulatory principle of permissionless innovation.[11] A permissionless innovation approach proposes that the default position for policymakers should be to allow experimentation and development with new technologies until demonstrable harms can be shown. That is, the regulation of new technologies should not be based on hypothetical future harms—which are easily conceivable and used by incumbent firms to lobby in their own private interest—but rather only once those harms have materialised as the technology is developed.

Of course such a permissionless innovation approach isn't perfect. It must be coupled with an effective property rights and court system, in order to remedy the inevitable harms that will arise. Further, a permissionless innovation approach relies heavily on a culture of public trust in policymakers to resist regulation. Nevertheless, such an approach to regulating new technologies helps to mitigate some of the challenges in how over-regulation and red tape holds back new technology.

Towards a dynamic approach to technology regulation
In this chapter we have explored the relationship between regulation and new technologies in both directions. What our analysis suggests is that on one hand technologies can decrease the compliance costs and enforcement costs of existing laws, and on the other hand regulation can impede the development and evolution of new technologies by holding back entrepreneurial discovery.

These understandings, however, exist within a dynamic economic system. Indeed, new technologies can shift what regulations can be considered red tape and those which can be considered minimally effective regulation. For example, the rise of ubiquitous information through ratings and reputation mechanisms in the 'sharing economy' are a type of self-regulation that may be comparatively more effective than state-based regulation.[12]

In this context, technologies may transform previously necessary or optimal regulations into red tape. Similarly, technologies such as blockchain, which is primarily a governance technology to facilitate coordination and exchange, shifts the boundaries at which regulation is an efficient solution. For this reason, it's important to adopt a permissionless innovation approach to public policy where new technologies are enabled by default: only then can we observe how technologies develop and shift the optimum level of regulation, and be sure not to unnecessarily inhibit technological change, the ulimate source of human prosperity.

References

CHAPTER ONE:
REGULATION IN A SMALL OPEN ECONOMY

1. John Howard, "Policy Speech", Sydney, 18 February 1996, http://electionspeeches.moadoph.gov.au/speeches/1996-john-howard.
2. Kevin Rudd, "Facing the Future", National Press Club, 17 April 2007, http://www.actu.org.au/media/172071/rudd-press-club-address.PDF.
3. Liberal Party of Australia, "Our Plan: Real Solutions for all Australians", (Liberal Party of Australia, 2013).
4. Shuyun May Li and Adam Hal Spencer, "Effectiveness of the Australian Fiscal Stimulus Package: A DSGE Analysis", *Economic Record*, Vol. 92 No. 296, (2015), 94-120; Philip Liu, "The Effects of International Shocks on Australia's Business Cycle", *Economic Record*, Vol. 86 No. 275, (2010), 486-503; Kristoffer P. Nimark, 'A Structural Model of Australia as a Small Open Economy', *Australian Economic Review*, Vol. 42 No. 1, (2009), 24-41.
5. ibid. Nimark (2009).

6. William O. Coleman, *Only in Australia: The History, Politics and Economics of Australian Exceptionalism*, (Oxford, United Kingdom: Oxford University Press, 2016); Ian W. McLean, *Why Australia Prospered: The Shifting Sources of Economic Growth*, (Princeton, NJ: Princeton University Press, 2013).

7. Chris Berg, *The Growth of Australia's Regulatory State: Ideology, Accountability and the Mega-regulators*, (Melbourne: Institute of Public Affairs, 2008); John Braithwaite, "Accountability and Governance Under the New Regulatory State', *Australian Journal of Public Administration*, Vol. 58 No. 1, (1999), 90-94; Edward L. Glaeser and Andrei Shleifer, "The Rise of the Regulatory State", *Journal of Economic Literature*, Vol. 41, No. 2, (2003), 401-425; Andrei Shleifer, *The Failure of Judges and the Rise of Regulators*, (Cambridge: MIT Press, 2012).

8. Mikayla Novak, *The Red Tape State*, (Melbourne: Institute of Public Affairs, 2016b).

9. Clyde Wayne Crews, "Tip of the Costberg: On the Invalidity of All Cost of Regulation Estimates and the Need to Compile Them Anyway, 2017 Edition", Working Paper, (2017), 20.

10. Commonwealth of Australia, *The Australian Government Annual Deregulation Report 2014*.

11. ibid. Clyde Wayne Crews, 20.

12. Deloitte, *Get Out of Your Own Way: Unleashing Productivity*, (Canberra, Deloitte, 2014).

13. Mark W. Crain and Nicole V. Crain, *The Cost of Federal Regulation to the US Economy, Manufacturing and Small Business*, (National Association of Manufacturers, 2014); Mikayla Novak, *The $176 Billion Tax on Our Prosperity*, (Melbourne: Institute of Public Affairs, 2016a).

14. Barry M. Mitnick, *The Political Economy of Regulation: Creating, Designing and Removing Regulatory Forms*, (New York: Columbia University Press, 1980).

15. Commonwealth Interdepartmental Committee on Quasi-regulation 1997, *Grey-Letter Law: Report of the Commonwealth Interdepartmental Committee on Quasi-regulation.*

16. Simeon Djankov, Edward Glaeser, Rafael La Porta, Florencia Lopez-de-Silanes and Andrei Shleifer, "The New Comparative Economics", *Journal of Comparative Economics*, Vol. 31 No. 4, (2003), 595-619.

17. Sinclair Davidson, "Productivity Enhancing Regulatory Reform", *Australia Adjusting: Optimising National Prosperity*, Vol. 66, (2013); Darcy W.E. Allen, "The Subjective Political Economy of Innovation Policy" SSRN (2016); Sinclair Davidson and Jason Potts, "Social Costs and the Institutions of Innovation Policy" SSRN; Sinclair Davidson and Jason Potts, "A New Institutional Approach to Innovation Policy", *Australian Economic Review*, Vol. 49 No. 2, (2016), 200-207; Chris Berg "An Institutional Theory of Free Speech" SSRN; Chris Berg and Sinclair Davidson, "Media Regulation: A Critique of Finkelstein and Tiffen" (2015); Chris Berg and Sinclair Davidson, "Section 18C, Human Rights, and Media Reform: An Institutional Analysis of the 2011-13 Australian Free Speech Debate", *Agenda: A Journal of Policy Analysis and Reform*, Vol. 23 No. 1, (2016), 5-30; Sinclair Davidson, "Environmental Protest: An Economics of Regulation Approach", *Australian Environment Review*, Vol. 29 No. 10, (2014), 283-286; Chris Berg, "Safety and Soundness: An Economic History of Prudential Bank Regulation in Australia, 1893-2008', *RMIT University Doctoral Thesis* (2016); Trent J. MacDonald "Theory of Unbundled and Non-territorial Governance: Studies in Evolutionary Political Economy", RMIT University Doctoral Thesis (2015).

18. Arthur C. Pigou, *The Economics of Welfare*, (London: Macmillan and Co, 1932).

19. Chris Hayes, "In Praise of Red Tape", *The Nation*, 21 June 2007.

20. Barry Bozeman, *Bureaucracy and Red Tape*, (Upper Saddle River, N.J: Prentice Hall, 2000).

21. Productivity Commission, *Trade and Assistance Review 2014-15*, (Commonwealth of Australia, 2016).

22. Simon Guttmann and Anthony Richards, "Trade Openness: An Australian Perspective", *Australian Economic Papers*, Vol. 45 No. 3, (2006), 188-203.

23. Geoffrey Blainey, *The Tyranny of Distance: How Distance Shaped Australia's History*, (Melbourne: Sun Books, 1966).

24. Ximena Clark, David Dollar, and Alejandro Micco, "Port Efficiency, Maritime Transport Costs, and Bilateral Trade," *Journal of Development Economics*, Vol. 75, No. 2, (2004), 417-450.

25. Jeffrey A. Frankel and David Romer, "Does Trade Cause Growth?", *American Economic Review*, Vol. 89 No. 3, (1999): 379-399; Romain Wacziarg and Karen H. Welch, "Trade Liberalization and Growth: New Evidence", *The World Bank Economic Review*, Vol. 22 No. 2, (2008), 187-231.

26. Chris Berg and Aaron Lane, *Coastal Shipping Reform: Industry Saviour or Regulatory Nightmare*, (Melbourne: Institute of Public Affairs, December 2013); see also Mary R. Brooks, "The Changing Regulation of Coastal Shipping in Australia", *Ocean Development & International Law*, Vol. 45 No. 1, (2014), 67-83; Aaron Lane, "Economic Vandalism on the Coast", *IPA Review*, Vol. 66, No. 1, 38; Jennifer Porter "Australian Coastal Shipping: Navigating Regulatory Reform", *Austl. & NZ Mar. LJ*, Vol. 29, (2015), 8.

27. Jan Walulik, "At the Core of Airline Foreign Investment Restrictions: A Study of 121 Countries", *Transport Policy*, Vol. 49, (2016) 234-251; Jan Walulik, *Progressive Commercialization of Airline Governance Culture*, (New York: Routledge, 2016).

28. ibid. Guttmann and Richards (2006).

29. Australian Government, *Australia in the Asian Century: White Paper*,

(Commonwealth of Australia, 2012).

30. Diane Coyle, *GDP: A Brief But Affectionate History*, (Princeton: Princeton University Press, 2014); Mikayla Novak, "A Partial Defence of GDP", *ABC The Drum*, 6 October 2014.

31. OECD, *Better Life Index*, accessed 19 April 2017, (2011), http://www.oecdbetterlifeindex.org/.

32. Commonwealth of Australia, *2015 Intergenerational Report: Australia in 2055*, (Canberra: Commonwealth of Australia, 2015a).

33. Chris Berg and Jason Potts, "The Economics of Zero Population Growth", *Quadrant*, Vol. 60 No. 4, (2016), 28.

34. Tony Makin, "Did Australia's Fiscal Stimulus Counter Recession?: Evidence from the National Accounts", *Agenda: A Journal of Policy Analysis and Reform*, Vol. 17 No. 2, (2010a), 5-16; Tony Makin, "How Should Macroeconomic Policy Respond to Foreign Financial Crises?", *Economic Papers: A Journal of Applied Economics and Policy*, Vol. 29 No. 2, (2010b), 99-108; Tony Makin, *The Effectiveness of Federal Fiscal Policy: A Review*, (Canberra: Australian Government, The Treasury, 2016). See also Sinclair Davidson and Ashton de Silva, *Submission to the Senate inquiry into Stimulus Packages*, (Melbourne: Institute of Public Affairs, 2009); Sinclair Davidson and Ashton de Silva, "Stimulating savings: An analysis of cash handouts in Australia and the United States", *Agenda: A Journal of Policy Analysis and Reform*, Vol. 20 No. 2, (2013), 39-57; Henry Ergas and Alex Robson, *The 2008–09 Fiscal Stimulus Packages: A Cost Benefit Analysis*, Submission to the Senate Inquiry into the Government's Economic Stimulus Initiatives, (2009).

35. Tony Makin and Julian Pearce, "Fiscal Consolidation and Australia's Public Debt", *Australian Journal of Public Administration*, Vol. 75 No. 4, (2016), 424-440.

36. James M. Buchanan and Richard E. Wagner, *Democracy in Deficit: the Political Legacy of Lord Keynes*, (New York: Academic Press, York, 1977).

37. Daniel Wild, *Business Investment in Australia Now Lower than Under Whitlam*, (Melbourne: Institute of Public Affairs, 2017).

38. Jim Minifie, *Stagnation Nation? Australian Investment in a Low-growth World*, (Melbourne: Grattan Institute, 2017).

39. Brett Hogan, *Where Have All the Entrepreneurs Gone? An Analysis of New Business Creation in Australia*, (Melbourne: Institute of Public Affairs, 2016)

40. *International Monetary Fund Australia: Staff report of the 2016 Article IV consultation*, (International Monetary Fund, 2017).

41. Joseph A. Schumpeter, *Capitalism, Socialism, and Democracy*, (New York, London: Harper & Brothers, 1942); Kenneth E. Boulding, *Evolutionary Economics*, (Beverly Hills, Calif.: Sage Publications, 1981).

42. Mancur Olson, *The Logic of Collective Action: Public Goods and the Theory of Groups*, Harvard Economic Studies, (Cambridge, Mass: Harvard University Press, 1971).

43. Sam Peltzman, "Toward a More General Theory of Regulation", *The Journal of Law and Economics,* Vol. 19 No. 2, (1976), 211-240; Richard A. Posner, *Theories of Economic Regulation*, (Cambridge, Mass., USA: National Bureau of Economic Research, 1974); George J. Stigler, "The Theory of Economic Regulation." *The Bell Journal of Economics and Management Science,* Vol. 2 No. 1 (1971), 3-21.

44. William A. Niskanen, Bureaucracy and representative government, (Aldine, Chicago: Transaction Publishers 1971); William A. Niskanen, "Bureaucracy: A Final Retrospective", in W.A. Niskanen (ed.), *Reflections of a Political Economist: Selected Articles on Government Policies and Political Processes*, Cato Institute, Washington, D.C., (2008), 189-206.

45. Anthony Downs, *An Economic Theory of Democracy*, (New York: Harper, 1957); James M. Buchanan and Gordon Tullock, *The Calculus of Consent*, (Michigan: The University of Michigan, 1960).

46. William J. Baumol, "Entrepreneurship: Productive, Unproductive, and Destructive", *Journal of Political Economy*, Vol. 98 No. 5, Part 1, (1990), 893-921.

47. Raquel Alexander, Stephen W. Mazza, and Susan Scholz. "Measuring Rates of Return on Lobbying Expenditures: An Empirical Case Study of Tax Breaks for Multinational Corporations." *Journal of Law and Politics*, Vol. 25 No. 401, (2009), 401.

48. Ike Mathur and Manohar Singh, "Corporate Political Strategies", *Accounting & Finance*, Vol. 51 No. 1, (2011), 252-277.

49. Truman F. Bewley, *Why Wages Don't Fall During a Recession*, (Cambridge, Mass.: Harvard University Press, 1999).

50. John Haltiwanger, Stefano Scarpetta, and Helena Schweiger. "Cross Country Differences in Job Reallocation: The Role of Industry, Firm Size and Regulations", *Labour Economics*, Vol. 26, (2014), 11-26.

51. Christian Bjørnskov, "Economic Freedom and Economic Crises", *European Journal of Political Economy*, Vol. 45 Supplement, (2016), 11-23.

52. Friedrich A. Hayek, "The Use of Knowledge in Society", *The American Economic Review*, Vol. 35 No. 4, (1945), 519-530.

53. Australian Chamber of Commerce and Industry, *National Red Tape Survey*, (Barton, Australian Capital Territory: Australian Chamber of Commerce and Industry, 2015).

54. Ken Henry, "Speech to Committee for Economic Development of Australia", paper presented to Committee for Economic Development of Australia, 23 February 2017, https://news.nab.com.au/nab-chairman-ken-henrys-speech-at-ceda/.

55. Sensis 2016, *Sensis Business Index*.

56. Wayne C. Crews, *Ten Thousand Commandments 2016*, (Washington D.C: Competitive Enterprise Institute, 2016).

57. United Nations Framework Convention on Climate Change Secretariat 2016, The Concept of Economic Diversification in the

Context of Response Measures, (Technical paper by the secretariat, 6 May 2016).

58. ibid. Berg (2008); ibid. Braithwaite (1999); Noralv Veggeland, *Taming the Regulatory State: Politics and Ethics*, (Cheltenham, UK; Northampton, Mass.: Edward Elgar, 1999).

59. Essential Research 2017, *Essential Report: Government regulation*, http://www.essentialvision.com.au/government-regulation-3.

60. ibid. Davidson (2013).

CHAPTER TWO:
THE BIG PICTURE

1. Robert G. Menzies, "The Measure of the Years", (Melbourne, Cassell, 1970), 8.

2. Alexis de Tocqueville, *Democracy in America*, (1835), ed. J.P. Mayer and M. Lerner, trans. G. Lawrence, (New York: Harper Collins, 1966); R. Bendix, *Work and Authority in Industry*, (New York: John Wiley & Sons, 1956) emphasised that ultimately authority depends on those subject to it.

3. Economist Intelligence Unit, *Democracy Index 2016: Revenge of the "Deplorables"*, (London: EIU, 2017); Mark Evans, Max Halupka, and Gerry Stoker, *How Australians Imagine Their Democracy*, (Canberra: University of Canberra, Museum of Australian Democracy, 2017).

4. Adam Smith, *An Inquiry into the Nature and Causes of the Wealth of Nations*, ed. R.H. Campbell, A.S. Skinner, (1776), Vol. I, 398-400.

5. John Stuart Mill, *On Liberty*, (Norwalk, Conn.: Easton Press, 1991 [1859]), 15.

6. Robert G. Menzies, "Speech is of Time", (London, Cassell, 1958), 211.

7. Adam Smith, *The Theory of Moral Sentiments*, (1759), ed. D.D. Ra-

phael, A.L. Macfie, (Oxford: Clarendon Press, 1976).

8. John Locke, *Two Treatises of Government*, (London, 1689).

9. Thomas Hobbes, *Leviathan*, (1651).

10. Tim Soutphommasane, "If We Relax the Racial Discrimination Act We Risk Condoning Racism", accessed 3 September 2017, http://www.huffingtonpost.com.au/ tim-soutphommasane/ if-we-relax-the-racial-discrimination-act-we-risk-condoning-rac_a_21714992/.

11. see John Hirst, *Freedom on the Fatal Shore: Australia's First Colony*, (Melbourne, Black Inc., 2008).

12. Alf Rattigan, *Industry Assistance: The Inside Story*, (Melbourne: Melbourne University Press, 1986), 11.

13. Frederic W. Eggleston, *State Socialism in Victoria*, (London: P.S. King & Son, 1932), 1.

14. Terry Miller and Anthony B. Kim, *2017 Index of Economic Freedom*, (Washington, The Heritage Foundation, 2017), 4.

15. Max Weber, *Economy and Society*, ed. G. Roth and C. Wittich (Berkeley: University of California Press, 1968); also Chester I. Barnard, *The Functions of the Executive*, (Cambridge: Harvard University Press, 1938); Robert A. Dahl and Charles E. Lindblom, *Politics, Economics and Welfare: Planning and Politico-Economic Systems Resolved into Basic Social Processes*, (New York: Harper, 1953).

16. ibid. Mill (1991), 22.

17. Charles E. Lindblom, *Politics and Markets: The World's Political-Economic Systems*, (New York: Basic Books, 1977); see also David A. Kemp, "Authority and Public Policy: Solving the Political Problem", in H. Redner (ed.), *An Heretical Heir of the Enlightenment: Politics, Policy and Science in the work of Charles E. Lindblom* (Boulder, Colorado: Westview Press, 1993), 155-186.

18. Charles E. Lindblom, *The Intelligence of Democracy: Decision-making through Mutual Adjustment*, (New York: Free Press, 1966), 207.

19. ibid. Kemp (1993), 166. Also see Friedrich A. Hayek, "The Use of Knowledge in Society", *The American Economic Review*, Vol. 35 No. 4, (1945), 519-530.

20. ibid, Tocqueville, 667; Also see David A. Kemp, *Foundations for Australian Political Analysis: Politics and Authority*, (Melbourne: Oxford University Press, 1987), esp. Ch.12 and Epilogue.

CHAPTER THREE:
AUSTRALIA'S ECONOMIC MALAISE

1. I thank Karla Pincott, Robert Carling, Pero Stojanovski, Matthew O'Donnell and an anonymous reviewer for comments on this chapter. Their comments have been of substantial assistance in improving the chapter.

2. There are many other factors that could also be harming Australia's economic performance, including tax and high energy costs, but the harmful effect of regulation is substantial as argued in this paper.

3. ABS, Australian National Accounts: National Income, Expenditure and Product, September 2017, Cat No 5206, Table 1. Figures are real quarterly growth, seasonally adjusted and smoothed by taking the 3 year centred moving average. The 1980s recession had 11 quarters (2.75 years) where quarterly smoothed growth was below 0.4 per cent, and the 1990s recession had 14 quarters (3.5 years) below 0.4 per cent; the current period of slow growth has to date lasted 37 quarters (9.25 years).

4. For example Scott Morrison, 'Address to the Higgins Budget Breakfast', Melbourne, 12 May 2017.

5. OECD.Stat, see: https://stats.oecd.org/index.aspx?queryid=60702

6. In the period 2010–2015, Australia's population growth rate was faster than growth in Japan, Korea, North America and almost all countries in Europe. See: United Nations *World Population Pros-*

pects 2017, available at: https://esa.un.org/unpd/wpp/Download/Standard/Population/

7. Using the standard definition that a recession is two consecutive quarters of negative real growth. Using trend growth in real GDP per person there were recessions in 2008 and 2000. Source: ABS, Australian National Accounts: National Income, Expenditure and Product, September 2017, Cat No 5206, Table 1.

8. The data source for Figure 1 is different from the source for Figure 2, explaining the differences in the two series for Australia. The OECD figures for most countries start in 1995, so no inference can be made about Australia's relative performance before 1995. The argument for using weighted rather than unweighted averages is presented in Michael Potter, *The Case Against Tax Increases in Australia: The Growing Burden*, (Sydney: CIS Research Report 15 in Box 2, 2016); and Peter Burn, *How Highly Taxed Are We?*, (Sydney: CIS Policy Monograph, 2004), 67. Figures are quarterly smoothed growth, using 3 year centred moving average. OECD average is weighted by economy size.

9. Grace Taylor and Rod Tyers, 'Secular Stagnation: Determinants and Consequences for Australia', *Economic Record*, Vol. 93 No. 303, (2017), 642.

10. Peter Tulip, "The Effect of the Mining Boom on the Australian Economy", *RBA Bulletin*, (2014), December Quarter, Graph 3. That paper estimates the boom would cause a short-term addition to GDP of 6 per cent, moderating to about 5 per cent in the long term.

11. ibid. Graph 3 of that paper indicates the decline in the level of GDP from the peak of the mining boom to the long-term figure is about 1 percentage point.

12. See Figure 3.9 of Jim Minifie, Ittima Cherastidtham, Daniel Mullerworth and James Savage, *The Mining Boom: Impacts and Prospects*,

(Melbourne: Grattan Institute, 2013). If this analysis is correct, excluding the effect of the mining boom will make the extent of the malaise since the end of the boom worse.

13. ABS, Wage Price Index, Australia, 2017, Cat No 6345.0, Table 1; and James Bishop and Natasha Cassidy "Insights into Low Wage Growth in Australia", *RBA Bulletin*, March Quarter, (2017), Graph 11.

14. Figures are seasonally adjusted. On this measure, real income per person was $13,883 in September 2008 and $14,318 in September 2017, a total increase over that period of 3.1 per cent, or an annualised growth rate of 0.3 per cent. Reference year for real income is 2014-15.

15. Over 400,000 new jobs were created in the 2017 calendar year, see Rachel Baxendale, "Turnbull Hails Record Job Figures", *The Australian*, 18 January 2018; Compensation of employees grew on average by 0.3 per cent per quarter in real terms over the past three years, compared to an average real growth of 0.8 per cent per quarter since 1992 (the last major recession). Source: ABS, Australian National Accounts: National Income, Expenditure and Product, September 2017, Cat No 5206, Table 1 and ABS, Consumer Price Index, Cat No 6401, Table 1.

16. The RBA paper cited earlier estimated the mining boom would lead to a boost to household incomes of 13 per cent and a boost to wages at its peak of about 6 per cent. The expected decline since the peak appears to be about 2 per cent for household incomes and 3 per cent for wages. Source: Section 5.1 and Figure 9 of Tulip (2014), *The Effect of the Mining Boom on the Australian Economy.*

17. Guy Debelle, "Global Influences on Domestic Monetary Policy", speech to Committee for Economic Development of Australia (CEDA) Mid-Year Economic Update, Adelaide, 21 July 2017, Graph 1.

18. See also David Uren, "Rising Cost of Essential Services Putting the Squeeze on Homes", *The Australian*, 15 January 2018.

19. Productivity Commission, *Shifting the Dial: 5 Year Productivity Review*, (Canberra: Productivity Commission Report No. 84, 2017, 34).

20. For example Mark Carney, "Policy Panel – Investment and Growth in Advanced Economies", *ECB Forum on Central Banking* 2017; and IMF, *World Economic Outlook: Uneven Growth—Short- and Long-term Factors*, (April 2017), Chapter 4.

21. The difference between Australia's investment to GDP ratio and the OECD weighted average is forecast to decline by 1.9 percentage points from 2017 to 2022.

22. A more detailed analysis of this issue, based on earlier data, is in Michael Potter, "The Looming Crisis in Business Investment", *Policy Magazine*, Vol. 4 No. 32, (2016).

23. Note the World Bank is revising these figures, see Josh Zumbrun and Ian Talley, "World Bank Unfairly Influenced Its Own Competitiveness Rankings", *Wall Street Journal*, 12 January 2018; Heritage Foundation, *Index of Economic Freedom*, various years; IMD World Competitiveness Center, *World Competitiveness Yearbook*, various years; and Fraser Institute *Economic Freedom of the World Annual Report*, various years. Australia's best rating was in 2010 on most measures (Except the World Bank Ease of Doing Business Index where our best performance was a rating of 5 in 2005; and the IMD Competitiveness Scorecard where our best performance was a rating of 4 in 2004.).

24. This refers to multifactor productivity based on labour inputs adjusted for quality. Source: ABS, Australian System of National Accounts 2016–17, Cat No 5204.0, Table 13.

25. ibid.

26. See Simon Campbell and Harry Withers, "Australian Productivity

Trends and the Effect of Structural Change", *Economic Roundup*, 28 August 2017; and Arif Syed, R Quentin Grafton, Kaliappa Kalirajan and Dean Parham, "Productivity in the Australian Mining Sector", *Australian Journal of Agricultural and Resource Economics*, Vol. 59 No. 4, (2015), 549-570.

27. "The HILDA Survey indicates there has been little net change in income inequality between 2001 and 2015. For example, the Gini coefficient, a common measure of overall inequality, has remained at approximately 0.3 over the entire 15 years of the HILDA Survey": Roger Wilkins, *The Household, Income and Labour Dynamics in Australia Survey: Selected Findings from Waves 1 to 15*, (Melbourne: Melbourne Institute, 2017), 29. The latest data from the ABS shows negligible change in inequality from 2007–08 to 2015–16, see ABS, Household Income and Wealth, Australia, 2015–16, Cat No 6523.0. For labour share of income, see Declan Trott, "Adjusting the Australian Wage Share for Depreciation, Housing, and Other Factors, 1960-2016", Paper presented to 2017 Australian Conference of Economists, (2017).

28. If the labour share has declined in Australia (see Footnote 33), then this could be a direct result of the capital deepening caused by the mining boom. See Dean Parham, *Labour's Share of Growth in Income and Prosperity*, Visiting Researcher Paper, (Canberra: Productivity Commission, 2013).

29. Since 1988, household net worth has increased by over 400 per cent, of which two thirds is attributable to increased dwelling prices, see: ABS, Australian National Accounts: Finance and Wealth, 2017, Cat No 5232.0, Table 34.

30. For example Christian Hilber and Wouter Vermeulen, "The Impact of Supply Constraints on House Prices in England", *Economic Journal*, Vol. 126 No. 591, (2015), 358-405; Edward Glaeser and Joseph Gyourko, "The Impact Of Building Restrictions On

Housing Affordability", *FRBNY Economic Policy Review*, Vol. 9 No. 2, June, (2003), 21-39; and Jason Furman, "Barriers to Shared Growth: The Case of Land Use Regulation and Economic Rents", Remarks to The Urban Institute, 20 November 2015. Furman was Chairman of the Whitehouse Council of Economic Advisers under President Obama.

31. The slowdown could be explained by factors common to many developed countries, for example the secular stagnation theory as outlined in Larry Summers, "The Age of Secular Stagnation: What It Is and What to Do About It", *Foreign Affairs*, February 2016. However, this cannot explain the decline in Australia's performance relative to other countries, as discussed earlier. Hence, Australia-specific factors will be major contributors to the slowdown.

32. This is the cumulative annual increase in the personal tax to GDP ratio per year from 2010–11 to 2016–17, based on figures in the 2017–18 Budget. Further discussion of bracket creep and fiscal drag, including definitions, are in Robert Carling and Michael Potter, *Exposing the Stealth Tax: The Bracket Creep Rip-off*, (Sydney: CIS Research Report 8, 2015).

33. Treasury, *Economic and Fiscal Effects of Rising Average Tax Rates*, (Treasury Ministerial Brief, 1 February 2016).

34. See Michael Potter, *Fix it or Fail: Why We Must Cut Company Tax Now*, (Sydney: CIS Research Report 20, 2016).

35. See Footnotes 11 and 12.

36. Deloitte, *Get Out of Your Own Way: Unleashing Productivity*, (Canberra: Deloitte, 2014).

37. ibid. Deloitte (2014), Chart 9.

38. Lucille Keen, "NAB Says Compliance Costs Unsustainable", *The Australian Financial Review*, 14 July 2014.

39. Justin Douglas, *Deregulation in Australia*, (Treasury Economic Roundup, 25 July 2014).

40. Daniel Wild, *Barriers to Prosperity: Red Tape and the Regulatory State in Australia*, (Melbourne: Institute of Public Affairs, 2017).

41. Mark Harrison, "Assessing the Impact of Regulatory Impact Assessments", *Agenda*, Vol. 3 No. 16, (2009), 41-49.

42. Productivity Commission, *Regulatory Impact Analysis: Benchmarking*, Productivity Commission Research Report (Canberra, Productivity Commission, 2012), 2.

43. Office of Best Practice Regulation, *Best Practice Regulation Report 2015–16*, (Canberra: Department of the Prime Minister and Cabinet, 2017).

44. The OBPR assessed the Major Bank Levy as compliant but not best practice because of poor consultation. Source: Wayne Poels, "Regulation Impact Statement – Second Pass Assessment – Major Bank Levy", Letter to Treasury, (Office of Best Practice Regulation, 2017).

45. The subsequent points are all from Michael Potter, *The Major Bank Levy: We're All Going to be Hit*, (Sydney: CIS Research Report 29, 2017).

46. John Lonsdale, "Regulatory Impact Statement – Final Assessment Second Pass", Letter to OBPR, OBPR ID 22319, (2017). The OBPR assessed the Levy breached consultation requirements, see Wayne Poels (2017).

47. See: Australian Government, "Cutting Red Tape", https://www.cuttingredtape.gov.au/

48. Sources for the list of harmful incentives include: Daniel Wild, *Barriers to Prosperity: Red Tape and the Regulatory State in Australia*, (Melbourne: Institute of Public Affairs, 2017); Business Council of Australia, *Action Plan for Enduring Prosperity: Rethinking our Approach to Regulation and Governance*, (July 2013); and Productivity Commission, *Regulatory Impact Analysis: Benchmarking*, (Research Report, Canberra, 2012).

49. This is not to say the financial incentives for the federal government are good—just the state government incentives are much worse.

50. Scott Morrison and Matthias Cormann, *Budget 2017–18: Budget Strategy and Outlook, Budget Paper 1*, Table 9, (2017), 5-18. FBT is included with personal tax; resource rent taxes and superannuation funds taxes are included with company tax.

51. As noted in Footnote 30, planning rules and regulations are a substantial cause of higher house prices. As a result, regulatory reform should lead to lower prices or reduced price growth.

52. See for example Hannah Leal, Stephanie Parsons, Graham White and Andrew Zurawski, "Housing Market Turnover", *RBA Bulletin*, March Quarter, (2017), 26.

53. Details of HFE are in John Brumby, Bruce Carter and Nick Greiner, *GST Distribution Review Interim Report*, (2012), Chapter 1; and Commonwealth Grants Commission, *How HFE Works*, available at: https://cgc.gov.au/index.php?option=com_content&view=article&id=258&Itemid=536

54. Two recent reports found the GST distribution formula in theory creates perverse incentives, discouraging economic reform. See John Brumby, Bruce Carter and Nick Greiner, *GST Distribution Review Final Report*, (2012), Chapter 9; and Productivity Commission, *Horizontal Fiscal Equalisation, Draft Report*, (Canberra: 2017). These reports were unable to list beneficial reforms that were discouraged because of the formula, but the Commission noted 'absence of evidence is not equivalent to evidence of absence' and the disincentives the formula creates for desirable policies 'when viewed cumulatively over time, could be at significant cost to the Australian economy' (p 13).

55. This is not to say that payroll tax is particularly efficient—instead the argument is payroll tax provides the right incentives to state governments for reform.

56. For dairy see David Harris, *Industry Adjustment to Policy Reform—A Case Study of the Australian Dairy Industry*, (Canberra: RIRDC, 2005); and for industry structural assistance more broadly see Productivity Commission, *Trade and Assistance Review 2015–16*, (2017), and the same report in earlier years.
57. See 2017-18 Budget, 8-19 to 8-20.
58. Minerals Council of Australia, *Submission to the Productivity Commission Inquiry on Horizontal Fiscal Equalisation in Australia*, (2017).
59. Productivity Commission, *Horizontal Fiscal Equalisation, Draft Report*, (2017), Chapter 8.
60. Peter Hendy, "Reforming Taxation Isn't About Increasing Taxes", *IPA Review*, Vol. 67 No. 2, (May 2015), 44-49; Tony Shepherd, Peter Boxall, Tony Cole, Robert Fisher and Amanda Vanstone, *Towards Responsible Government—The Report of the National Commission of Audit*, Part One, (February, 2014).
61. Productivity Commission, *Review of National Competition Policy Arrangements, Inquiry Report*, (2005), 152-157. The Commission supported the incentive payments while also proposing various technical improvements to the payment system.
62. ibid. Productivity Commission (2005), 381 and 387.
63. The ending of the incentive payments in 2005-2006 is stated on the National Competition Council website: http://ncp.ncc.gov.au/pages/about
64. Australian Government, *Reducing Pressure on Housing Affordability: Fact Sheet 1.7—A New National Housing and Homelessness Agreement*, (Canberra: 2017).
65. For more details, see ibid. Productivity Commission, (2005).
66. Business Council of Australia, *Action Plan for Enduring Prosperity: Rethinking Our Approach to Regulation and Governance*, (July, 2013); and Productivity Commission, *Regulatory Impact Analysis: Benchmarking*, (Canberra: Productivity Commission Research Report, 2012).

References

67. John Uhrig, *Review of the Corporate Governance of Statutory Authorities and Office Holders*, (2003), 67-68. This proposal was also supported in ibid. Business Council of Australia (2013).
68. ibid. Productivity Commission (2012), 27.
69. See ibid. Business Council of Australia (2013), 13; ibid. Productivity Commission (2012), 24.
70. ibid. Business Council of Australia (2013), 13.
71. ibid. Productivity Commission (2012), 23.
72. ibid. Business Council of Australia (2013), 14.
73. Australian Government, *Australian Government Guide to Regulation*, (Canberra: 2014). See also the proposal for a 'red tape trading scheme' involving a stocktake of existing regulatory costs and setting a limit on total costs below this original level. This would mean departments and agencies will need to cut regulation over time. See Oliver Marc Hartwich, *Towards a Red Tape Trading Scheme: Treating Excessive Bureaucracy as Just Another Kind of Pollution*, (Sydney: CIS Issue Analysis No 121, 2010).
74. See for example a requirement for one in two out in The White House, "Presidential Executive Order on Reducing Regulation and Controlling Regulatory Costs", Office of the Press Secretary, (2017).
75. As part of the series of Productivity Commission inquiries into Performance Benchmarking of Australian Business Regulation, see https://www.pc.gov.au/inquiries/completed/regulation-benchmarking
76. The onus of proof is discussed in ibid. Productivity Commission (2005), 134-137.
77. See for example ibid. Productivity Commission (2012), Table 1, 5, showing most jurisdictions fall well behind best practice for regulatory assessment.

CHAPTER FOUR:
SOME (MICRO)ECONOMICS OF RED TAPE AND
REGULATION

1. This chapter relies on material I have previously published in Davidson (2010) and Davidson (2013).

2. Edward Glaeser and Andrei Shleifer, "The Rise of the Regulatory State", *Journal of Economic Literature*, Vol. 41 No. 2, (2003), 401-425.

3. Andrei Shleifer, "Understanding Regulation", *European Financial Management*, Vol. 11 No. 4, (2005), 439-451.

4. Rafael La Porta, Florencio Lopez-de-Silanes and Andrei Shleifer, "What Works in Security Laws?", *The Journal of Finance*, Vol. 61 No. 1, (2006), 1-32.

5. James Barth, Gerard Caprio, Jr. and Ross Levine, *Rethinking Bank Regulation: Till Angels Govern*, (Cambridge: Cambridge University Press, 2006).

6. Edward Glaeser and Andrei Shleifer, "Legal Origins", *The Quarterly Journal of Economics*, Vol. 117 No. 4, (2002), 1193-1229.

7. Jonathan Klick, "Shleifer's Failure", *Texas Law Review*, Vol. 91 No. 4, (2013), 899-909.

8. Simeon Djankov, Edward Glaeser, Rafael La Porta, Florencia Lopez-de-Silanes and Andrei Shleifer, "The New Comparative Economics", *Journal of Comparative Economics*, Vol. 31 No. 4, (2003), 595-619.

9. Sinclair Davidson and Jason Potts, "A New Institutional Approach to Innovation Policy", *Australian Economic Review*, Vol. 49 No. 2, (2016a), 200-207; Sinclair Davidson and Jason Potts, "The Social Costs of Innovation Policy", *Economic Affairs*, Vol. 36 No. 3, (2016b), 282-293.

10. Chris Berg and Sinclair Davidson, "Media Regulation: A Critique

of Finkelstein and Tiffen", SSRN (2015); Chris Berg and Sinclair Davidson, "Section 18C, Human Rights, and Media Reform: An Institutional Analysis of the 2011–13 Australian Free Speech Debate", *Agenda: A Journal of Policy Analysis and Reform*, Vol. 23 No. 1, (2016), 5-30.

11. Bryan Caplan, *The Myth of the Rational Voter: Why Democracies Choose Bad Policies*, (Princeton University Press, 2007).

12. Harold Demsetz, "Information and Efficiency: Another Viewpoint", *Journal of Law and Economics*, Vol. 12 No. 1, (1969), 1-22.

13. Chris Berg, *The Growth of Australia's Regulatory State: Ideology, Accountability and the Mega-regulators*, (Melbourne: Institute of Public Affairs, 2008).

CHAPTER FIVE:
THE POLITICS OF RED TAPE

1. Australian Greens, "Cutting Red Tape is One Thing, Cutting Taxes For Small Business is Another," accessed 19 June 2017, https://greens.org.au/cutting-red-tape-one-thing-cutting-taxes-small-business-another.

2. Senate Economics Committee dissenting report by the Australian Greens, accessed 19 June 2017, http://www.aph.gov.au/Parliamentary_Business/Committees/Senate/Economics/ACNC/Report/d02.

3. Australian Greens Leader Dr Richard Di Natale said "With this latest round of regulations, the Government has tried to add unnecessary time, stress, and difficulty for terminally ill patients to access medicinal cannabis. This is something the Australian Greens will not accept." in Richard Di Natale, "Greens Take Action in the Senate to Make it Easier to Access Medicinal Cannabis," *Australian Greens Media Release*, accessed 19 June 2017, https://greens.org.au/

news/vic/greens-take-action-senate-make-it-easier-access-medic-inal-cannabis.

4. Australian Greens, "Solar Red Tape Scrapped," *Australian Greens Media Release,* accessed 19 June 2017, https://greens.org.au/news/solar-red-tape-scrapped.

5. Australian Greens, *Living Reefs, Dying Coal: After Coal: The Clean Economy*, accessed 19 June 2017, https://greens.org.au/sites/greens.org.au/files/20160428_Living%20Reefs-Dying%20Coal.pdf.

6. Klaus Schwab, *The Global Competitiveness Report 2013–2014* (World Economic Forum, 2014), accessed 1 September 2017, http://www3.weforum.org/docs/WEF_GlobalCompetitiveness-Report_2013-14.pdf.

7. Australian Government, *Annual Red Tape Reduction Report 2015*, accessed 1 September 2017, https://www.cuttingredtape.gov.au/annual-red-tape-reduction-report-2015.

8. Australian Government, "Budget 2017-18 Stronger Growth," accessed 1 September 2017, http://budget.gov.au/2017-18/content/glossies/jobs-growth/html/jobs-growth-00.htm.

9. Chris Berg, *The Growth of Australia's Regulatory State: Ideology, Accountability and the Mega-regulators*, (Melbourne: Institute of Public Affairs, 2008), 81.

10. Richard Gluyas, "Banks Brace for Red Tape as Financial Reforms loom," *The Australian,*13 April 2017, accessed 19 June 2017, http://www.theaustralian.com.au/business/opinion/richard-gluyas-banking/banks-brace-for-red-tape-as-financial-reforms-loom/news-story/d4d5e8fae16caeab32ce1a5fb2a69eab.

11. ibid. Berg (2008).

12. ibid. Berg (2008), 39.

13. ibid. Berg (2008), 39.

14. Tony Blair, "Common Sense Culture, Not a Compensation Culture," Speech to Institute for Public Policy Research, 26 May 2005.

15. Section 391, *Environment Protection and Biodiversity Conservation Act (Cth) 1999.*

16. Robert Boutilier and Ian Thomson, "Modeling and Measuring the Social License to Operate: Fruits of a Dialogue between Theory and Practice" (2011), accessed 1 September 2017, https://socialicense.com/publications/Modelling%20and%20Measuring%20the%20SLO.pdf.

17. Convention of Biological Diversity, "The Nagoya Protocol on Access and Benefit-sharing," accessed on 19 June 2017, https://www.cbd.int/abs/.

18. Daniel Cressey, "Biopiracy Ban Stirs Red-tape Fears", *Nature*, Vol. 514, (2014), accessed 19 June 2017, 14-15. http://www.nature.com/news/biopiracy-ban-stirs-red-tape-fears-1.16028.

19. Climate Action Moreland, *Submission on Tax Deductable Status of Environmental Organisations*, (2017), https://climateactionmoreland.org/2017/08/04/submission-on-tax-deductible-status-of-environmental-organisations/.

20. ibid. Climate Action Moreland (2017).

CHAPTER SIX:
A REGULATORY CULTURE?

1. Michael Koziol, "Nanny State Rules Making Australia 'World's Dumbest Nation': Tyler Brûlé," *Canberra Times*, 27 May 2015, http://www.canberratimes.com.au/nsw/nanny-state-rules-making-australia-worlds-dumbest-nation-tyler-brl-20150526-gh9myx.html.

2. For further discussion of Australia's 'safety ethic,' see Glenn Jessop, "Victoria's Unique Approach to Road Safety: A History of Government Regulation*," *Australian Journal of Politics & History*, Vol. 55 No. 2, (2009), 190-200.

3. Brian Galligan, "Federalism," in *The Oxford Companion to Australian Politics*, eds. Brian Galligan and Winsome Roberts (South Melbourne: Oxford University Press, 2007).

4. Department of Finance, "Australian Government Organisations Register," September 2017, https://www.finance.gov.au/resource-management/governance/agor/; Daniel Wild, "Barriers to Prosperity: Red Tape and the Regulatory State in Australia" (Melbourne: Institute of Public Affairs, 2017).

5. OECD, "Government at a Glance 2017", (Paris, France: Organisation for Economic Co-operation and Development, July 13, 2017), 103, http://www.oecd-ilibrary.org/governance/government-at-a-glance_22214399;jsessionid=7spqq3k2jps-gg.x-oecd-live-02.

6. W. K. Hancock, *Australia*, (London: Ernest Benn, 1930), 72.

7. Michelle Grattan and Paul Austin, "Three Amigos from the Sunshine State," *The Age*, 9 February 2008, http://www.theage.com.au/news/in-depth/three-amigos-from-the-sunshine-state/2008/02/08/1202234164888.html?page=fullpage#contentSwap1.

8. See Paul Pierson, "Increasing Returns, Path Dependence, and the Study of Politics", *The American Political Science Review*, Vol. 94 No. 2, (2000), 251-267.

9. Mikayla Novak, *The $176 Billion Tax on Our Prosperity*, (Melbourne: Institute of Public Affairs, 2016), 178.

10. Dan Sperber, *Explaining Culture: A Naturalistic Approach*, (Wiley, 1996).

11. For further discussion of culture and human evolution, see Steven Pinker, *The Blank Slate: The Modern Denial of Human Nature*, (Penguin, 2003), 70.

12. Ronald Inglehart, "The Renaissance of Political Culture", *The American Political Science Review*, Vol. 82, No. 4, (1988), 1205-1230.

REFERENCES

13. For further discussion of the concept see Lucian W. Pye, "Introduction: Political Culture and Political Development", in *Political Culture and Political Development*, eds. Lucian W. Pye and Sidney Verba, (Princeton, N.J: Princeton University Press, 1965), 8.

14. Sidney Verba, "Comparative Political Culture", in *Political Culture and Political Development*, eds. Lucian W. Pye and Sidney Verba, (Princeton, N.J: Princeton University Press, 1965), 521.

15. Alexander Hamilton, James Madison, and John Jay, *The Federalist Papers*, The Avalon Project (Yale Law School), accessed 13 November 2017, http://avalon.law.yale.edu/subject_menus/fed.asp.

16. The Constitution of the Commonwealth of Australia.

17. Helen Irving, "A Nation Built on Words: The Constitution and National Identity in America and Australia", *Journal of Australian Studies*, Vol. 33 No. 2, (June 2009), 211–225.

18. Donald Horne, *The Lucky Country: Australia in the Sixties*, 2nd ed. (Melbourne: Penguin, 1964), 15.

19. Michael Foley, *American Credo: The Place of Ideas in US Politics*, (Oxford: Oxford University Press, 2007); Richard Ellis, *American Political Cultures*, (New York: Oxford University Press, 1993).

20. There is extensive discussion of Australian and American political differences, see Dennis Altman, *51st State?*, Scribe Short Books, (Carlton North, Vic: Scribe Short Books, 2006), 115; H. C. Allen, *Bush and Backwoods: A Comparison of the Frontier in Australia and the United States*, (East Lansing, Mich.: Michigan State University Press, 1959); Russel Ward, *The Australian Legend*, (Melbourne: Oxford University Press, 1958); Henry Mayer, *Australian Politics: A Reader*, (Melbourne: Cheshire, 1966). Mayer 1966; Ward 1958; Altman 2006, 115; Allen 1959.

21. Altman, *51st State?*, 15; Lyn Spillman, "Imagining Community and Hoping for Recognition: Bicentennial Celebrations in 1976 and 1988", *Qualitative Sociology*, Vol. 17 No. 1, (March 1, 1994), 3-28;

Altman 2006, p.15; Spillman 1994; Irving 2009, 215.

22. Rodney Smith, *Australian Political Culture*, (Frenchs Forest, N.S.W: Longman, 2001).

23. William Coleman, "Theories of Australian Exceptionalism", in *Only in Australia: The History, Politics, and Economics of Australian Exceptionalism*, (Oxford University Press, 2016).

24. Chris Berg, "Adam Smith and Jeremy Bentham in the Australian Colonies," *History of Economics Review*, (2018).

25. James Walter, *What Were They Thinking?: The Politics of Ideas in Australia*, (UNSW Press, 2010), 64.

26. John Gascoigne, *The Enlightenment and the Origins of European Australia*, (Cambridge University Press, 2002), 35.

27. Hugh Collins, "Political Ideology in Australia: The Distinctiveness of a Benthamite Society", *Daedalus*, Vol. 114 No. 1, (1985), 147–169.

28. ibid. Collins (1985), 148.

29. ibid. Collins (1985), 152.

30. ibid. Collins (1985), 150.

31. Jeremy Bentham, *The Collected Works of Jeremy Bentham*, (Charlottesville, Va: InteLex Corporation, 2000).

32. For introductions to utilitarianism see John Stuart Mill, *Utilitarianism* (Longmans, Green, 1870); Julia Driver, "The History of Utilitarianism", in *The Stanford Encyclopedia of Philosophy*, ed. Edward N. Zalta, Winter 2014 (Metaphysics Research Lab, Stanford University, 2014); William Sweet, "Bentham, Jeremy", in *Internet Encyclopedia of Philosophy* (Martin, Tennesse: The University of Tennesse), accessed November 13, 2017, http://www.iep.utm.edu/bentham/.

33. L.J. Hume, *Bentham and Bureaucracy*, (Cambridge University Press, 2004), 100.

34. This is quoted in W. H. Greenleaf, *Rise Collectivism*, (Taylor & Francis, 2003), 963.

35. ibid. Collins (1985), 157.
36. ibid. Hancock (1930), 73.
37. ibid. Hancock (1930), 73.
38. For further discussion of political culture and Australia's lack of bill of rights see Paul Kildea, "The Bill of Rights Debate in Australian Political Culture", *Australian Journal of Human Rights*, Vol. 9 No. 1 (2003), 65-117.
39. ibid. Walter, 55; ibid. Gascoigne, 35.
40. For further discussion of chartism see Malcolm Chase, *Chartism: A New History*, (Manchester: Manchester University Press, 2007).
41. David G. M. Llewellyn, "Australia Felix: Jeremy Bentham and Australian Colonial Democracy" (University of Melbourne, 2016), 57, http://minerva-access.unimelb.edu.au/handle/11343/108748; John Charlton, *The Chartists: The First National Workers' Movement*, (Pluto Press, 1997), 12.
42. Llewellyn, "Australia Felix"; Paul A. Pickering, "A Wider Field in a New Country: Chartism in Colonial Australia", in *Elections: Full, Free & Fair*, ed. Marian Sawer (Federation Press, 2001); Roy MacLeod and John Eddy, eds., "The Technique of Government: Governing Mid-Victorian Australia," in *Government and Expertise: Specialists, Administrators and Professionals, 1860-1919* (Cambridge University Press, 2003); Andrew Messner, "Contesting Chartism from Afar: Edward Hawksley and the People's Advocate", *Journal of Australian Colonial History*, Vol. 1 No. 1, (1999), 62.
43. William Bramwell Withers, *The History of Ballarat*, (Carlton, Vic: Queensberry Hill Press, 1980), 83.
44. Ian McAllister, "Political Culture and National Identity", in *New Developments in Australian Politics*, ed. Brian Galligan, Ian McAllister, and John Ravenhill (South Melbourne: Macmillan Education Australia Pty Ltd, 1997), 8.
45. ibid. Hancock (1930), 71.

46. ibid. Llewellyn, "Australia Felix".

47. ibid. Gascoigne (2002), 35.

48. A. Atkinson, "Jeremy Bentham and the Rum Rebellion", *Journal of the Royal Australian Historical Society,* Vol. 64, (1978), 1-13.

49. Gregory Melleuish, "Christianity and Australian Political Thought", *St Mark's Review,* No. 181, (2000), 24-32.

50. ibid. Melleuish.

51. Gascoigne (2002), 71; Walter, 58.

52. ISSP Research Group, "International Social Survey Programme: Role of Government IV—ISSP 2006", *GESIS Data Archive,* 2008, 2006, http://dx.doi.org/10.4232/1.4700.

53. Halévy Elie, *The Growth of Philosophic Radicalism,* (London: Faber & Faber, 1934).

54. ibid. Sweet (2017).

55. Friedrich A. Hayek, "The Use of Knowledge in Society", *The American Economic Review,* Vol. 35 No. 4, (1945), 519-530.

56. ibid. Hayek (1945).

57. Herbert A. Simon, "Rational Decision Making in Business Organizations", *The American Economic Review,* Vol. 69 No. 4, (1979), 493-513.

58. See, for example, William A. Niskanen, "The Peculiar Economics of Bureaucracy", *The American Economic Review,* Vol. 58 No. 2, (1968), 293-305.

59. ibid. Greenleaf (2003).

60. Werner Stark, *Jeremy Bentham's Economic Writings,* (Routledge, 2004), 202, 234, 252.

61. Alasdair MacIntyre, "Utilitarianism and Cost-Benefit Analysis: An Essay on the Relevance of Moral Philosophy to Bureaucratic Theory", in *The Moral Dimensions of Public Policy Choice,* ed. John Martin Gillroy and Maurice L. Wade, (University of Pittsburgh Press, 1992).

62. The consistent failure of major project cost-benefit analysis is a case in point, see Bent Flyvbjerg, "Over Budget, Over Time, Over and Over Again: Managing Major Projects", *SSRN Scholarly Paper* (Rochester, NY: Social Science Research Network, April 1, 2011), https://papers.ssrn.com/abstract=2278226.
63. Quoted in Bhikhu C. Parekh, *Jeremy Bentham: Critical Assessments*, (Taylor & Francis, 1993), 918.
64. ibid. Llewellyn (1997), 221-222.
65. Albert Venn Dicey, *Lectures on the Relation Between Law and Public Opinion in England During the Nineteenth Century*, (Online Library of Liberty, 1917), 218.
66. ibid. Llewellyn (1997).
67. As Adam Smith wrote in The Wealth of Nations that 'Little else is requisite to carry a state to the highest degree of opulence from the lowest barbarism, but peace, easy taxes, and a tolerable administration of justice,' see Adam Smith, *An Inquiry into the Nature and Causes of the Wealth of Nations*, (London, United Kingdom: W. Strahan and T. Cadell, London, 1776).
68. George J. Stigler, "The Theory of Economic Regulation", *The Bell Journal of Economics and Management Science*, Vol. 2 No. 1, (1971), 3-21.
69. J. J. Pincus, "Pressure Groups and the Pattern of Tariffs", *Journal of Political Economy*, Vol. 83 No. 4, (1975), 757-778.
70. Mary P. Mack, *Jeremy Bentham; An Odyssey of Ideas*, First Edition (Columbia University Press, 1963).
71. ibid. Greenleaf (2003), 532.
72. Paul Kelly, *The End of Certainty: The Story of the 1980s*, (St. Leonards, N.S.W: Allen & Unwin, 1992).
73. ibid. Melleuish, 27.
74. ibid. Collins; ibid. Melleuish, 27; Colin Hughes, "Political Culture", in *Australian Politics: A Third Reader, ed. Henry Mayer and Helen*

Nelson, (Melbourne: Cheshire, 1973), 140.

75. Giandomenico Majone, "The Rise of the Regulatory State in Europe", *West European Politics*, Vol. 17 No. 3, (1994), 77-101.

76. Chris Berg, *The Growth Of Australia's Regulatory State: Ideology, Accountability and the Mega-Regulators*, (Melbourne, VIC: Institute of Public Affairs, 2008).

77. ibid. Berg (2008).

78. John Maynard Keynes, *The General Theory of Employment, Interest and Money*, (London: Palgrave Macmillan, 1936), 383-84.

79. ibid. Greenleaf (2003), 248.

80. John Stuart Mill, *On Liberty*, (Project Gutenberg, 2011).

81. Mikayla Novak, "Road Safety Remuneration Tribunal Costs More than it Saves", On Line Opinion (blog), 18 April 2016, https://westerncivilisation.ipa.org.au/sectors/work-reform-and-productivity-unit/news/3452/road-safety-remuneration-tribunal-costs-more-than-it-saves/pg/87.

82. SkyNews Australia, "Turnbull Government Scraps Road Tribunal," 19 April 2016, http://www.skynews.com.au/news/top-stories/2016/04/19/turnbull-government-scraps-road-tribunal.html.

CHAPTER SEVEN:
1901: FEDERATION AS BUREAUCRATISATION

1. In its wake of the 1890s crisis there did germinate a feeling that legislation over banking might be usefully continental. But such a feeling cannot be felt very strongly, because, beyond a Commonwealth Bank, the Commonwealth produced no banking legislation for 40 years.

2. See K.T. Livingston, "Anticipating Federation: The Federalising in Telecommunications in Australia", *Australian Historical Studies*, Vol. 26 No. 102, (1994), 111.

3. Doug Buckley, *Cutting Green Hay: Friendships, Movements and Cultural Conflicts in Australia's Great Decades*, (Melbourne: Penguin, 1983), 126.

4. Stanley J. Stein and Barbara H. Stein, *The Colonial Heritage of Latin America: Essays on Economic Dependence in Perspective*, (New York: Oxford University Press, 1970), 68.

5. Douglas Pike, *Paradise of Dissent: South Australia 1829-1857*, (Melbourne: Melbourne University Press, 1967), 35.

6. Patrick Morgan, *The Vandemonian Trail: Convicts and Bushrangers in Early Victoria*, (Redland Bay: Connor Court, 2016), 13.

7. See John M. Ward, "'The Germ of Federation' in Australia", *Australian Historical Studies*, Vol. 4 No. 15, (1950), 214-223.

8. The recommendation that the states reconstitute simply as administrative agencies of the Commonwealth is found explicitly in Garran's autobiography, and has been welcomed even from a former Premier. See John Bannon, "Overcoming The Unintended Consequences of Federation", *Australian Journal of Public Administration*, Vol. 46 No. 1, (1987), 1-9.

9. A.J. Brown, "The Constitution We Were Meant To Have", *Papers on Parliament*, No. 44, (Canberra: Parliament of Australia, 2006).

10. J.D.Lang, http://nla.gov.au/nla.obj-88843869/view?partId=nla.obj-88843915#page/n0/mode/1up, (1850), accessed 4 September 2017.

11. A.C.V. Melbourne, *Early Constitutional Development in Australia*, (Melbourne: University of Queensland Press, 1963), 349.

12. Deakin is an exception, but only partly. Not quite all political careers end in defeat, but Deakin's certainly did, in two electoral routs that reduced his 25 parliamentary adherents of 1903 to 4 by 1910. Forrest may also be cited as Federationist with a successful post-Federation career, even if he lost his attempt to succeed Deakin as Prime Minister. But 'Forrest was, above all, an administrator and master of

files. ... Forrest's occupancy of the ministerial offices of PMG, Defence, Home Affairs and Treasurer were perhaps more a measure of his skill as an administrator than of his standing as a politician'. See Martyn Webb, "John Forrest: Architect and Founder of Modern Western Australia", *Early Days: Journal of the Royal Western Australian Historical Society*, Vol. 12 No. 3, (2003), 250-272.

13. Attorney-General's Department, "GARRAN, Robert Randolph", http://legalopinions.ags.gov.au/opinionauthor/garran-robert-randolph?page=5, sighted 4 September 2017.

14. Robert Randolph Garran, *Prosper the Commonwealth*, (Sydney: Angus and Robertson, 1958), 109.

15. In this account of the Federation movement, Robert Garran clearly grants Thomson's priority in mooting federation. Thomson was a friend of his father, Andrew. Could Thomson's priority be part of Garran family lore?

16. The *Naturalization Act of 1903* recognized all the previous naturalisations of the six States, but ordained henceforth 'aboriginal natives of Asia, Africa or Islands of the Pacific [save New Zealand]' would be ineligible for naturalization.

17. So that the State with the most lenient requirement would not become the de facto standard of all, there would clearly need to be a clause that voided mutual recognition in cases where naturalisation in one state was undertaken for the purpose of residing in another with the rights of a naturalised subject.

18. Livingston, op.cit.

19. See Postal and Telegraph Conference, 1893, Report of the Conference Held in Brisbane (Brisbane: James C. Beal, 1893) and the Report of the Proceedings and Debates of the Postal and Telegraph Conference held in New Zealand (1894). See also the account of Graeme Davison in *The Unforgiving Minute* (Melbourne: Oxford University Press, 1993), 72-73.

20. Don Dignan, "McIlwraith, Sir Thomas (1835-1900)", *Australian Dictionary of Biography*, Vol. 5, (Melbourne: Melbourne University Press, 1974).

21. John Nethercote, "Australia's 'Talent for Bureaucracy' and the Atrophy of Federalism", *Only in Australia. The History, Politics and Economics of Australian Exceptionalism*, ed. Coleman, W., (Oxford: Oxford University Press, 2016)

22. The disquieted permanent secretary was Atlee Hunt. 'Like Garran, Hunt was a barrister from New South Wales, and a disciple of Barton, who had worked strenuously in Federation campaigns'. J.A. La Nauze, *Alfred Deakin: A Biography*, Vol 1. (Melbourne: Melbourne University Press, 1965), 271.

23. Jeremy C. Martens, "Pioneering the Dictation Test? The Creation and Administration of Western Australia's Immigration Restriction Act 1897-1901", *Studies in Western Australian History*, Vol. 28, (2013), 47-67.

24. *Plus ca change* ... Consider the Oppel case of 2017, in which Linda Oppel was refused a Remaining Relative Visa—intended for those 'whose only near relatives are living in Australia'—despite her having a sister living in Australia, and no near relatives in her country of citizenship. The Migration Review Tribunal rejected her application on the grounds that as a child she had been adopted by a half-sister, following the murder of her parents. In the brutal legalism of bureaucracy, this rendered Oppel no longer the sister of her sister, and in a one line letter ordered her to leave Australia within weeks. (The order was overturned by the Minister for Immigration).

25. One illustration of bureaucratisation by pseudo-federalism was the asphyxiating organisation of Australian soccer into national, state and 'district' levels, in undeniable imitation of her falsely conceived federation. This was only overthrown in the late 1950s, by the emer-

gence of grass roots soccer clubs; from then dates the revival of Australian soccer. Trevor Thompson, *One Fantastic Goal: A Complete History of Football in Australia*, (Sydney: ABC books, 2006).

26. See Francis Mines, *Premiers' Conferences and Other Intercolonial Conferences in Australasia before Federation*, (Canberra: Arrow, 1976).

27. It is no surprise that one of the very earliest of these 'intercolonials' was the Conference of Statisticians of 1861, concerned to obtain an 'indispenable' 'uniformity in collection and compilation of statistics'.

CHAPTER EIGHT:
RED TAPE: TETHERING AUSTRALIA
TO THE WORLD

1. Cyril Pearl and WEP, *The Best of Lennie Lower*, (Melbourne: Landsdowne Press, 1963), 112.

2. For 'cultural patterning' see Marshall G. S. Hodgson, *Rethinking World History: Essays on Europe, Islam and World History*, Ed. Edmund Burke III, (Cambridge: Cambridge University Press), 1993, chapter 8.

3. Michael Cook, *A Short History of the Human Race*, (New York: Norton), 2005, 63-8.

4. Procopius, *The Anecdota or Secret History*, Trans. H. B. Dewing, (Cambridge: Harvard University Press, 1935), XII.

5. Harold J. Berman, *Law and Revolution: The Formation of the Western Legal Tradition*, (Cambridge: Harvard University Press, 1983), Part 1.

6. Molly Greene, *A Shared World: Christians and Muslims in the Early Modern Mediterranean*, (Princeton: Princeton University Press, 2000).

7. Anthony Grafton, "Commentary", in Anthony Grafton et al, *The Classical Tradition*, (Cambridge: Harvard University Press, 2010), 225-233.

REFERENCES

8. Michael Mann, *The Sources of Social Power, Volume I, A History of Power From the Beginning to A.D. 1760*, (Cambridge: Cambridge University Press, 1986), 524-527.

9. F. W. Mote, *Imperial China: 900-1800*, (Cambridge: Harvard University Press, 1999), 746.

10. Hilary Golder, *Politics, Patronage and Public Works: The Administration of New South Wales Volume 1 1842-1900*, (Sydney: UNSW Press, 2005), 142-148.

11. Golder, 155-7.

12. William Coleman, Selwyn Cornish, and Alf Hagger, *Giblin's Platoon: The Trials and Triumph of the Economist in Australian Public Life*, (Canberra: ANU E Press, 2006), 160-164.

13. Charles E. W. Bean, *On the Wool Track: Pioneering Days of the Wool Industry*, (Sydney: Angus and Robertson, 1985), 63, 74, 79.

14. Henry Lawson, *The Roaring Days*, visited 20 July 2017, https://www.poetrylibrary.edu.au/poets/lawson-henry/the-roaring-days-0002004.

15. Norman Stone, *Europe Transformed 1878–1919*, (Glasgow: Collins, 1983), 129-139.

16. See for example, George H. Knibbs, "Miscellaneous Notes on Australia, Its People and Their Activities", in George H. Knibbs (ed.) *Federal Handbook Prepared in connection with the Eighty-Fourth Meeting of the British Association for the Advancement of Science held in Australia August, 1914*, (Melbourne: Government Printer, 1914), 581-598.

17. Banjo Paterson, *Clancy of the Overflow*, http://www.wallisandmatilda.com.au/clancy-of-the-overflow.shtml Visited 20 July, 2017.

18. Stephen Kern, *The Culture of Time and Space, 1880-1918*, (Cambridge Mass, Harvard University Press, 2005), Chapter 1.

19. Arthur Mitzman, *The Iron Cage: An Historical Interpretation of Max Weber*, (New York: Alfred A Knopf, 1970), 148-163.

20. Henry B. Higgins, *A New Province for Law and Order*, (Melbourne: Anderson Gowan, 1921).

21. William M. Hughes, *The Case for Labor*, (Sydney: Sydney University Press, 1967), 61.

22. Sir Robert Menzies, *Central Power in the Australian Commonwealth*, (London: Cassell, 1967), 68.

CHAPTER NINE:
ENVIRONMENTAL REGULATION
AND RED TAPE

1. Morgan Begg, *The Growth of Federal Environmental Law 1971 to 2016*, (Institute of Public Affairs: April 2017), accessed 21 September 2017, https://www.ipa.org.au/wp-content/uploads/2017/05/IPA_Report_Growth_Of_Federal_Environmental_Law_170430.pdf.

2. Productivity Commission, *Major Project Development Assessment Processes*, (Productivity Commission: December 2013), accessed 23 October 2017, https://www.pc.gov.au/inquiries/completed/major-projects.

3. Australian Government, *Environment Protection and Biodiversity Conservation Act 1999*, (Australian Government: 1 July 2016), accessed 23 October 2017, https://www.legislation.gov.au/Details/C2016C00777.

4. Daniel Wild, *Section 487: How Activists use Red Tape to Stop Development and Jobs*, (Melbourne: Institute of Public Affairs: October 2016), accessed 22 September 2017, https://ipa.org.au/wp-content/uploads/2016/11/26Oct16-DW-Section487-How_activists_use_red_tape.pdf

5. Greenpeace Australia Pacific, *Stopping the Australian Coal Export Boom: Funding Proposal for the Australian Anti-Coal Movement* (November 2011), accessed 22 September 2017, http://www.abc.net.au/mediawatch/transcripts/1206_greenpeace.pdf.

References

6. ibid. Wild (2017).
7. The Hon. Tony Burke, *Environment Protection and Biodiversity Conservation Amendment Bill 2013: Second Reading*, (Parliament of Australia: 2013), accessed 22 September 2017.
8. Babs McHugh and Tom Nightingale, "Water Trigger has no 'environmental dividend'", *The ABC*, 27 September 2013, accessed 11 October 2017, http://www.abc.net.au/news/rural/2013-09-27/water-trigger-for-coal-csg/4985026.
9. The Australian Petroleum Production and Exploration Association, "'Water Trigger'—A Political Fix For a Non-existent Problem," https://www.appea.com.au/media_release/water-trigger-a-political-fix-for-a-non-existent-problem/.
10. Babs McHugh, "Labor and Greens Battle Over Proposals to Extend Water Trigger Legislation to Include Shale and Other Gas Operations", *The ABC*, 27 May 2016, accessed 23 October 2017, http://www.abc.net.au/news/rural/2016-05-27/alp-water-trigger-promise-a-rerun-of-greens-policy/7445142.
11. Commonwealth Government, *Independent Review of the Environment Protection and Biodiversity Conservation Act 1999: Interim Report*, (Commonwealth Government: 2009), accessed 23 October 2017, http://www.environment.gov.au/resource/independent-review-environment-protection-and-biodiversity-conservation-act-1999-interim.
12. Productivity Commission, *Impacts of Native Vegetation and Biodiversity Regulations*, (Productivity Commission: August 2004), accessed 25 September 2017, https://www.pc.gov.au/inquiries/completed/native-vegetation.
13. Australian Parliament, *The Constitution of Australia*, (Commonwealth Government: 2010), accessed 25 September 2017, http://www.aph.gov.au/About_Parliament/Senate/Powers_practice_n_procedures/Constitution.

14. Australian Network of Environmental Defenders Office, *Submission to the Senate Committee on Native Vegetation Laws, Greenhouse Gas Abatement and Climate Change Matters*, (Commonwealth Government: April 2010), http://www.edonsw.org.au/anedo_submission_on_native_vegetation_laws_greenhouse_gas_abatement_and_climate_change_measures.

15. Commonwealth Government, *Environment Protection and Biodiversity Conservation Bill 1998: Explanatory Memorandum*, (Commonwealth Government: 1998), accessed 23 October 2017, https://www.legislation.gov.au/Details/C2004B00223/Explanatory%20Memorandum/Text.

16. Commonwealth Treasury, *Public Good Conservation and the Impact of Environmental Measures Imposed on Landholders*, (Commonwealth Government: 2001), accessed 23 October 2017, https://archive.treasury.gov.au/documents/110/PDF/round5.pdf.

17. Alison Burrell, *Evaluating Policies for Delivering Agri-environmental Public Goods*, (OECD: 2011), accessed 23 October 2017, https://www.oecd.org/tad/sustainable-agriculture/48281102.pdf.

18. Friedrich Hayek, "The Use of Knowledge in Society", *The American Economic Review*, Vol. xxxv No. 4, (1945), 519-530.

19. ibid.

20. See, for example, James M. Buchanan and Gordon Tullock, *The Calculus of Consent*, (Michigan: The University of Michigan, 1960).

21. Daniel Wild, *Five Reasons to Abolish the Renewable Energy Target*, (Melbourne: Institute of Public Affairs: 2017), accessed 1 November 2017, https://ipa.org.au/publications-ipa/research-papers/5-reasons-abolish-ret.

22. Deloitte, *Assessing the Impact of the Renewable Energy Target*, (2014), accessed 1 November 2017, http://www.bca.com.au/publications/assessing-the-impact-of-the-renewable-energy-target.

23. ACIL Allen, *RET Review Modelling: Market Modelling of Various*

RET Policy Options, (2014), accessed 1 November 2017, http://www.acilallen.com.au/projects/3/energy/135/ret-review-modelling-market-modelling-of-various-ret-policy-options. Analysis assumes all of the costs of the renewable energy certificates are passed on as higher energy prices.

CHAPTER TEN:
HOUSING AFFORDABILITY
AND RED TAPE

1. Nicole Gurran and Peter Phibbs, "'Boulevard of Broken Dreams': Planning, Housing Supply and Affordability in Urban Australia", *Built Environment*, Vol. 42 No. 1, (2016), 55-71.

2. Senate Standing Committee on Economics Inquiry into Affordale Housing, accessed 9 August 2017, http://www.aph.gov.au/Parliamentary_Business/Committees/Senate/Economics/Affordable_housing_2013/Submissions.

3. Robert Menzies, "The Forgotten People", speech 22 May 1942, accessed 13 December 2017, https://menziesvirtualmuseum.org.au/transcripts/the-forgotten-people/59-chapter-1-the-forgotten-people.

4. Abraham H. Maslow, "A Theory of Human Motivation", *Psychological Review*, Vol. 50 No. 4, (1943), 370-396.

5. Morris A. Davis and Stijn Van Nieuwerburgh, "Housing, Finance and the Macroeconomy", *NBER Working Paper No. 20287*, (2014).

6. Ashton de Silva, Sarah Sinclair and Sveta Angelopoulos. "Retirees, Creatives and Housing Market Complexity: Challenges for Policy-Makers", *Australian Economic Review*, Vol. 49 No. 3, (2016), 340-351.

7. ABS, Housing Occupancy and Costs, Catalogue 4130.0, Table 1, accessed 22 November 2017.

8. A selected history of mortgage product development is found in:

Ashton de Silva, Jonathan Boymal, Stuart Thomas and Jason Potts. "The Residential Mortgage (De) Regulation—Innovation Nexus." *Munich Personal RePEc Archive Paper No. 62549*, (2015).

9. Productivity Commission, First Home Ownership, Productivity Commission Inquiry Report Number 28 (March 2004).

10. At the margin governments may be able to reduce immigration flows—however immigration, particularly skilled immigration, is likely to lead to a more prosperous society.

11. ibid. Productivity Commission (2004), Figure 1.1, 39.

12. Gavin Wood, Richard Watson and Paul Flatau, "Microsimulation Modelling of Tenure Choice and Grants to Promote Home Ownership", *Australian Economic Review*, Vol. 39 No. 1, (2006), 14-34.

13. Judith Yates, "Policy Forum: Housing Affordability: What are the Policy Issues? Australia's Housing Affordability Crisis", *The Australian Economic Review*, Vol. 41 No. 2, (2008), 200-214.

14. HSAR (2012). Housing Supply and Affordability Reform. Retrieved from http://webarchive.nationalarchives.gov.uk/20120919132719/www.communities.gov.uk/documents/507390/pdf/1436960.pdf.

15. Australian Building Codes Board, "About", accessed 3 October 2017, https://www.abcb.gov.au/NCC/About.

16. John Stuart Mill, On Liberty, Library of Economics and Liberty, accessed 12 December 2017, (1869), http://www.econlib.org/library/Mill/mlLbty1.html.

17. Property Council, Development Assessment Report Card, (2015), https://www.propertycouncil.com.au/downloads/submissions/DAreportcard2015.pdf.

18. HSAR (2012). Housing Supply and Affordability Reform, http://webarchive.nationalarchives.gov.uk/20120919132719/www.communities.gov.uk/documents/507390/pdf/1436960.pdf

19. Rachel Ong, Gavin Wood, Stephen Whelan, Melek Cigdem, Kadir Atalay and Jago Dodson, Inquiry into Housing Policies, Labour

Force Participation and Economic Growth, *AHURI Final Report 285*, (Melbourne: Australian Housing and Urban Research Institute, 2017), http://www.ahuri.edu.au/research/final-reports/285, doi:10.18408/ahuri-8107001

20. The views expressed in this discussion are strictly the view of this author only. The author acknowledges and appreciates the permission received from co-investigators to use the transcripts for this discussion. See: Jago Dodson, Ashton de Silva, Tony Dalton and Sarah Sinclair, Housing, Multi-level Governance and Economic Productivity, *AHURI Final Report 284*, (Melbourne: Australian Housing and Urban Research Institute Limited, 2017).

21. ibid. Dodson et al. (2017), 66.

22. James H. Boren, *When in Doubt, Mumble: A Bureaucrat's Handbook*, (1972).

23. ibid. de Silva et al (2016).

24. ibid. Dodson et al (2017).

CHAPTER ELEVEN: OVER-CRIMINALISATION AS RED TAPE

1. Consider Blackstone's Commentaries on the Laws of England, originally published in 1765, in which he defends the idea of crime as part of the natural law: "The case is the same as to crimes and misdemeanours, that are forbidden by the superior laws, and therefore styled mala in se, such as murder, theft, and perjury; which contract no additional turpitude from being declared unlawful by the inferior legislature." (p. 54). Blackstone goes on to distinguish the criminal law from the civil law by declaring it to govern "public wrongs, which being a breach of general and public rights, affect the whole community, and are called crimes and misdemeanours" (p. 93). Sir William Blackstone

[1893], *Commentaries on the Laws of England in Four Books*. Notes selected from the editions of Archibold, Christian, Coleridge, Chitty, Stewart, Kerr, and others, Barron Field's Analysis, and Additional Notes, and a *Life of the Author* by George Sharswood. In Two Volumes. Philadelphia: JB Lippincott Co. available online at http://files.libertyfund.org/files/2140/Blackstone_1387-01_EBk_ v6.0.pdf, accessed 6 November 2017.

2. See for example, David Brown, "Criminalisation and normative theory" in *Current Issues in Criminal Justice*, Vol. 25 No. 2, (2013), 605-626. For a broader discussion of the theoretical basis of the criminal law, see Antony Duff, "Theories of Criminal Law", in *The Stanford Encyclopedia of Philosophy* (Summer 2013 Edition), Edward N. Zalta (ed.) https://plato.stanford.edu/archives/sum2013/entries/criminal-law, accessed 6 November 2017.

3. In the words of David Friedman, "If muggers are rational [in this sense], we do not have to make mugging impossible in order to prevent it, merely unprofitable". David Friedman, "Rational Criminals and Profit-Maximising Police" (davidfriedman.com, accessed 31 October 2017, 1995).

4. Gary S. Becker, "Crime and Punishment: An Economic Approach", in Gary S. Becker and William M. Landes (eds.) *Essays in the Economics of Crime and Punishment*, (Columbia University Press, 1974), 2.

5. ibid. Friedman.

6. There is a distinction between 'strict liability' and 'absolute liability'. The former permits an accused the defence of reasonable mistake, meaning that he acted in the reasonable belief about facts that, if true, would have made his actions innocent, whereas the latter does not. In this chapter, for brevity I will refer only to strict liability but it should be noted that some parts of some criminal offences are absolute liability, which amplifies the points that I make.

REFERENCES

7. In the United States, criminal justice reformers have made the restoration of mens rea to criminal statutes a key goal. They argue, as Blackstone above, that the singular aspect of the criminal law is its role in punishing moral wrongs, and this can only be done justly where the culpability of the accused is established. See, for example, John Malcolm and Michael B. Mukasey, "The Importance of Meaningful Mens Rea Reform", 2016, http://www.heritage.org/crime-and-justice/commentary/the-importance-meaningful-mens-rea-reform (accessed 6 November 2017) and Ilya Shapiro, "You Shouldn't Have to be Criminally Liable if You Don't Have a Guilty Mind", Cato at Liberty, 14 February 2017, https://www.cato.org/blog/you-shouldnt-be-criminally-liable-you-dont-have-guilty-mind (accessed 6 November 2017).

8. Corporations Act 2001 (Cth) section 588G, accessed 6 November 2017, http://www8.austlii.edu.au/cgi-bin/viewdoc/au/legis/cth/consol_act/ca2001172/s588g.html.

9. Claire Finkelstein, "The Inefficiency of Mens Rea", in *California Law Review*, Vol. 88 No. 3, (2000), 895-920. Note though that Finkelstein's argument is that concerns about the efficiency of strict liability are part of the reason that the utilitarian turn in the criminal law has been resisted, with many arguing that the moral importance of demonstrating culpability trumps the desirability of efficiency.

10. George J. Stigler, "The Optimum Enforcement of Laws", in Becker and Landes, ibid., (1974), 62.

11. Australian Law Reform Commission, *Traditional Rights and Freedoms—Encroachments by Commonwealth Laws Final Report*, (Canberra: Australian Government, 2015), 295.

12. Economic References Committee (2017), "Lifting the fear and suppressing the greed", Penalties for White Collar Crime and Corporate and Financial Misconduct in Australia, (Canberra: The Senate, 2017), 52.

13. Corporations Act 2001 (Cth) section 588G(3); Environment Protection and Biodiversity Conservation Act 1999 (Cth) section 17B(1).

14. See, for example, Alex Tabarrok, "What was Gary Becker's Biggest Mistake?", *Marginal Revolution*, 16 September 2015, accessed 6 November 2017, http://marginalrevolution.com/marginalrevolution/2015/09/what-was-gary-beckers-biggest-mistake.html.

15. ibid. Economic Reference Committee, 48.

16. It is also worth noting that if regulators ever did start frequently using the regulatory criminal law to its fullest extent, they would be contributing to Australia's growing incarceration costs. Between 2007 and 2016, the Australian prison population grew by 43 percent. Expenditure on prisons across the country now exceeds $3.8 billion. The most serious offence of up to 46 percent of Australian prisoners was a nonviolent offence, indicating that Australia already has an inefficient punishment mix. See: Australian Bureau of Statistics (2016), *Prisoners in Australia 2007 and 2016*; Productivity Commission (2017), *Report on Government Services 2017*; Andrew Bushnell and Daniel Wild, *The Use of Prisons in Australia: Reform Directions*, (Melbourne: Institute of Public Affairs, 2016), 16.

17. Jonathan Shapiro (2016), "Will Criminal Penalties for Benchmark Riggers Dry Up Markets?", *The Australian Financial Review*, 4 October 2016.

18. Emily Glazer, "The Most Thankless Job on Wall Street Gets a New Worry", *The Wall Street Journal*, 11 February 2016.

19. Deloitte (2014), *Get Out of Your Own Way: Unleash Productivity*, accessed 6 November 2017, 5, https://www2.deloitte.com/au/en/pages/building-lucky-country/articles/get-out-of-your-own-way.html. Note that this number refers to both public and private compliance; even though a lot of companies' internal regulation is in response to legal liability, not all of it is.

20. ibid. Khanna, 1500.
21. See for example, Jonathan Clough, "Improving the Effectiveness of Corporate Criminal Liability", in Rony Levy et al. (eds.), *New Directions for Law in Australia*, (Canberra: ANU Press, 2017), 163-172, 168.
22. ibid. Khanna, 1484-1485.
23. John T. Byam, "The Economic Inefficiency of Corporate criminal liability", *The Journal of Criminal Law and Criminology*, Vol. 73 No. 2, (1982), 582-598, 587.
24. ACCC, "NYK Convicted of Criminal Cartel Conduct and Fined $25 Million", *Release Number MR 126/17* (2017).
25. ibid. Byam, 600.
26. ABC News, "Arthur Andersen Goes Out of Business", 31 August 2002, (accessed 6 November 2017), http://abcnews.go.com/Business/Decade/arthur-andersen-business/story?id=9279255.
27. Criminal sentencing is guided by the principle of proportionality, as captured in the maxim, 'Let the punishment fit the crime'. In the economic analysis, proportionality and efficiency are linked, with a proper proportion being that which secures maximum deterrent value at the lowest cost to the economy.
28. ibid. Khanna, 1503-1504.
29. Steven Mufson, "BP Settles Criminal Charges for $4 Billion in Spill: Supervisors Indicted on Manslaughter", *The Washington Post*, 15 November 2012, accessed 6 November 2017, https://www.washingtonpost.com/business/economy/bp-to-pay-billions-in-gulf-oil-spill-settlement/2012/11/15/ba0b783a-2f2e-11e2-9f50-0308e1e75445_story.html?utm_term=.0f494e709467.
30. "BP plc Common Stock Historical Stock Prices", Nasdaq, accessed 3 November 2017, available at http://www.nasdaq.com/symbol/bp/historical.
31. While BP's overall market capitalisation has not recovered,

that is not a consequence of the criminal proceedings, but of the disaster. The total cost to BP of the disaster was estimated in 2016 to be almost US$61.6 billion. BP paid US$14 billion in civil penalties compared to $4 billion in criminal penalties. Steven Mufson, "BP's Bill for the World's Largest Oil Spill Now Reaches $81 Billion", *The Sydney Morning Herald*, 15 July 2016.

32. For example, under the Corporations Act 2001 (Cth), it is a crime punishable by up to two years' imprisonment to provide financial advice without a licence. Being branded a criminal in such a circumstance may well cost a person more than money. Corporations Act 2001 (Cth). ASIC (2013), *Regulatory Guide 36—Licensing: Financial product advice and dealing*, accessed 6 November 2017, 27, http://download.asic.gov.au/media/1238108/rg36-published-20-august-2013.pdf.
33. ibid. Becker (1974), 31. Becker suggests that this might be one way to distinguish the criminal law from the civil law on utilitarian grounds. See also Friedman (1995), as above, for his explanation of Becker's point.
34. Attorney-General's Department, *A Guide to Framing Commonwealth Offences, Civil Penalties and Enforcement Powers*.
35. The 2007 Treasury Review of Sanctions in Corporate Law, for example, endorsed a model of 'responsive regulation': '[A]lthough the regulator should have access to severe punishments, they should rarely need to use them in practice if they ensure that it is economically rational for the regulated to cooperate. Where breaches occur, the initial response should be to persuade and educate the transgressor on appropriate behaviour—this promotes self-regulation and the wish to preserve reputation.' Similarly, the Department of the Environment's policy guidance on the enforcement of the EPBC Act states: 'In the first instance, we support responsible self-regulation by encouraging the community to act in accordance with the EPBC Act.'

The Treasury, *Review of Sanctions in Corporate Law*, (2007), accessed 6 November 2017, 6, https://archive.treasury.gov.au/documents/1182/PDF/Review_of_Sanctions.pdf. Department of the Environment (2013), Compliance and Enforcement Policy: Environment Protection and Biodiversity Conservation Act 1999, accessed 6 November 2017, 6, https://www.environment.gov.au/.../epbc-act-compliance-enforcement-policy_1.pdf.

36. Matthew Goode, "Corporate Criminal Liability", in *Environmental Crime: Proceedings of a Conference Held 1-3 September 1993, Hobart*, (1995), accessed 6 November 2017, 8, http://www.aic.gov.au/media_library/publications/proceedings/26/goode.pdf.

CHAPTER TWELVE:
OVER-REGULATION IN PUBLIC SERVICES

1. Ben Bommert, "Collaborative Innovation in the Public Sector", *International Public Management Review*, Vol. 11 No. 1, (2010), 15-33.
2. Ludwig von Mises, *Bureaucracy*, (New Haven: Yale University Press, 1944), 1.
3. Productivity Commission, *Report on Government Services—Chapter 1 Approach to Performance Measurement*, accessed 11 September 2017, http://www.pc.gov.au/research/ongoing/report-on-government-services/2017/approach/performance-measurement.
4. ibid.
5. Productivity Commission, *Report on Government Services—Chapter 4 School Education*, accessed 4 September 2017, http://www.pc.gov.au/research/ongoing/report-on-government-services/2017/child-care-education-and-training/school-education/rogs-2017-volumeb-chapter4.pdf.
6. For example see: Thomas Jefferson, 1818, in *Early History of the University of Virginia, as Contained in the Letters of Thomas Jefferson*

and Joseph C. Cabell, Hitherto Unpublished, ed. JW Randolph, accessed 19 January 2017.

7. Alan Barcan, *A History of Australian Education*, (Melbourne: Oxford University Press, 1980), 12.

8. ibid. Barcan.

9. ibid. Barcan.

10. State of Victoria, *Regulatory Impact Statement: Education and Training Regulations 2017*, (Melbourne: Department of Education and Training, 2016), 14, accessed 15 September 2017, http://www.education.vic.gov.au/Documents/about/department/legislation/RegulatoryImpactStatementEduTrainReformReg2017.pdf.

11. Friedrich Hayek, *Constitution of Liberty*, (London: University of Chicago Press, 1960 [1963]), 378.

12. ibid. Barcan.

13. As cited in Alan Barcan, *A History of Australian Education*, (Melbourne: Oxford University Press, 1980), 51.

14. ibid. Barcan.

15. Milton Friedman, "The Role of Government in Education", in *Economics and the Public Interest*, ed. RA Solo, (New Brunswick: Rutgers University Press, 1955), 2.

16. Friedman was not the first liberal scholar to put forward this contention. See: Adam Smith, *An Inquiry into the Nature and Causes of the Wealth of Nations*, (1776 [1904]), accessed 11 September 2017, http://www.econlib.org/library/Smith/smWN20.html; and see also: John Stuart Mill, On Liberty (Kitchener: Cartouche Books, 1859 [2001]).

17. For example, see: Andrew Young and Walter Block, "Enterprising Education: Doing Away With the Public School System", *International Journal of Value-Based Management*, Vol. 12 No. 3, (1999), 195-207.

18. For example, see: Chris Bonnor and Jane Caro, *The Stupid Country:*

How Australia is Dismantling Public Education, (Sydney: University of New South Wales Press, 2007); Amanda Keddie, "Maintaining the Integrity of Public Education: A Comparative Analysis of School Autonomy in the United States and Australia", *Comparative Education Review*, Vol. 60 No. 2, (2015), 249-270.

19. For example, see: Pape v Commission of Taxation (2010) 238 CLR 1; Williams v Commonwealth of Australia (2012) 248 CLR 156.

20. ibid. Mises, 41.

21. ibid. Mises, 45.

22. Gordon Tullock, *The Politics of Bureaucracy*, (New York: Longman, 1965).

23. William Niskanen, *Bureaucracy and Representative Government*, (Chicago: Aldine Atherton, 1971).

24. George Stigler, "The Theory of Economic Regulation", *The Bell Journal of Economics and Management Science*, Vol. 2 No. 1, (1971), 3-21.

25. National Education Board Act 1848 (NSW); NSW Government Gazette, 7 January, 1848, 23.

26. A more robust measure is RegData, developed by researchers at the Mercatus Centre at George Mason University, which counts the number of restrictive clauses within legislation. This methodology is not yet available in Australia. See: Omar Al-Ubaydli and Patrick McLaughlin, "RegData: A numerical database on industry-specific regulations for all United States industries and federal regulations, 1997–2012", *Regulation & Governance*, Vol. 11, (2017), 109-123.

27. Incorporating amendments as at 5 April 2005.

28. Historical consolidations of the Education Act 1958 (Vic) obtained from the Victorian Legislation and Parliamentary Documents database, accessed 4 September 2017, http://www.legislation.vic.gov.au.

29. Incorporating amendments as at 1 July 2017.

30. Australian Bureau of Statistics, *4221.0—Schools—Australia—2016*,

2 February 2017, accessed 4 September 2017, http://www.abs.gov.au/AUSSTATS/abs@.nsf/Lookup/4221.0Main+Features12016?OpenDocument.

31. Barry Bozeman, *Bureaucracy and Red Tape*, (Upper Saddle River: Prentice Hall, 2000, p. 12).

32. Incorporating amendments as at 27 June 2017. Further amendments passed in 2017 will commence in January 2018.

33. Australian Education Amendment Act 2017; Schedule 1.

34. Australian Public Service Commission, *APS Statistical Bulletin: December 2016*, (31 March 2017), Table 2, accessed 23 September 2017, http://www.apsc.gov.au/publications-and-media/parliamentary/aps-statistical-bulletin/december-2016/table2.

35. Bronwyn Hinz, *Federalism and schooling reforms in Australia*, Doctoral Thesis, (Melbourne: University of Melbourne, 2016).

36. Brian Caldwell and Donald Hayward, *The Future of Schools: Lessons From the Reform of Public Education*, (London: Falmer Press, 1998); ibid. Hinz.

37. ibid. Caldwell and Hayward.

38. Victorian Commission of Audit, *Report of the Victorian Commission of Audit*, (Melbourne: Victorian Government, 1993).

39. ibid. Caldwell and Hayward, 46.

40. ibid. Caldwell and Hayward, 46.

41. Liberal Party of WA, 2008, "Empowering School Communities", accessed 26 September 2017, https://www.academia.edu/32176504/2008_Liberal_Party_Policy_Empowering_School_Communities.

42. Education and Health Standing Committee, *IPS Report Card: The Report of the Inquiry into the Independent Public Schools initiative*, (Perth: Parliament of Western Australia, 2016), i.

43. Department of Education, *Independent Public Schools*, accessed 26 September 2017, https://www.education.wa.edu.au/web/our-

schools/independent-public-schools.

44. Centre for Program Evaluation, *Evaluation of the Independent Public Schools Initiative Final Report*, (Department of Education, May 2013), 74, accessed 14 November 2017, https://www.education. wa.edu.au/documents/2548175/2664299/Evaluation+of+the+Independent+Public+Schools+initiative+%28Full+report%29.pdf/ aafae012-c595-4447-943f-caf982c75785.

45. ibid, Centre for Program Evaluation, 32.

46. Hamilton Associates, *School Autonomy: Building the Conditions for Student Success*, (Department of Education, October 2015), 33, accessed 14 November 2017, https://www.education.wa.edu. au/documents/2548175/2664299/FINAL+School+Autonomy+Building+the+conditions+for+the+student+success.pdf/e6d-0bc09-423b-4a1e-b569-fb1b596c462e.

47. Centre for Program Evaluation, *Evaluation of the Independent Public Schools Initiative Final Report*, (Department of Education, May 2013), accessed 14 November 2017, https://www.education. wa.edu.au/documents/2548175/2664299/Evaluation+of+the+Independent+Public+Schools+initiative+%28Full+report%29.pdf/ aafae012-c595-4447-943f-caf982c75785.

48. Department of Education and Training, *Independent Public Schools: Driving Local Decision Making and Innovation*, (Queensland Government, 2012), 2.

49. ibid, Department of Education and Training, 6.

50. Daniel Hurst, "Independent School Push May Trigger 'Bitter' Strikes", *Brisbane Times*, 29 November 2011, accessed 14 November 2017, http://www.queenslandcountrylife.com.au/story/3614579/ independent-school-push-may-trigger-bitter-strikes/?cs=4698#!.

51. Kevin Donnelly, "The Australian Education Union: A History of Opposing School Choice and School Autonomy Down-Under", *Journal of School Choice*, Vol. 9 No. 6, (2015), 626-641.

52. Aaron Lane, "Innovation in Public Sector Services: A Case Study on Queensland's Independent Public School Program to Examine Regulatory Constraints", Presented to the 2017 Australian Centre for Entrepreneurship Research Exchange Conference, Melbourne, February 2017.

53. Christopher Pyne, "Launch of the Australian Government's Independent Public Schools Initiative", Media Release, 3 February 2014, accessed 14 November 2017, https://ministers.education.gov.au/pyne/launch-australian-governments-independent-public-schools-initiative.

54. Hamilton Associates, *School Autonomy: Building the Conditions for Student Success*, (Department of Education, October 2015, p. 41), accessed 14 November 2017, https://www.education.wa.edu.au/documents/2548175/2664299/FINAL+School+Autonomy+Building+the+conditions+for+the+student+success.pdf/e6d-0bc09-423b-4a1e-b569-fb1b596c462e.

55. Brad Gobby, "Enacting the Independent Public Schools program in Western Australia", *Issues in Educational Research*, Vol. 23 No. 1, (2013), 19-34.

56. ibid. Hamilton Associates, 41.

57. ibid. Hamilton Associates, 41.

58. Vicki Stanley, Darcy Allen and Aaron Lane, *Freedom to Teach: A Research Report of the Work and Conditions of Teachers in Australia*, (Melbourne: Institute of Public Affairs, December 2014), accessed 14 November 2017.

59. Andrew Burrell, "WA Teachers' Union Hails Curbs on Hiring by Principals", *The Australian*, 1 November 2017, accessed 14 November 2017, http://www.theaustralian.com.au/national-affairs/state-politics/wa-teachers-union-hails-curbs-on-hiring-by-principals/news-story/4ed9f86a4b0a5475350d5561174318ae.

60. These are the five forms of innovation proposed by Joseph Schumpeter.

61. Ian Harper, Peter Anderson, Su McCluskey, and Michael O'Brien, *Competition Policy Review Final Report*, (Department of Treasury, March 2015, p. 254), accessed 14 November 2017, http://competitionpolicyreview.gov.au/files/2015/03/Competition-policy-review-report_online.pdf.

62. Australian Government, "Australian Government response to the Competition Policy Review", (Department of Treasury, 2015), accessed 14 November 2017, https://static.treasury.gov.au/uploads/sites/1/2017/06/Govt_response_CPR.pdf.

63. Productivity Commission, *Introducing Competition and Informed User Choice into Human Services: Identifying Sectors for Reform* (Productivity Commission, November 2016), 49, accessed 14 November 2017, https://www.pc.gov.au/inquiries/completed/human-services/identifying-reform/report/human-services-identifying-reform.pdf.

CHAPTER THIRTEEN:
RED TAPE REDUCTION:
A NEW APPROACH

1. Peter Carroll and Brian Head, "Regulatory reform and the management of intergovernmental relations in Australia", *Australian Journal of Political Science,* Vol. 45 No. 3, (2010), 407-424.

2. Peter Boettke and Peter Leeson, "An 'Austrian' perspective on public choice", In *The Encyclopedia of Public Choice*, 351-356, Springer US (2004); Mancur Olson, *The Logic of Collective Action,* (Harvard University Press, 2009).

3. For public choice theory see: James M. Buchanan and Gordon Tullock, *The Calculus of Consent,* (Vol. 3, Ann Arbor: University of Michigan Press, 1962). For the economics of regulation see: George J. Stigler, "The Theory of Economic Regulation." *The Bell Journal of Economics and Management Science,* Vol. 2 No. 1 (1971), 3-21. Sam Peltzman, "Toward

a More General Theory of Regulation", *The Journal of Law and Economics*, Vol. 19 No. 2, (1976), 211-240.

4. Herbert A. Simon, *Models of Man: Social and Rational*. (New york: John Wiley and Sons, 1957).

5. Patrick A. McLaughlin and Richard Williams, *The Consequences of Regulatory Accumulation and a Proposed Solution*, (Mercatus Working Paper, Mercatus Center at George Mason University, Arlington, VA, 2014).

6. See Douglass C. North, *Institutions, Institutional Change and Economic Performance*, (Cambridge: Cambridge University Press, 1990).

7. ibid. Buchanan and Tullock.

8. Note that this is an optimistic analysis, with various criticisms of red tape reduction policies as a form of signalling to in effect avoid reform.

9. Cary Coglianese and Evan Mendelson, "Meta-regulation and Self-regulation", *Penn Law School Public Law and Legal Theory Research Paper No. 12-11*, (2010).

10. John Braithwaite, "Enforced Self-regulation: A New Strategy for Corporate Crime Control", *Michigan Law Review*, Vol. 80 No. 7, (1982), 1466-1507.

11. Productivity Commission, *Microeconomic Reforms and Australian Productivity: Exploring the Links*, (Productivity Commission: 1999).

12. Dean Parham, "Microeconomic Reforms and the Revival in Australia's Growth in Productivity and Living Standards", In *Conference of Economists, Adelaide*, Vol. 1, (2002).

13. Chris Berg, *The Growth of Australia's Regulatory State: Ideology, Accountability and the Mega-Regulators*, (Melbourne: Institute of Public Affairs, 2008).

14. Commonwealth Government, *Time for Business*, (Report of the Small Business Deregulation Taskforce, 1996).

15. Regulation Taskforce, *Rethinking Regulation: Report of the Taskforce on Reducing Regulatory Burdens on Business*, (Canberra: Report to the Prime Minister and Treasurer, 2006).

16. ibid. Regulation Taskforce, 146.

17. Cary Coglianese, "Empirical Analysis and Administrative Law." *Faculty Scholarship Paper*, no. 978, (2002), 1111-1138.

18. Australian Government, *The Australian Government Annual Deregulation Report 2014*, (Canberra, 2014).

19. Portfolios were to use the Regulatory Burden Measurement Framework to estimate the administrative costs, substantive costs and delay costs of Commonwealth regulations.

20. Mikayla Novak, *The $176 Billion Tax on Our Prosperity*, (Melbourne: Institute of Public Affairs, 2016).

21. Sid Maher, "Success Makes Red Tape Repeal Days Redundant", *The Australian*, 4 February 2016.

22. Commonwealth of Australia, *Australian Red Tape Reduction Report*, (Canberra: Department of the Prime Minister and Cabinet, 2015).

23. James M. Buchanan, "Opportunity Cost", in *The World of Economics*, (UK: Palgrave Macmillan, 1991), 520-525.

24. ibid. Novak (2016).

25. James Broughel, *A Step-by-step Guide to Using Mercatus Tools to Reduce State Regulation Levels*, (Mercatus on Policy Guidance Note, 2017).

26. Commonwealth of Australia, *Regulatory Burden Measurement Framework*, (Canberra: Department of Prime Minister and Cabinet Guidance Note, July 2014).

27. Meave P. Carey, *Methods of Estimating the Total Cost of Regulations*, (Congressional Research Service Paper, January 2016).

28. Joe Kelly, "Rising Tide of Red Tape a Threat: IPA", *The Australian*, 2 January 2017.

29. Casey B. Mulligan and Andrei Shleifer, "The Extent of the Market

and the Supply of Regulation", *Quarterly Journal of Economics*, Vol. 120 No. 4, (2005), 1445-1473.

30. Ministry of Small Business and Red Tape Reduction, "Regulatory Reform Policy", British Columbia, 2016.

31. British Columbia Regulatory Reform BC, "Count Overview Report: Regulatory Requirement Count as at 31 March 2017".

32. Laura Jones, *Cutting Red Tape in Canada: A Regulatory Reform Model for the United States?*, (Mercatus Research: Mercatus Center at George Mason University, November 2015).

33. Government of Canada, *Backgrounder — Legislating the One-for-one rule*, (Canadian Government, 2015).

34. Queensland Competition Authority, *Measuring and Reducing the Burden of Regulation*, (Interim Report of the Queensland Competition Authority, October 2012).

35. Queensland Competition Authority, 2.

36. Queensland Competition Authority, *Queensland's Regulatory Requirements Count Methodology*, (July 2013).

37. Anthony Templeton, "Opposition Leader Tim Nicholls Pledges 20 Per Cent Reduction in Red Tape Over 6 Years", *The Courier Mail*, 15 May 2017.

38. Omar Ahmad Al-Ubaydli and Patrick A. McLaughlin, *RegData: A Numerical Database on Industry-Specific Regulations for All US Industries and Federal Regulations, 1997–2012*, (Mercatus Working Paper, 2014).

39. Bentley Coffey, Patrick A. McLaughlin and Pietro Peretto, *The Cumulative Cost of Regulations*, (Arlington, VA: Mercatus Working Paper, Mercatus Center at George Mason University, April 2016).

CHAPTER FOURTEEN: REGULATION AND TECHNOLOGICAL CHANGE

1. Jeffrey Friedman and Wladimir Kraus, *Engineering the Financial Crisis: Systemic Risk and the Failure of Regulation*, (University of Pennsylvania Press, 2011).
2. Emma Connors, "NAB Buys US Software for Basel Accord", *Australian Financial Review*, 20 December 2004.
3. Duff & Phelps, *Global Regulatory Outlook 2017*. https://www.duffandphelps.com/-/media/assets/pdfs/publications/compliance-and-regulatory-consulting/2017-global-regulatory-outlook-viewpoint.ashx
4. Baumol, William J. "Entrepreneurship: Productive, Unproductive, and destructive", *Journal of Business Venturing*, Vol. 11 No. 1, (1996), 3-22.
5. On the topic of private governance see: Edward Stringham, *Private Governance: Creating Order in Economic and Social Life*, (USA: Oxford University Press, 2015).
6. Alex Tabarrok and Tyler Cowen, "The End of Asymmetric Information", Cato Unbound, 6 April 2015
7. For example, see: Calestous Juma, *Innovation and its Enemies: Why People Resist New Technologies*, (Oxford University Press, 2016).
8. Richard Allsop, "How Government Holds Back Technological Change", *IPA Review* 2014; Darcy Allen and Jason Potts, *Innovation Strangled by Red Tape*, Submission to the Productivity Commission Inquiry into business set-up, transfer and closure, (Melbourne: Institute of Public Affairs, 2015).
9. Senate Standing Committee on Rural and Regional Affairs and Transport, Regulatory Requirements that Impact on the Safe Use of Remotely Piloted Aircraft Systems, Unmanned Aerial Systems and Associated Systems.

10. Darcy Allen, *The Case for Cutting Red Tape on Drones,* IPA Research Paper, (Melbourne: Institute of Public Affairs, 2016).

11. Adam Thierer, *Permissionless Innovation: The Continuing Case for Comprehensive Technological Freedom*, (Mercatus Center at George Mason University, 2016).

12. Darcy Allen and Chris Berg, *The Sharing Economy: How Over-regulation Could Destroy an Economic Revolution*, (Melbourne: Institute of Public Affairs, 2014).

Contributors

Darcy Allen is a Postdoctoral Research Fellow in the Blockchain Innovation Hub at RMIT University and an Adjunct Fellow with the Institute of Public Affairs. Dr Allen's work focuses on the institutional economics of entrepreneurship and new technologies.

Chris Berg is a Senior Research Fellow at the RMIT Blockchain Innovation Hub at RMIT University, a Senior Fellow with the Institute of Public Affairs and an Academic Fellow with the Australian Taxpayers' Alliance. He is author of six books including *The Libertarian Alternative* and *The Growth of Australia's Regulatory State*.

Andrew Bushnell is a Research Fellow at the Institute of Public Affairs, where he leads the *Criminal Justice Project*. He holds degrees in law and arts and is a PhD candidate in philosophy at the University of Melbourne.

William Coleman is a Reader in the School of Economics at the Australian National University. He has written extensively on the history of economics, and it's contested place in society. He is editor of the recently published *Only in Australia: The History, Politics and Economics of Australian Exceptionalism* (2016). He is currently researching a revisionist history of Australian Federation.

Sinclair Davidson is a Professor of Institutional Economics in the School of Economics, Finance and Marketing at RMIT University, a Senior Research Fellow at the Institute of Public Affairs and an Academic Fellow at the Australian Taxpayers' Alliance.

Georgina Downer is an Adjunct Fellow at the Institute of Public Affairs. Georgina has extensive experience in foreign policy. She has degrees in Commerce and Law from the University of Melbourne. She was awarded a UK Foreign and Commonwealth Office Chevening Scholarship and holds a Masters in Public International Law from the London School of Economics.

David Kemp is a former Cabinet Minister in the Howard Government, and former Professor of Politics at Monash University. He has a Ph.D. from Yale University.

Aaron M. Lane is a Lecturer in Law at RMIT University and is a Legal Fellow at the Institute of Public Affairs. His doctoral research in economics at RMIT focuses on the relationship between regulation and public sector innovation.

CONTRIBUTORS

Matthew Lesh is a Research Fellow at the Institute of Public Affairs. His research interests include economic and social freedom, the foundations of western civilisation, and university intellectual freedom. He holds a Bachelor of Arts from the University of Melbourne and an MSc in Public Policy and Administration from the London School of Economics.

Gregory Melleuish is a Professor in the School of Humanities and Social Inquiry at the University of Wollongong where he teaches Australian politics, political theory and ancient history. His books include *Cultural Liberalism in Australia* (1995), *The Packaging of Australia* (1998) and *Despotic State or Free Individual?* (2014).

Michael Potter works as an economist in the financial services sector. He is the author of five research papers for the Centre for Independent Studies including *Fix it or Fail: Why we must cut company tax now* and *Exposing the Stealth Tax: the Bracket Creep rip-off*.

Ashton De Silva is an Associate Professor in the School of Economics, Finance and Marketing at RMIT University. He is an applied economist and econometrician specialising in the analysis of the property (including housing) sector, natural resources, credit and financial markets, and government policy.

Daniel Wild is a Research Fellow at the Institute of Public Affairs. He specialises in economic policy, with a focus on regulation, red tape, and taxation. Daniel holds an honors qualification in economics from the University of Adelaide.

www.ingramcontent.com/pod-product-compliance
Lightning Source LLC
Chambersburg PA
CBHW021945220326
41599CB00012BA/1183